Routledge Revivals

The Constitution of Parliaments in England Deduced from the Time of King Edward the Second, Illustrated by King Charles the Second in his Parliament Summon'd the 18 of February 1660/1. And Dissolved the 24 of January 1678/9 (1680)

The Constitution of Parliaments in England Deduced from the Time of King Edward the Second, Illustrated by King Charles the Second in his Parliament Summon'd the 18 of February 1660/1. And Dissolved the 24 of January 1678/9 (1680)

John Pettus

First published in 1680 by Thomas Basset

This edition first published in 2018 by Routledge
2 Park Square, Milton Park, Abingdon, Oxon, OX14 4RN
and by Routledge
52 Vanderbilt Avenue, New York, NY 10017, USA

Routledge is an imprint of the Taylor & Francis Group, an informa business

Publisher's Note
The publisher has gone to great lengths to ensure the quality of this reprint but points out that some imperfections in the original copies may be apparent.

Disclaimer
The publisher has made every effort to trace copyright holders and welcomes correspondence from those they have been unable to contact.

A Library of Congress record exists under ISBN:

ISBN 13: 978-0-367-18089-8 (hbk)
ISBN 13: 978-0-367-18090-4 (pbk)
ISBN 13: 978-0-429-05946-9 (ebk)

The constitution of parliaments in England deduced from the time of King Edward the Second, illustrated by King Charles the Second in his Parliament summon'd the 18 of February 1660/1. And dissolved the 24 of January 1678/9 (1680)

John Pettus

Early English Books Online (EEBO) Editions

Imagine holding history in your hands.

Now you can. Digitally preserved and previously accessible only through libraries as Early English Books Online, this rare material is now available in single print editions. Thousands of books written between 1475 and 1700 and ranging from religion to astronomy, medicine to music, can be delivered to your doorstep in individual volumes of high-quality historical reproductions.

We have been compiling these historic treasures for more than 70 years. Long before such a thing as "digital" even existed, ProQuest founder Eugene Power began the noble task of preserving the British Museum's collection on microfilm. He then sought out other rare and endangered titles, providing unparalleled access to these works and collaborating with the world's top academic institutions to make them widely available for the first time. This project furthers that original vision.

These texts have now made the full journey -- from their original printing-press versions available only in rare-book rooms to online library access to new single volumes made possible by the partnership between artifact preservation and modern printing technology. A portion of the proceeds from every book sold supports the libraries and institutions that made this collection possible, and that still work to preserve these invaluable treasures passed down through time.

This is history, traveling through time since the dawn of printing to your own personal library.

Initial Proquest EEBO Print Editions collections include:

Early Literature

This comprehensive collection begins with the famous Elizabethan Era that saw such literary giants as Chaucer, Shakespeare and Marlowe, as well as the introduction of the sonnet. Traveling through Jacobean and Restoration literature, the highlight of this series is the Pollard and Redgrave 1475-1640 selection of the rarest works from the English Renaissance.

Early Documents of World History

This collection combines early English perspectives on world history with documentation of Parliament records, royal decrees and military documents that reveal the delicate balance of Church and State in early English government. For social historians, almanacs and calendars offer insight into daily life of common citizens. This exhaustively complete series presents a thorough picture of history through the English Civil War.

Historical Almanacs

Historically, almanacs served a variety of purposes from the more practical, such as planting and harvesting crops and plotting nautical routes, to predicting the future through the movements of the stars. This collection provides a wide range of consecutive years of "almanacks" and calendars that depict a vast array of everyday life as it was several hundred years ago.

Early History of Astronomy & Space

Humankind has studied the skies for centuries, seeking to find our place in the universe. Some of the most important discoveries in the field of astronomy were made in these texts recorded by ancient stargazers, but almost as impactful were the perspectives of those who considered their discoveries to be heresy. Any independent astronomer will find this an invaluable collection of titles arguing the truth of the cosmic system.

Early History of Industry & Science

Acting as a kind of historical Wall Street, this collection of industry manuals and records explores the thriving industries of construction; textile, especially wool and linen; salt; livestock; and many more.

Early English Wit, Poetry & Satire

The power of literary device was never more in its prime than during this period of history, where a wide array of political and religious satire mocked the status quo and poetry called humankind to transcend the rigors of daily life through love, God or principle. This series comments on historical patterns of the human condition that are still visible today.

Early English Drama & Theatre

This collection needs no introduction, combining the works of some of the greatest canonical writers of all time, including many plays composed for royalty such as Queen Elizabeth I and King Edward VI. In addition, this series includes history and criticism of drama, as well as examinations of technique.

Early History of Travel & Geography

Offering a fascinating view into the perception of the world during the sixteenth and seventeenth centuries, this collection includes accounts of Columbus's discovery of the Americas and encompasses most of the Age of Discovery, during which Europeans and their descendants intensively explored and mapped the world. This series is a wealth of information from some the most groundbreaking explorers.

Early Fables & Fairy Tales

This series includes many translations, some illustrated, of some of the most well-known mythologies of today, including Aesop's Fables and English fairy tales, as well as many Greek, Latin and even Oriental parables and criticism and interpretation on the subject.

Early Documents of Language & Linguistics

The evolution of English and foreign languages is documented in these original texts studying and recording early philology from the study of a variety of languages including Greek, Latin and Chinese, as well as multilingual volumes, to current slang and obscure words. Translations from Latin, Hebrew and Aramaic, grammar treatises and even dictionaries and guides to translation make this collection rich in cultures from around the world.

Early History of the Law

With extensive collections of land tenure and business law "forms" in Great Britain, this is a comprehensive resource for all kinds of early English legal precedents from feudal to constitutional law, Jewish and Jesuit law, laws about public finance to food supply and forestry, and even "immoral conditions." An abundance of law dictionaries, philosophy and history and criticism completes this series.

Early History of Kings, Queens and Royalty

This collection includes debates on the divine right of kings, royal statutes and proclamations, and political ballads and songs as related to a number of English kings and queens, with notable concentrations on foreign rulers King Louis IX and King Louis XIV of France, and King Philip II of Spain. Writings on ancient rulers and royal tradition focus on Scottish and Roman kings, Cleopatra and the Biblical kings Nebuchadnezzar and Solomon.

Early History of Love, Marriage & Sex

Human relationships intrigued and baffled thinkers and writers well before the postmodern age of psychology and self-help. Now readers can access the insights and intricacies of Anglo-Saxon interactions in sex and love, marriage and politics, and the truth that lies somewhere in between action and thought.

Early History of Medicine, Health & Disease

This series includes fascinating studies on the human brain from as early as the 16th century, as well as early studies on the physiological effects of tobacco use. Anatomy texts, medical treatises and wound treatment are also discussed, revealing the exponential development of medical theory and practice over more than two hundred years.

Early History of Logic, Science and Math

The "hard sciences" developed exponentially during the 16th and 17th centuries, both relying upon centuries of tradition and adding to the foundation of modern application, as is evidenced by this extensive collection. This is a rich collection of practical mathematics as applied to business, carpentry and geography as well as explorations of mathematical instruments and arithmetic; logic and logicians such as Aristotle and Socrates; and a number of scientific disciplines from natural history to physics.

Early History of Military, War and Weaponry

Any professional or amateur student of war will thrill at the untold riches in this collection of war theory and practice in the early Western World. The Age of Discovery and Enlightenment was also a time of great political and religious unrest, revealed in accounts of conflicts such as the Wars of the Roses.

Early History of Food

This collection combines the commercial aspects of food handling, preservation and supply to the more specific aspects of canning and preserving, meat carving, brewing beer and even candy-making with fruits and flowers, with a large resource of cookery and recipe books. Not to be forgotten is a "the great eater of Kent," a study in food habits.

Early History of Religion

From the beginning of recorded history we have looked to the heavens for inspiration and guidance. In these early religious documents, sermons, and pamphlets, we see the spiritual impact on the lives of both royalty and the commoner. We also get insights into a clergy that was growing ever more powerful as a political force. This is one of the world's largest collections of religious works of this type, revealing much about our interpretation of the modern church and spirituality.

Early Social Customs

Social customs, human interaction and leisure are the driving force of any culture. These unique and quirky works give us a glimpse of interesting aspects of day-to-day life as it existed in an earlier time. With books on games, sports, traditions, festivals, and hobbies it is one of the most fascinating collections in the series.

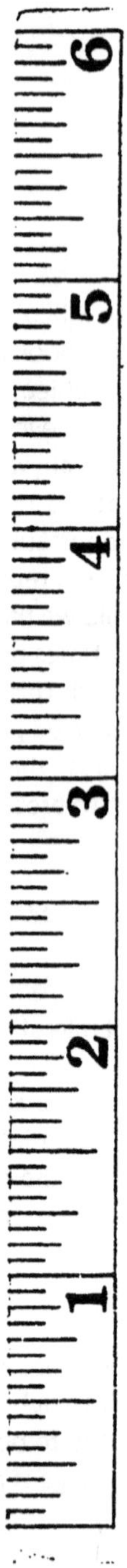
1
2
3
4
5
6

THE CONSTITUTION OF Parliaments IN ENGLAND,

Deduced from the time of King *Edward* the Second,

Illuſtrated by King *Charles* the Second In His Parliament Summon'd the 18 of *February* $166\frac{0}{1}$. And Diſſolved the 24 of *January* $167\frac{8}{9}$.

Obſerved by Sr. *John Pettus* of *Suffolk*, Knight.

LONDON,

Printed for *Thomas Baſſet*, at the *George* in *Fleetſtreet*, 1680.

The Epistle

To the Generous

READER.

HAving the Honor of Consanguinity to some of the *House* of *Lords*, and free access to most of the Rest who make up the Harmony of that Noble *Judicature*, I thought it not convenient (as well to prevent exceptions as dissatisfactions) to dedicate this to any one of their particular Lordships, well knowing that to offer any addition to their Universal *Intuitions* had been needless.

But I devote it in General to such whose Youth, or diversions (by other Imployments) have made them unknowing, or leſs knowing in this Subject, which I have brancht out into 16 parts, whereof 12 conſiſt of *Precognita* or things fit to be known or done after Summons and before the ſitting of any *Parliament*, the 13. 14. and 15. are of matters to be known or done only during the ſitting of a *Parliament*, the 16*th*. hath a relation, and is a Supplement of ſuch matters as could not well be Inſerted to the foregoing 15 Parts.

'Tis true, this ſubject of *Parliaments* hath been treated on by many Learned writers, but becauſe none of them have proceeded in ſuch a due *Series* as they might have done (for they were more for the *Modus tenendi*, than *Inchoandi*) I have partly from them, and partly from my own obſervations (having been a member of the *Houſe* of *Commons* about

bout 12 years, and thereby had intercourſe with the *Houſe* of *Lords*) and partly by the help of ſome worthy Friends) digeſted this Conſtitution into as clear a Method as my leſſer abilities could perform.

Firſt I ſhew the Gradations and Progreſſes to a *Parliament*, from the Fountain. *viz.* the Kings Warrant to the *Lord Chancellor* Impowering him to Summon it in Generals by *Writs.*

Next I ſhew his Lordſhips Warrant to the Clerks of the *Pettibag*, for framing (according to former Precedents) Writs of Summons in Particulars.

Thirdly, I ſhew that theſe Clerks did Anciently and do ſtill uſe a Method therein, which Method (being fairly ingroſt on one large *Parchment*) is called a *Parliament Pawn.*

I doe not find that any writers

before

before me have made any mention of theſe *Pawns* (nor doe I put any weight on them, but in their Method whereby they are compos'd) becauſe I find that the Clerks not conferring with the *Heraulds* have committed many miſtakes in Chriſtian and Surnames, in Titles and Orthography.

However the Method therein hath continued for many Ages, as will be ſhewn, and though I have tried many ways to frame this Treatiſe, yet none pleaſed me ſo well as the Method uſed in the framing of a *Pawn*, which I have herein purſued.

The Writs which are contain'd and Methodiz'd in all *Pawns* have two Appellations *viz.* *Exemplars* and *Conſimilars*, and from thoſe do ariſe the Method of this Treatiſe. But as the *Pawn* doth only recite one Writ of one ſort, (as an Example for *Conſimilar Writs* of the

the ſame ſort to be iſſued, yet are not therein mentioned;) So I by that Method do take occaſion only to Treat of the *Exemplars* (except in ſome few places (for to Treat of all the *Conſimilars* had been too great a task) by which means I have here only five Writs, which gives me opportunity to treat of the *Blood Royal*, of the *Lords Spiritual*, of the State Officers, of the *Lords Temporal*, and of the moſt Eminent *Togati* as the Aſſiſtants in that noble *Houſe*, the other ſeven concerning the *Houſe* of *Commons* I ſhall treat of in a diſtinct Part.

And though my deſign is wholly to treat of what concerns that noble *Houſe* in this part, yet I could not avoid the Intermixtures of ſome neceſſary hints of what properly concerns the *Houſe* of *Commons*, which I intend (*aſſ-vente Deo*) to publiſh by it ſelf.

It was ſcarce poſſible that a Subject, which ſpreads it ſelf into ſuch varieties, ſhould be ſo collected as not to have Omiſſions, ſome of which were purpoſely done, Firſt, that I might not injure the Reader nor my Method by two long diverſions, and yet ſatisfy him in concluſion. 2*ly.* I have been as careful as I could to prevent miſtakes, but ſome will be, yet thoſe which are neceſſary to be corrected (*viz.* my own overſights, or the Printers) I have added them to the end of this Epiſtle, but as for the Printers Omiſſions of Marginal Authorities, and diſtinctions of Sections, and obſervations (which were in my Copy) and for his not putting ſome words into *Italick* Letters, and for want of *Comma's*, *Points* &c. the Ingenious Reader, may Eaſily pardon them.

I have ſo order'd this Impreſ-

ſion

ſion, that you have a Syſtem or the Contents of an Introduction and of 20 ſubſequent *Chapters*, *Sections* and Obſervations which I thought fit to exhibit, that thoſe who have not the Leiſure to read all the *Chapters*, may turn to ſuch parts as moſt ſuit with their Genius.

I begin the proper matter of this Treatiſe with the Kings Warrant in *Feb.* 166$^{0}_{1}$ for Summoning that *Parliament*, and I ſhall End all with His *Proclamation* for its Diſſolution in 167$^{8}_{9}$.

In theſe diſcourſes I take the liberty to look back into former Ages, but not forward beyond the Diſſolution of that *Parliament*; Only as an *Appendix*, I ſhall ſpeak of ſome things that are to be done with *Records*, *Leidger Books* &c. and Allowances to *Knights*, *Citizens* and *Burgeſſes* after any one *Parliament* is ended.

Corrigenda.

Pag. 20 l. 25 d. are, read, or, P. 79 l. 23 after *Seal*, read till of Late years, P. 100 l. 17 r. *Hertford*. P. 124 l. 16. r. forgeting the Title of Knight P. 129 fill up the blanck thus.

L. 15	*Ric.* 3	11	38	o	38		
L. 16	*Hen.* 7	10	42	1	29		
L. 17	*Hen.* 8	37	45	1	36	dele. 28	44

P. 137 d. son, r. Heir to Blanch the Wife of *John* P. 139 l. 6 d. and 6. P. 383 l. 7 read by this.

The Reader may also take notice that after the Contents, there are observations Printed, concerning the Names and Titles of our *English Kings*, especially of the Name *Carolus* or *Charles*, with some Prophetick Interpretations of it, which should have been plac'd next the 14 Page of this Treatise, but being omitted by an Accident he is desir'd to read them after that Page, if he please.

THE

THE

CONTENTS

of this

TREATIS.

The Introduction.

Hewing the Original of Councils, and the several Names of Councils in other Nations *and in this* Kingdom, *How and when the Name of* Parliament *began; Of its* Etymology *and Definition; That a* Parliament *is the Abstract, yet includes the whole Constitution and* Fabrick *of the Government of the* Kingdom; *That it Consists of a King and three Estates, and of three assisting Interests to those three Estates.*

The rest is divided into twenty Chapters *with several* Sections *and Observations in them, as followes.* Chap-

The Contents.

CHAP.

The Contents.

Chap. II.

Chap. III.

The Contents.

lesser

Sect. II.

Of the Princes of the Blood.

Sect. III.

Of the Kings Vicegerent.

Sect. IV.

Of Bishops.

the Convocation Houses *where they sit, as* Bishops, *and in* Parliament *upon a* Baronial *account, How plac'd, Call'd* Lords Spiritual, *Anciently they did manage the Chief Offices of the* Kingdom, *Of their Priviledge in the* Lords House.

SECT. V.

Of the *Lord Chancellor* or *Lord Keeper*, Referred to Chap. the 8*th*.

SECT. VI.

Of the *Lord Treasurer* Referred to Chap. the 9*th*.

SECT. VII.

Of the *Lord President* of the Kings Council.

Of it's Antiquity, Discontinuance, and Supply, Of other Lords Presidents.

SECT. VIII.

Of the Lord Privy Seal

It's Antiquity and several Titles, How granted, Considered as Master of Requests, *Of his* Seals, *and other* Seals, *Of his*

Clerks

The Contents.

into three, the Majores *makes the Lords House, the* Minores *the Commons House.*

SECT. II.

Of Dukes.

Duke from the Latin word Duco & Dux, *Antiently Earls were Prior to Dukes in* England, *How Dukes got the Priority: Of the several Titles attributed to Dukes; Duke and Earl promiscuously us'd, And of the name Grace apply'd to Dukes in* England: *Dukes were in* England *before they were formally Created; The time when Created, Of two sorts of Dukes how distinguisht, (A Duke as Generall) is not provided for in the* Act *of* Precedency *as other degrees of officiall honors are.*

SECT. III.

Of Marquesses.

When begun in the Empire, *and in* France, *When in* England: *the reason of placing him between Duke and Earl: From whence the Title is suppos'd to come, Noble Actions caus'd Noble Titles, and by some Hereditary.*

SECT.

The Contents.

SECT. IV.

Of Earls.

SECT. V.

Of Viscounts.

The Contents.

Sect. VI.

Of a Baron.

Of the word Baron, the Baronial Tenures were the foundation of the Superior Tenures and Degrees, Of Contributions to the King from Barons Spiritual: Barons how Exempted from Contributions, Of ſeveral other ſorts of Barons, The advantages of Created Barons.

Chap. VI.

Of the Writ to Princes of the Blood Royal.

Of the Writ to Edward *Earl of* Cheſter *Eldeſt Son to King* Edward *the 2d.* Anno 15. Ed. 2. *And the Writ to* James *Duke of* York 13. Car. 2. *Compar'd, Obſervations on both Writs, A Recital or Numeration of the Exemplars of Earls, Princes, and Dukes of the Blood from* Edward *the 2d. to this* Parliament 1661. *Obſervations on the Title of* York, *the* Conſimilar *to the Duke of* York, *Obſervations on the* Conſimilars.

Chap.

The Contents.

CHAP. VII.

Of the Writ to the Arch-Bishop and Bishops with Observations.

Reasons for incerting this Exemplar in this Place, . *shewing that the Idolatrous* Jews *brought in* Paganism *into* Britain, *manag'd by* Druids *and* Bards, *after by* Arch-Flamins, *and* Flamins (*which were* Pagan Priests) *Afterwards* Christ *Himself or his Apostles, or Disciples, or some of them brought in Christianity into* Britain: *Bishops had Eleven several Titles* (*according to several Regions*) *given to the first managers of Christian Religion: All included in the Word Bishop as Inspector or Father: Of the Antiquity of the word Bishop*, Aristobulus *the first Bishop of* Britain, *who were his Successors, Of King* Lucius *his message to Pope* Eleutherius *and the Popes answer about the first ordering of Christian affairs in* Britain : *Of* Linus *the first Bishop of* Rome *and his Successors till the time of* Lucius *and* Eleutherius (*all subsequent to* Aristobulus) *The Amity between the Bishop of* Britain, *and the Bishop of* Rome, (*in that time without any discord about Supremacy*) *Afterwards the Bishop of* Rome *assum'd the Title of Pope, and also a*

The Contents.

Degrees of Nobles (viz.) *Dukes, Marquesses, Earls, Viscounts, and Barons*) *and Titles of the Officers of State are still intermixt in the Writs with some of those five Degrees, Which of these Degrees are usually made* Exemplars, *Of the Antiquity of the method us'd herein, Of their* Consimilars, *Observations concerning the various applications of the Titles*, Chevaleer, Dominus, Miles, Eques Auratus, & Bannerettus.

Chap. X.

Of Patents, of Creation enabling the Lords Patentees to sit in *Parliament*.

The difference between Writs and Patents and advantages of Patents, what the word signifies, Patents of 3. sorts viz. *of Confirming, Reviving and Creating, (that is, given where none was before,) The form of those 3. sort of Patents, Their ellegant preambles, The Patents consisting of 4. parts, Of the distinct form of the Patents to Dukes, Marquesses, Earls, Viscounts, and Barons, impowring them to sit in* Parliaments, *Of the Consies of Antient Patents, Of Creation money, Of the difference in the former and late value of moneys.*

Chap.

The Contents.

Chap. XI.

Of Lords and Peers.

Of the words Dominus & Pares,*or Lords and Peers, what the words signifie, When Peers us'd in* France, *and of their number there: when in* England *and of their number there, Of the words* Prælates, Magnates & Proceres *how to be appy'd, Who properly called Peers, how placed in the Lords House, the words Generally applyed and promiscuously us'd, the number, increase or decrease according to the pleasure of the King, a Corrollary on the Subject.*

Chap. XII.

Of *Proxies* in the Lords House.

Of the word Procurator, Proxie & Proctor *considered as distinct appellation,* Proxie *only proper in the Lords House, Licenced by the King, and to whom, and sometimes denied, A* Proxies *double vote, when* Proxie *made, sometimes before, and sometimes in time of* Parliament, *and how many allow'd, the Antient way to be Licenced upon any petition to the King, Of the Licence where to be entred, Of* Tacit *Licences,*

Of

The Contents.

Of the form of Licences at this day for a Lord Spiritual, as also for a Lord Temporal, how to be return'd, Of the Titles which intitle Proxors *and* Proxes *to be such, The difference of* Proxe *Writs, before the siting of a* Parliament *and after* Prorogations, *How long they continue, Of their places in the Lords House.*

Chap. XIII.

Of Assistants in the Lords House.

The Assistants are generally professors of the Laws *the vertues arising from that Profession, it is the path to wisdom: How call'd* Laws: *The antient way of distributing them; The benefit of good* Laws *in any State, The Revenues, Honors, Profits, Places, and other Rewards given to the Professors of them: Intituled* Justices *and* Judges &c. *Divided into 3* Orbs *or degrees; The several sorts of* Laws *in which they are to be conversant; of the Titles of the chief professors, 1st. Of the Chief* Justice *of the Kings* Bench *with general observations on his Writ of Summons to* Parliaments, *Of his* Patent *and Jurisdiction. 2ly. Of the Master of the* Rolls *with observations on his* Patent *and Writ and Office: Of the chief* Justice *of the* Common Pleas *with observations*

CHAP.

The Contents.

CHAP.

Observations

Observations on the Names and Titles of our English *Kings.*

THe Learned Mr. *Selden* having bestowed an Excellent Addition to Libraries, by his book of the Titles of Honour, and Sr. *Edward Cook* thinking it a necessary part of his Institutes, for a Student to be well vers'd in the several Titles of our Kings, and knowing that the substance flowing from those Titles are the chief Subjects which are handled in *Parliaments*, I think fit to give a light touch (by way of Preface) to the seueral words of the Title in the Kings *Warrant*, as also in the Title of his Latin *Writs*, which are mentioned so often in the following discourses. *viz.*

Charles the Second by the Grace of *God*, King of *England*, *Scotland*, *France*, and *Ireland*, Defender of the Faith, *&c.*

Carolus Secundus Dei Gratia Rex Angliæ, Scotiæ, Franciæ, & Hiberniæ, Defensor Fidei, &c.

First, It may be observed that all our Kings before, and since the coming in of the *Normans*, have been Usher'd into that

Regal

Regal Dignity by their *Christian* Names, whereof from that time we have Ten several Appellations. *viz.*

One *Stephen*, 1 *John*, 1 *Mary*, 1 *Elizabeth*, 1 *James*. 2 *Williams*, 3 *Richards*, 6 *Edwards*, 8 *Henrys*, 2 *Charles*, but of all these Ten Names *Charles* must have the Honour of Priority given to it.

To prove this, I shall trace their Progresses through *Empires*, *Kingdoms*, *Principalities*, and *States*, under Secular Governours, (not medling with Ecclesiastical) and first of the Name *Carolus*, *or Charles*, Concerning which, I shall not goe so far back as *Charellus Prince* of *Lacedemon*, but since *Christianity* was first, I find that the Name *Charles* or *Carolus* (for they are agreed to be the same) had its first splendor from *Charles* Surnam'd *Martill* (a *French* King) in *Anno* 714. (who was the first that had the Title of Most *Christian* King and from whom came *Caroloman* and *Charlemain* in *Anno* 778) and after *viz.* in *Anno* 800 the Name of *Charles* went into the *Empire*, and in *Anno* 1119 into *Flanders*, In *Anno* 1150 into *Swethland*, In *Anno* 1263 into *Naples* and *Sicily*, In *Anno* 1310 into *Hungary*, In *Anno* 1346 into *Bohemia*, In *Anno* 1601 into *Scotland*, (King *Charles* the first being there Born,) And in *Anno* 1625 into *England*, (the *Charles* I.

*

(the same *Charles* being then King) so as our Present King *Charles* the 2d Immediate Heir to *Charles* the 1*st*. is the Second King of that Name in *England*, and *Scotland*, and that Name of *Charles* is the first of any of the aforesaid Ten Names affixt to any *Diadem* in *Europe*.

Edward II. *Edwardus* or *Edward*, began but in the time of *Edward* the Elder, who was the 24*th*. King of the *Saxon* Race and 25*th*. *Monarch* of *England*, And he in *Anno* 901 gave the first reputation to it, In *Anno* 1332 it went into *Scotland*, And in *Anno* 1334 Carried into *France* by our *Edward* the third (who laid Claim to that *Crown*) And in *Anno* 1433 it went into *Portugal*, continuing still in *England* (with some interpositions of other Names) till Queen *Mary* came to the *Crown* in *Anno* 1553.

Henry III. *Henricus* or *Henry* began in the *Empire* of the *East*, *Anno* 919, and in *Anno* 1101 came into *England*, from thence *Anno* 1192 it went into *Bohemia*, thence *Anno* 1206 to the *Emperour* then at *Constantinople* in *Greece*, In *Anno* 1214 to the Kingdoms of *Leo*, and *Castile*, In *Anno* 1271 to the Kingdom of *Navarr*, In *Anno* 1422 carried into *France* by our *Henry* the 6*th*. (who was then Crown'd in *Paris* King of *France*) And in *Anno* 1573 it went into *Poland*; so as this Regal Name of *Henry*

con-

continued in *England* from *Anno* 1100 (with some interpositions) till *Edward* the 6*th*. *Anno* 1546.

Stephanus or *Stephen* the 1*st*. that made his Name famous was *Stephen* a *Martyr* for *Christianity*, but it was not annext to any Regal Title, till *Anno* 997 in *Hungary*, and thence in *Anno* 1135 it came into *England*, (yet never fixt there, but on one King) And in *Anno* 1576 it went into *Poland*. *Stepten* IV.

Guilielmus or *William* began first as a Regal Title in *Sicily* and *Naples*, *Anno* 1023 and thence, and in *Anno* 1066 it came into *England*, where it never fixt but on two Kings. *William* V.

Johannes or *John*, the first who made this Name famous was *John* the *Baptist* and *John* the *Evangelist*, but it was not a Regal Title till *Anno* 1118 and then the *Emperour* of the *East* assum'd it, And in *Anno* 1199 it came into *England*, (determining in one King) from thence in *Anno* 1222 it went to the *Emperour* at *Adrianople*, And thence in *Anno* 1303 into *Scotland*, In *Anno* 1310 into *Bohemia*, In *Anno* 1350 into *France*, In *Anno* 1379 Into *Leon* and *Castile*, In *Anno* 1383 into *Arragon*, In *Anno* 1387 into *Portugal*, In *Anno* 1405 into *Flanders*, In *Anno* 1418 to *Navarr*, In *Anno* 1478 to *Denmark*, and *John* VI.

way, In *Anno* 1492 to *Poland*, And in *Anno* 1597 to *Hungary*.

Note, that there were 23 *Popes* of this Name *John*, and 10 *Stephens*, but I here ſpeak only of the Regal Names of Secular, not Eccleſiaſtick Princes, and it may be obſerved, that none of the *Popes* have taken on them any of our 10 Regal Names Except *John* and *Stephen*.

Richard VII. *Richardus* or *Richard*, was not a Regal Title till *Anno* 1189 and then it came firſt into *England*, and continued (with ſome interpoſitions) till *Anno* 1485 when *Hen.* the *7th.* came to the Crown, nor was the Name of *Richard* either before or after thoſe years, fixt to any Regal Title in *Europe*, unleſs *Ricarodos* in *Spaniſh* do ſignifie *Richard* in *Engliſh*.

James VIII. *Jacobus* or *James*, (not medling with *Jacob* the father of the Twelve *Patriarchs*, or *James* the Apoſtle but upon a Regal account it was not fixt to any King till *Anno* 1213, then it began with the King of *Arragon*, Thence in *Anno* 1286 into *Sicily*, and *Naples*, In *Anno* 1423 to *Scotland*, In *Anno* 1603 to *England*, given a Title to that happy Union of *England*, and *Scotland* by King *James*.

Mary IX. *Maria* or *Mary*, had the ſuprem Honour to be Mother of our Saviour but it was not annext to any other Regal Title, till

till *Anno* 1310 in *Hungary*, and from thence *Anno* 1476 to *Flanders*, Then in *Anno* 1542 to *Scotland*, And in *Anno* 1553 to *England*.

Elizabetha or *Elizabeth*, had the Honour to be Mother to *John* the *Baptist*, but was not annext to any Regall Title till *Anno* 1438 in *Hungary* and from thence *Anno* 1538 it came into *England*. *Elizabeth* X.

Thus having trac'd the Perambulation of their Ten Names through most parts of *Europe* I shall pass to the next Epithet in the Kings Title, *viz.*

Secundus or Second, and see when a Numeral Appellation was first made Titular to our Kings, and here it may be observed that our Kings had Anciently Adjuncts to their *Christian* Names; to distinguish them from others of the same Name, as *Edward* the Elder, *Edward* the Confessor, in the *Saxons* time, and in the *Normans*, *William* the *Conquerour*, and *William Rufus* and after him (other Titles signifying their tempers) but not Numeral, till *Henry* (who was the *8th.* of that Regal Name in *England*) and he in the *10th.* year of his Reign did first begin to write himself Numerally *Henricus Octavus*: And after him *Edward* his Son did write himself *Edwardus Sextus*, and ever since in our *Histories* and *Records*, where there *Second* II.

 hath

hath been ſince *William* the firſt, two or more Kings of the ſame *Chriſtian* Names; the Numeral Appellation is added, and there upon our preſent King Stiles himſelf in all *Writs* and *Warrants*, as well *Parliamentary* as otherwiſe, *Carolus Secundus* or *Charles* the Second.

Grace of God. III. *Gratia Dei* by the Grace of *God*; Neither the Letters *D. G.* (denoting *Dei Gratia*) nor the words *Dei Gratia* (or the Grace of God) were uſed as Adjuncts to our Kings Titles, till *William Rufus* his time and after that, there were ſome intermixtures (as Sr. *Edward Coke* ſaith) but according to Mr. *Speeds Medals* and ſome others; the Letters *D. G.* and the words *Dei Gratia* were firſt us'd by *Edward* the Confeſſor, and conſtantly after *William Rufus* by every ſucceeding King without omiſſion;

King IV. King or Cuning according to the *Britiſh* or *Saxon* Dialect (ſignifying the ſame with *Rex*) and is not us'd in any *Parliamentary* Writs, nor in any Circumſcription of our Coins, but *Rex* (being a word as Ancient as the Latine Tongue is us'd in all our *Writs*, as well *Parliamentary* as *Judicial*) and may be traced in our *Coines* from the begining of our *Saxon* Kings to the *Danes* with addition only of the *Chriſtian* Name and then alſo *Canutus* the firſt of the *Danes* here, Stil'd himſelf only

only *Canutus Rex*; and others who succeeded him, and *Edward* the Confessor (the fourth *Danish* King) and 37 Monarchs of *England* sometimes wrot *Edwardus Rex*, sometimes *Edwardus Anglorum Rex*, and sometimes *Edwardus Anglorum Basilicus* (according to the Greek word for King) so as the word *Rex* did goe along from the *Britains* to the *Romans*, *Saxons*, and *Danes*: *Herald* the last of that Race, and those before him writing only *Rex* with their Names, and so when the *Normans* Entred. *William* the first Stiled himself only *Willielmus Rex*, and so did the succeeding Kings seldom using the word *Basilicus* till King *James* time.

As to the Etymologies and Originalls of these and other words in this Title I shall leave them to my Annotations, but sometime our Kings wrote *Rex Angliæ*, and some times *Rex Anglorum* (ever from *Edw.* the Confessors time) Now what *Anglia* or *England* contains, every *Geographer* tels us that it is surrounded by the sea Except towards *Scotland*, and as to the diversity of Names several Chronologers tell us that it was Anciently call'd *Albion* by the *Greeks*; *Iniswen* by the *Welch* Poets, *Insula Cæruly* & *Insula Florum* by other Poets, and *Britannia* by the *Greeks* and *Romans*, *Romania* & *Valentia* only by the *Romans* England V.

 Angle-

Angleand, *England* and *Britain* by the *Saxons*, but when the *Saxon Heptarchy* was United under King *Egbert*, he by his Edict *Anno* 819 ordain'd it more solemnly to be call'd *Britain* (containing *England*, *Scotland*, and *Wales*, yet notwithstanding this Edict, it was sometimes call'd *Albion*, sometimes *Britain*, and sometimes *England*, and these various Appellations were us'd (as appears by *History*) under Ten successive Kings after that Edict, and then King *Canutus* the 10*th*. King from *Egbert*, and the first of the *Danish* Race, fixt the Name of *England* & that Name hath continued ever since, according to the *English* dialect; and *Anglia* according to the *Latine* (considered as disjoynted from *Scotland*, and *Wales*) but upon reduction of *Wales* by *Henry* the 8*th*. and by the happy Union with *Scotland* by King *James*: the Kings Title hath been more general, *viz. Rex Magnæ Britanniæ*, comprehending *England*, *Scotland*, and *Wales*, but not to be so understood in our *Parliamentary Writs* for they are applicable only to *England* and *Wales*, and not to *Scotland* though *Scotland* be mentioned in the *Writs*, and it may be observed that this distinction of *England* and *Scotland* were united under the Name of *Britain* by King *Egbert Anno* 819 but after that they were again

again disjoynted, and though both did continue so disjoynted neere 800 years yet now the Ancient Name of *Britain* is restor'd (being bound by one Ocean and Govern'd by one King as it was 800 years before) and though it is now thus intire, yet *England* hath a distinct *Parliament* for its *Laws*, and *Scotland* a distinct *Parliament* for its *Laws*, and both distinctly consisting of 3 Estates under one King, so as in all *Writs* for Summoning an *English Parliament*, though *Scotland* be mentioned yet the operation of the *Writs* can only be applyed to *England*.

The addition of *Scotland* in the Title of our *Parliament Writs*, did begin with King *James* who happily united both Kingdoms as I said under one King, and so wrot himself *Rex Angliæ Scotiæ* &c. But they never send any Representative to our *Parliaments* nor we to theirs yet the King of *Scots* before the union had a Chair allotted for him in the House of Lords but never sat there yet he was sometimes Summon'd as Earl of *Huntington* and so by vertue of that *English* Title might have sat there but not by his Regal Title untill the said union. *Scotland* VI.

Although we had several inlets to *France* by *Normandy*, *Anjoy Poictors-Tourny Mayne* &c. yet the addition of King of *France* to the Title of *English* Kings was not *France* VII.

not till *Edward* the 3*ds.* time, who had a Just Title to it, and there upon did Quarter the Armies of *France*, But *Hen.* the 6*th.* was actually Crown'd King of *France* in *Paris*, and from these two, the Title and right hath continued ever since (though dispossest) and as I shall shew in the second Part of this Treatise that *Callis* did send Burgesses to our *English Parliaments*, for many years till it was Lost by Qu. *Mary.*

Ireland VIII. The Title of *Rex Hiberniæ* was as Ancient as our King *Hen.* the 2*d.* who created his Son *John* the King thereof, yet for what reason of State (otherwise then what I shall mention) in the 7*th.* Chapter) that Title of the King of *Ireland* was never annext to the regal Title of the Kings of *England* till the 33*d.* of *Hen.* the 8*th.* and then to his other Titles he added *Rex Hiberniæ*, before it was only *Dominus*, and their *Parliaments*, are fram'd like our *English Parliaments*, yet Subject to the Kings pleasure in confirming of their *Laws* here in *England*, See more of this in Chap. 7*th.*

Defender IX. As to this part of the Kings Title *viz.* Defender of the Faith, I shall speak more fully of it in the 7*th.* Chapter, Or &c. *id est* other Titles which were formerly, and may still be added as you may Read also in the 7*th.* Chapter, Section the 11 and 12.

&c. X. Thus having past through the General words

words of the Kings Titles in his *Warrants* and *Writs*: now in observance to Sr. *Edward Coke*, I shall make a Summary of the particular Titles of our several Kings, from *William* the first Inclusive to this time, shewing what words were added or withdrawn.

When the *Normans* entred, *William* the first stil'd himself sometimes *Willielmus Rex*, and sometimes *Rex Angliæ & Anglorum*, (as other former Kings) Omitting *Dei Gratia* (as the Institutor saith though I am not satisfied therein) and not adding *Primus*. *William* I.

William surnamed *Rufus* had the same Title, yet sometimes adding *Dei Gratia*, not adding *Secundus*. *William* II.

Henry stil'd himself *Rex Anglorum*, and sometimes *Dei Gratia Rex*, not adding *Primus*. *Henry* I.

Stephen did the like. *Stephen* I.

Henry did the like but Omitted *Dei Gratia* (as Sr. *Edward Coke* saith) but in the Coins which Mr. *Speed* Exhibits to us his stile was *Dei Gratia Rex Angliæ Dux Normaniæ & Aquitaniæ & Comes Andegaviæ*, not adding *Secundus*. *Henry* II.

Richard not adding *primus* us'd the same sometimes Changing the Declension, and the singular Number into the plural, *viz. Dei Gratia*, *Rex Anglorum*, *Dux Normanorum* *Richard* I.

rum & Aquitaniarum & Comes Andegaviarum.

John

John us'd the same with Addition of *Dominus Hiberniæ.*

Henry III.

Henry stil'd himself like his Father King *John*, till the 44 of his Reign, and then he left out *Normaniæ & Andegaviæ*, and writ only *Dei Gratia, Rex Angliæ, & Dominus Hiberniæ, & Dux Aquitaniæ*, not adding *tertius.*

Edward I. *Edward* II.

Edward the 1*st.* and *Edward* the 2*d.* stil'd themselves like *Henry* the 3*d.*

Edward III.

Edward us'd also the same stile till the 13 of his Reign and then having, and Challenging a Just Title to all *France* he left out the parts of it (before mention'd) and stil'd himself *Dei Gratia Rex Angliæ, Franciæ, & Dominus Hiberniæ*, not adding *Tertius.*

Richard II. *Henry* IV.

Richard and *Henry*, not adding *Secundus* or *Quartus* stil'd themselves like *Edward* the 3*d.* from the 13 of his Reign.

Henry V.

Henry not adding *Quintus* us'd the same stile till the 8*th.* of his Reign, and then writ himself *Dei Gratia Hæres & regens Franciæ & Dominus Hiberniæ.*

Henry VI.

Henry not adding *Sextus* being Crown'd King of *France* in *Paris* wrote *Dei Gratia Rex Angliæ, Franciæ, & Dominus Hiberniæ.*

Edward IV. *Richard* III. *Henry* VII.

Edward, Richard and *Henry* not adding *Quartus,*

Quartus Tertius vel Septimus, stile themselves *Dei Gratia Rex Angliæ Franciæ & Dominus Hiberniæ.*

Henry writ also the same till the 10*th*. of his Reign as I said and then, and not before, he added a Numeral word to his Title and so made it, *Henricus Octavus Dei Gratia Rex Angliæ Franciæ & Dominus Hiberniæ*; Now as to the Additional Titles to *Henry* the 8*th*. after his 10 years they Consisted of so many varieties that I shall refer them to the 7*th*. Chapter of this Treatise Section the 11) As also the Titles of *Ed.* the 6*th*. Q. *Mary*, Q. *Elizabeth*, K. *James*, and K. *Charles* the first. *Henry* VIII.

In which Chapter and Section I conclude with the Title of our present King *Charles* the 2*d*. *viz. Carolus Secundus Dei Gratia, Rex Angliæ, Scotiæ, Franciæ, & Hiberniæ, Fidei Defensor. viz.* as in the *Warrant*.

And so having shown how the ten Names of our Kings from the *Normans* have been dignified by Kings, *Emperours* &c. Especially the Name of *Charles* by its Priority which is the more remarkable, because that by Transposition only of its Letters it doth Anagrammatise and render it

O CLARUS }
CAROLUS } Anagram.

This Anagram may be applyd generally to

to all of that Royal Name, and it may be one reason why so many Kings in *Europe* do at this day own that Name, and possibly another reason of assuming it, may be to amuse the World about *Grebners* Prophecy, *viz.* that *Carolus E stirpe Caroli, Erit Carolo Magno Major*, but none can pretend to a greater interest in that Prophecy, then our present King *Charles* the 2*d.* being so punctually and Signally *ex stirpe Caroli.*

How ever I am sure nothing can be more particularly Prognostical and Applycable to any Regal *Charles* (then this following Anagram) to him being made when he was born Prince of *Wales*, which I have ever since kept safe by me.

CHARLES PRINCE OF WALES.

Anagram.

AL FRAVNCE CRIES O HELP VS.

As to the uses which shall be made on these regal Names, their Progresses and Anagrams (being not the proper Subject of this place) I shall refer them to my Annotations and proceed to Observations on the *Warrant* of another Nature.

THE

THE
INTRODUCTION
Shewing how a
Parliament
CONSISTS,

Section I.

Hen *Families* increaſt into *Villages*, *Towns*, *Cities*, large *Countreys*, *Kingdoms*, and *Empires*, under one *Father* or *Conductor*, (for all other Governments are collateral to *Paternal* and *Monarchical*) there was a neceſſity to Conſtitute a *Supream Council* of the chiefeſt and wiſeſt men ſelected from the multitude, as might keep ſuch extended Dominions in a perfect Unity and Obedience to their Original *Father* or *Monarch*.

The end of this *Conſtitution* was both for Conſervation of the *Original Family* or *Potentate*, who did thus Conſtitute them, or for his own eaſe in managing the common intereſt of *Safety* and *Plenty*.

II. That their proceedings in their *Councils* might have the more ſolemn Effects and *Veneration*, ſeveral Nations in imitation have ſince given diſtinct names to their *Supream Council* erected, as diſtinctions to thoſe which were more *Subordinate*.

Thus the *Jews* (from whom we derive our moſt credible Memoires of Antiquity) had their *Supream Council* called the *Sanhedrim*, conſiſting of ſecular Perſons, *viz.* One *Prince*, (as their chief Head) beſides Seventy others of mixt natures, they had alſo another *great Council* altogether *Eccleſiaſtical*, called a *Synagogue*, and other leſſer, in the nature of our *Convocations*, and ſometimes all did meet at the great *Sanhedrim*, (which was only kept in *Jeruſalem*) and this was the *Supream Council*, as may be ſeen in the *26th. ch.* of *Jeremiah*, *v.* 8. who was condemned by the *Eccleſiaſtical Conſiſtory* of *Prieſts*, and abſolved by the *Temporal* or great *Sanhedrim* of *Princes*, or chief *Council*, as may be more fully ſeen in that Chapter and in the *Jew's* Antiquities.

And to paſs the *Ariopagus* among the *Athenians*, we read that the *Old Romans* alſo had their *Great Council* called a Sea *Senate*, consisting of 300. Laicks chosen out of the *Nobiles Majores & Minores*, and their *Consistoriani*, where their *Senate* did sit: and their *Comites* and *Consistoriani* (as Members thereof) did somewhat resemble the *Constitution* of a Parliament: they had also a *Pontifical Colledge* consisting of *Ecclesiasticks*; but the name of *Senate* at *Rome*, hath been long since drown'd, since the fall of that old *Roman Empire*; for at *Rome* the name of *Senate* is now altered into that of *Consistory*, (and in the vacancy of the *Pope*, or *See* of *new Rome*, it is called a *Conclave*) and now the *Empire* of *Germany* (which did arise from the ashes of the *old Roman Empire*) being shiver'd into several *Proprietors* (lest it should grow again too great) was brought to a *Dyet*, for so the *chief Council* of that *Empire* is called.

Yet the old *State of Venice* still keeps the name of *Senate* for her *great Council*, and the chief *Council* in *France* is called an *Assembly of States*.

III. But here in *England* we have the name of our *chief Council* from *Romans*, *Saxons*, *Normans*, and lastly from the *French*, for it hath been called by those, *Senatus*, *Curia altissima*, *Michel Synoth*,

Assisa Generalis, and many more names, some of which I think fit to render in *English*, viz. *Senate*, the *great Synod* (or meeting of the *King*, and of the *Wise-men*) the *highest Judicatory*, the *General Pleas*, the *Great Court*, the *Common Council* of the Kingdom, and the *General Assize*.

At last, in the time of *Henry* the Third, or *Edward* the Second, all these Names were reduced to the word *Parliament*, which was then borrowed from the Language and Name of the chief *Councils* in *France* (in many of which *Provinces* and *Parliaments* our *Kings* had then a considerable interest.)

IV. I do here mention, that the *Original* of this Name did begin with us in *Henry* the Third, or *Edward* the Second's time, but Sir *Edward Coke*, in his *Institutes*, is pleas'd to cite one Precedent before the *Conquest*: When (saith he) the word *Parliament* was here us'd, but it seems it did not continue a fix'd name of *Parliament* from thence; for at the *great Council*, held by *Henry* the First at *Salisbury*, consisting of the three Estates, *viz. Lords Spiritual*, *Lords Temporal*, and *Commons*, it is called by the Name of *Council*, and not *Parliament*, (as some other Writers have

mistaken,)

mistaken,) However, it was not us'd again; till once in *Henry* the Third's time, as some say; but we are certain, that it was us'd in the 15*th* of *Edward* the Second, (as I shall shew from safe *Records*) and after *Edward* the Third was Crowned *King* of *France*, then, and ever since, this great Council of the whole *Kingdom* hath, without variation, gone by the Name of *Parliament*.

V. And though, as that learned *Institutor* observes, That the *French Parliaments* were lesser *Courts* subject to the Assembly of *Estates*, yet that Assembly of *Estates* was but originally a *grand Parliament*, constituted of those lesser *Estates* or *Parliaments*, and those did anciently consist of *Lords Temporal*, *Commons*, and *Clergy*, (for in that rank they are cited by *Comines*, (an approved Author.) However, since the 15*th* of *Edward* the Second, we have not altered its name, only a little in Orthography (which hath made work for that learned *Institutor* and other grave Writers on this Subject about its *Etymology*) so by Example of those *Worthies*, I may venture to cull out one, (intending to speak of the rest in my Annotations,) *viz.* *Parliament*, i. e. *a Parly of minds*; and to this *Etymology* I may add this definition,

Comines, p. 226.

nition, That *our Parliament consists of a certain number of Men, of certain Degrees and Qualities, Summoned by Writs from the King, to meet together in some place appointed by those Writs, to parly or confer their minds to each other for the good of the Publick.*

VI. This *Definition* will be more fully proved in this following Treatise; yet, before I confirm it at large, I think fit to give a brief and intelligible *Explanation* of it (in relation to a Parliament here in *England.*) To that end I shall first set down the Nature of our *Monarchical Government*, and then we shall more easily underſtand the *Constitution* of our *Parliaments*.

It is generally held, That the frame of this *Monarchy* consists of a *King*, and of *three Estates subordinate to him.*

The *first Estate*, mentioned in all our *Acts* of *Parliament*, is *Spiritual* and *Ecclesiastical*, govern'd by the *Lords Spiritual*; and this *Estate* hath *Jurisdiction* over the whole *Kingdom*, not only considering the effects upon our *Souls*, but in its civil *latitude* and *dimensions*, as having an influence and interest in every individual *Man*, *Woman*, and *Child*, and in most of the Products of the *Earth* from their first *Being* to their

Disso-

Diſſolution; and this in all the fifty two *Counties* of *England* and *Wales*; but for the diſtinction of the *Civil* and *Eccleſiaſtical Juriſdiction*, theſe are compriſed into a leſſer number, *viz.* of twenty ſix, and are call'd *Dioceſſes*, as being given to them from *God* by the hands of the *King*, to whom they acknowledge a *ſubordination*.

The *ſecond Eſtate* (and ſo mention'd in our *Laws*) is the *Lords Temporal*, or rather *Militial*, having the *Lieutenancies* of all the *Counties* of *England* and *Wales* comitted to their Truſt, Care, and Charge; and to theſe belong the managing of *Embaſſies*, *Treaties* of *War* or *Peace*, and all honorary Actions, both *Foreign* and *Domeſtick*, as the *King* (who is the Fountain of *Honour*) does uſually confer upon them.

The *third Eſtate* is the *Commons*, (alſo mentioned in our Laws) and this alſo *ſubordinate* to the *King*; and theſe conſiſt of *Gentry* (Men of fixt and ſetled Fortunes, deſigned for things of *Gallantry* and *Hoſpitality*) and of the *Yeomanry*, compriſed under ſeveral appellations, *viz.* *Husbandmen*, *Artificers*, and *Labourers*, all driving on a *Commutative Commerce*, as well to ſupply themſelves as others with what the *Land* or

Sea affords, either *necessary*, *convenient*, *ornamental*, or *superfluous*.

VII. Besides these three, there are three very great Interests, which are not call'd *Estates*, but *Assistances*, and in truth they are the very *Supporters* of these three *Estates*: *viz.*

The first, *Religion*, the second, *Law*, the third, *Trade*.

1. *Religion* is to be managed by the *Clergy* of several *Degrees* (as will be shewn) some neither *Freeholders*, nor *Freemen*) by their winning of men with a *persuasive* or *exemplary Power*, into all Pious and Virtuous Actions, whereby the Souls and Minds of Men may be united to Love and Obedience; and this is the cement of *Unity* (to the three Estates.)

2. The *Laws* are manag'd by *Lawyers* of several degrees (some neither *Freeholders*, nor *Freemen*) by instructing *Magistrates* in their compulsory Power, when occasion requires, so as both the *Laws* of *God* and *Man* may be duely observed, and that such whom the *Clergy* cannot invite to Piety, and Virtue, by Precept, and Example, may be compelled to it by the *Rigour* of the *Laws*, and this is the cement of *Severity* to the *three Estates*.

3. *Trade*

3. *Trade* is manag'd chiefly by *Merchants*, (ſome alſo neither *Freeholders*, nor *Freemen*) theſe give life to *Induſtry*, whereby the *Rich* do help the *Poor*, and the *Poor* the *Rich*, and thus *Trade*, *Commerce*, and *Induſtry*, are as neceſſary Cements to the Three *Eſtates*, as either *Religion* or *Law* (reſpecting only what morally concerns Juſtice and Obedience) and this is the Cement of *Proſperity* to the whole Fabrick.

So we ſee that as there are Three *Eſſential Eſtates*, ſo there are alſo Three *Eſſential Aſſiſtances* or *Supportations* of thoſe *Eſtates*, and without which thoſe *Eſtates* cannot well ſubſiſt.

Now out of theſe Three *Eſtates* in VII. *general* the *King* doth abſtract a Parliament. For when *He* gives notice of his intentions to have one, he orders *Writs* to *Archbiſhops* and *Biſhops*, who are chiefly to manage the concerns of the *Clergy*.

At the ſame time *He* alſo orders *Writs* to ſuch of the *Nobility* as *He* or *His Predeceſſors* have either by *Patent created* to that employment, or otherwiſe inveſted with ſome right thereunto, who are chiefly to manage the concerns of the *Nobility* and *Kingdom*. At the ſame time *He* alſo orders *Writs* for *Electing* ſuch a number

number of *Commons* out of *Counties*, *Shires*, *Cities*, and *Burroughs*, as may manage the concerns of the *Commonalty*, and yet these *three Estates* thus distinctly *Summoned*, are so admirably intermixt in this *Supream Council* or *Parliament*, that these *three Estates* in that *Council* seem to have an interchangable power and check on each other, in the more Safe and Wise carrying on the Affairs of the whole *Kingdom*, considered either at *Home* or *Abroad*.

IX. And as the Government of the Kingdom hath three sorts of Assistances, (as is before shewn) so those three sorts of Assistances are disposed into three sorts of Assistants. For the *Bishops* have a certain number of *Deans*, *Archdeacons*, and *Proctors*, cull'd out of *Prebends*, *Parsons*, *Vicars*, and the *Clergy* in general, as may be *Assistants* to the Episcopal Interest.

The *Nobility* have a certain number of *Lawyers*, (*viz.* Justices of the Respective *Benches* and Courts of Judicature in *Westminster-Hall*, (as will be shewn) cull'd out of the Profession of *Lawyers*, to be Assistants to them.

The *Commons* have the bulk of every *County* contracted into Two *Knights*, or one, for each County, and of Two *Mer-*

chants

chants for each *City*, and of Two leſſer *Traders* for each *Burrough*, and yet the *Electors* of them are not ſo confined to the Perſons *Eligible*,but that ſuch as they hold fit to manage ſuch *Imployment*, are capable to be *Elected*,though they be not *Knights*, *Merchants*, or *Traders*, yet they are confined to a ſet *number*, (as I ſaid) and of *qualifi'd Perſons*, as well to preſerve the *Honor* of it, as to prevent a *ſurcharge* of too great a concourſe to this Aſſembling of a Parliament.

By this eaſie demonſtration it is evident that the *Lords Spiritual* (conſiſting of *Archbiſhops* and *Biſhops*, (*Succeſſive* but not *Hereditary*) do Sit in the *Lords Houſe*, and there Repreſent the whole *Clergy* of this Kingdom.

The *Lords Temporal* conſiſting of *Dukes*, *Marqueſſes*, *Earls*, *Viſcounts*, and *Barons*, which Five *Degrees* by a *Nobilitated Intereſt*, *Hereditary* and *Succeſſive*, do Sit there alſo, Repreſenting all the *Nobility* of thoſe *Degrees* in the Kingdom.

The *Commons* conſiſting of *Knights*, *Citizens* and *Burgeſſes*, (by an *Elective Intereſt*, neither *Hereditary* nor *Succeſſive*) do Sit in the *Houſe* of *Commons*, Repreſenting all the *Commonalty* of this *Kingdom*. Over

Over which Three Eſtates, the *King* for the time being ever was and ſtill is eſteemed by an *Hereditary* and *Succeſſive* Right, the *Supream*, and in the *Eye* of the *Law*, the *Immortal Balance* of theſe Three *Eſſential* yet *Subordinate Parts*, *Intereſts* or *Eſtates* of this *Kingdom*; I ſay *Immortal*, becauſe our *Laws* do ſay that *Rex nunquam moritur*, and thereby gives him a clear *diſtinction* from the Three Eſtates.

X. Now to undeceive ſome that would have the Three Eſtates to conſiſt of *King*, *Lords*, and *Commons*, becauſe our *Government* ſeems to be framed of *Monarchy*, *Ariſtocracy*, and *Democracy*: To clear their Judgments, the *Monarchy* ſtands *ſingle*, but the *Ariſtocracy* is *double*, *viz.* An *Ariſtocracy* of the *Lords Spiritual*, and an *Ariſtocracy* of the *Lords Temporal*, to which add the *Democracy* of the *Commons*, and all is reconciled into *Two Ariſtocratical Eſtates*, and one *Democratical*, and the *Monarchical* as *Superintendent* to thoſe *Three*, and ſo this *Unity* with the *Triplicity*, is the due *conſtitution* of our *Engliſh Parliament*, and indeed of the *Kingdom* it ſelf.

THE

THE

CONSTITUTION OF PARLIAMENTS.

CHAP. I.

The King's Warrant *to the* Lord Chancellor *for* Summoning *the* Parliament *begun the* 8*th of* May, 1661.

CHARLES *the Second*, *by the* *Grace of God King of* England, Scotland, France, *and* Ireland, *Defender of the Faith*, &c. *To Our right Trusty and well beloved* Counsellor, *Sir* Edward Hide, Knight, Chancellour of England, *Greeting*; *Whereas We by our* Council *for certain great and urgent Causes, concerning Us, the good Estate and Common-wealth of this our* Realm, *and of the* Church *of* England, *and for the good Order and Continuance of the same, have appoint-* CHAP. I.

CHAP. I. *appointed and ordain'd a* Parliament *to be holden at our City of* Westminster *the eighth day of* May *next ensuing; In which Case divers and sundry* Writs *are to be directed forth under our* Great Seal *of* England, *as well for the* Nobility *of this our* Realm, *as also for the* Election *of* Knights, Citizens *and* Burgesses *of the several* Counties, Cities, *and* Burrough Towns *of the same, to be present at the said* Parliament *at the* Day *and* Place *aforesaid. Wherefore* We Will *and* Command *you forthwith upon receipt hereof, and by* Warrant *of the same, to cause such, and so many* Writs *to be* made *and* sealed *under our* great Seal, *for accomplishment of the same, as in* like Cases *have been heretofore used and accustomed. And this* Bill *signed with our Hand shall be as well to* you *as to every* Clerk *or* Clerks *as shall make or pass the same, a* sufficient Warrant *in that behalf.*

Given at Our Palace *at* White-hall *this Eighteenth Day of* February, *in the Twelfth Year of Our* Reign, *and in the Year of our* Lord *One Thousand Six Hundred Sixty and One.*

Obser-

CHAP. I.

Observations and Proceedings on this Warrant.

THe *King* of *England* by his undoubted *Prerogative* hath (and his *Predecessors* ever had) in himself the Power of *Summoning* (as also to appoint the *times* of *beginning*, *continuing*, *discontinuing*, or *dissolving*) of *Parliaments*. I.

This *Summoning* (for I shall speak of the rest in order) or Uniting the chiefest Parts of his *Kingdom* into a *Parliament*, (or *Representation* of the *Kingdom* in a *less Body* than it self) is performed by the *King's Warrant*, in *his Name*, and by *his Authority only*, as *Supreme*, not only of *his Kingdom*, but of its *Representation*; and from this *Warrant* all *Writs* of *Summons* for a *Parliament* are deriv'd. II.

The *Warrant* is in *English*, Sign'd by the *King's* own *Hand*, and Seal'd with his *Privy Seal*, or *Signet*; but the *Writs* are always in *Latin* (or anciently some few in *French*) and are Seal'd with the *King's Great Seal* in his *Name*, with a *Teste* of his Approbation (though not manually Sign'd or Seal'd by him.) III.

The

CHAP. I. The *Warrant* is *General*, *viz.* for *ſummoning* the *Nobility*, as alſo for *Elections* of *Knights*, *Citizens*, and *Burgeſſes*, but the *Writs* deriv'd from thoſe *Warrants* are to *particular perſons*, of *particular degrees* (as will be ſhewn.)

IV.

V. The *Form* of this *Warrant* is ancient, and hath had little or no variation (except in the leaving out of *Abbots* and *Priors*) ever ſince the 36 of *Henry* the 8*th*, and except in leaving out *Prelates* and *Biſhops* in this very *Warrant*, whereby the *Biſhops* had no *particular Writs*, before the ſitting of this *Parliament*, but within three Months after, for which *Omiſſion* Reaſons will be given in the 7*th* Chapter.

VI. Before this *Warrant* was iſſued, the *King* (and ſo *former Kings*) did adviſe with their *Privy Council* (which is maniſeſted by the Words of the *Warrant*, *viz. Whereas We, by our* Council) yet if theſe words had been omitted at any time, and not inſerted in the *Warrant*, the *Warrant* was held good and ſufficient for due *Summons*.

VII. However, (for publick ſatisfaction) the words of every *Writ* are always (*Quia de advizamento & aſſenſu Concilij noſtri*) and this *Council* is call'd the *King's Privy*, or *Private Council*, (of which

which I ſhall ſpeak more) and is the *King's* conſtant or ſtanding *Council*, as well in time of *Parliament* as when there is none ſitting: ſo as before this *Magnum Concilium*, or *Parliament*, is ſummon'd, this *Privy Council conſults* and *deliberates* concerning the Motives and *Reaſons* for calling it, and after ſuch *deliberations* and *reſults*, doth adviſe the King to ſend out a *Warrant*. CHAP. I.

And therefore I conceive it uſeful to ſet down the Names of ſuch as were of the *King's Privy Council*, when the calling of this *Parliament* was adviſ'd and reſolv'd upon.

At the Court *of* White-hall, *Feb.* $166\frac{0}{1}$.

The KING Preſent.

His *Royal Highneſs* the *Duke* of *York*.
His *Highneſs Prince Rupert*.
William, Lord Arch-Biſhop of *Canterbury*, (*Juxon.*)
Edward, Earl of *Clarendon*, Lord Chancellor of *England*, (*Hide*)
Thomas, Earl of *Southampton*, Lord Treaſurer of *England*, (*Wriotheſley.*)
John, Lord *Roberts*, Lord Privy-Seal, (Baron of *Truro.*)

C *John*,

CHAP. I.

John, Duke of *Latherdale*, (*Maitland*,) Earl of *Guilford*.

James, Duke of *Ormond*, Lord Steward of the King's Houſe, (*Butler*.)

George, Duke of *Albemarle*, (*Monk*.)

Henry, Marqueſs of *Dorcheſter*, (*Pierpoint*.)

Montague, Earl of *Lindſey*, Lord great Camberlain, (*Bertie*.)

Edward, Earl of *Mancheſter*, the King's Chamberlain, (*Montague*.)

Aldjernoone, Earl of *Northumberland*, (*Piercy*.)

Robert, Earl of *Leiceſter*, (*Sydny*.)

Charles, Earl of *Berkſhire*, (*Howard*.)

Thomas, Earl of *Cleveland*, (*Wentworth*.)

George, Earl of *Norwich*, (*Goring*.)

Henry, Earl of St. *Albans*, (*Jermin*.)

Edward, Earl of *Sandwich*, (*Montague*.)

Arthur, Earl of *Angleſey*, (*Anneſly*.)

Charles, Earl of *Carlile*, (*Howard*.)

William, Viſcount *Say* and *Seal*, (*Fiennes*.)

Francis, Lord *Seymour*, (Baron of *Troubridge*.)

Frederick, Lord *Cornwallis*, (Baron of *Ai*.)

Anthony, Lord *Aſhley*, (*Cooper*.)

Charles Berkley, Knight and Baronet.

Sir *George Carteret*, Knight, Vice-Chamberlain.

Sir *Edw. Nicholas*, } Knights, { Secretaries
Sir *Will. Morrice*, } { of State.

After

After the *Warrant* is *sign'd* and *seal'd* by the *King*, it is sent from the *Signet-Office* to the *Lord Chancellor*, or *Lord Keeper*, and Directions are given to the *Heralds*, to make *Proclamation* (at the *Court-gate*, and Capital City of *London*,) of the King's Resolutions (of which I shall speak more in the Chapter of Proclamations.) CHAP. I.

The *Lord Chancellor*, &c. upon the receipt of this *Warrant*, doth issue out his *Warrant* also to the *Master* of the *Rolls*, as the chief Clerk of the *Pettibag-Office*, in this Form:

YOu *are hereby requir'd forthwith to prepare for the* great Seal *of* England *the several* Writs *of* Summons *for the* Lords Temporal; *As also for the* Judges *and others to appear at the* Parliament, *to be holden the 8th of* May *next, together with the several* Writs *of* Election *of the several* Knights, Citizens, *and* Burgesses *of the several* Counties, Cities, Towns, *and* Burroughs *within the* Kingdom *of* England, Dominion *of* Wales, *and* Town of Berwick *upon* Tweed, *as also of the several* Barons *of the* Cinque-Ports *to serve in the said* Parliament, *in such* Method *and* Form, *and* directed *to such* persons *as are and have*

CHAP. I. *been* uſual *in ſuch Caſes, all which ſaid* Writs *are to bear* date *this preſent* eighteenth *of* February, 1661. *and for the ſo doing, this ſhall be your* Warrant.

Dated, *&c.*

Upon receipt of the *Lord Chancellor's Warrant*, the Clerks of the *Pettibag*, by the aſſiſtance of the former *Precedents* of *Writs* (and anciently by help of the *Maſters* of *Chancery*) and by advice with the *Heralds* (as to Titles and true Names of Perſons) do fix a *Schedule*, or *digeſt*, or *Forms of Writs* to be iſſued.

Which *Schedule*, or *digeſt*, they keep fairly ingroſt in Parchment, as a *Record* in this *Office*, and this *Record* is then entituled the *Parliament Pawn*, and hath no other Name, which is, as they ſay, the *awarding* of *ſeveral Writs* for a *Parliament*. And this *methodical Record* is very ancient, (as may be collected, by comparing this with thoſe which remain in the *Pettibag*.) And with the like Endorſments are the *Clauſe Rolls* in the *Tower*; but there are no more *Pawns* at preſent in this *Office*, than from the 21 of *Hen.* 8. to this of the 31 of *Car.* 2. making twenty in all.

Formerly theſe *Pawns*, (or *Records*) ſome time after the *diſſolution* of every *Parlia-*

Parliament (as will be ſhewn) were carried to the *Inrolment Office*, and then among many other *Parliamentary Matters* (of weighty concern) tranſcrib'd into *Parchment Rolls*, and from thence (for more ſafety) carried to the *Tower* of *London*, where they loſt the name of *Pawns*, and were and are ſtill call'd *Parliament Clauſe* (*or Cloſe*) *Rolls*: which I mention becauſe I ſhall have often occaſion in this Treatiſe to recite ſuch *Clauſe-Rolls*, wherein the *Pawns* were for the moſt part inſerted or endors'd. And in reſpect I do not find that any who have writ before me of *Parliaments*, have taken notice of *thoſe Parliament Pawns*, (although they are *Recorded* and kept in the *Pettibag*, an ancient *Office of Record*) I have cull'd out one of the twenty, and made it the foundation of the whole Scheme of this Treatiſe. CHAP. I.

That there are no more *Parliament Pawns* in the *Pettibag*, than (as I ſaid) from the 21. of *Hen.* the 8*th.* to the 13. *Car.* 2*d.* this reaſon may be given, that when they were again Enroll'd and tranſmitted to the *Tower*, or *Rolls Chappel*, it might be thought needleſs to preſerve them, in reſpect that from *Ed.* the 2.*d.* to *Ed.* the 4.*th. Incluſive*, they are ſafely kept inroll'd among the *Records* in the *Tower*, and from *Ed.* the 4*th.* to the 21 of *Hen.*

 the

CHAP. I. the 8. *Excluſive*, they are kept ſafe amongſt the *Records* in the *Rolls Chappel*, and from the 21 of *Hen.* the 8*th.* to the 13 *Car.* 2*d.* they are preſerved amongſt the *Records* in the *Pettibag Office*, and of theſe which remain in the *Pettibag*, that of the 31 of *Hen.* the 8*th.* is much defaced and interlin'd, but that of the 21 and all the reſt from the 36 *Hen.* 8. are farely ingroſt and Legible, and Tyed up in one great *Bundle*, the laſt of which made up for this *Parliament* of 13 *Car.* 2*d.* is here *Verbatim* Tranſcribed. In which, for want of Application to the *Herraulds*, the *Clerks* have Committed many miſtakes (I ſuppoſe (by long diſcontinuance of Methodical *Parliaments*) not being well inſtructed *viz.* In the Titles of the Lord *Stourton*, Lord *Vaux*, Lord *Wharton*, Lord *Pagit*, Lord *Shandois*, Lord *Stanhop*, Lord *Charles Howard*, Ld. *Roberts*, Ld. *John Pawlet*, Ld. *Coventry*, Ld. *Frances Seymour*, Ld. *Bruce*, Ld. *Newport*, Ld. *Colpeper*, Ld. *Gerrard*, Ld. *Langdale*, Ld. *Hollis*, Ld. *Cornwallis*, Ld. *Delamare*, Ld. *Townſend*, Ld. *Aſhly*, Ld. *Crew*, and ſome others which ſhall be rectified in the 4*th.* part of this *Treatiſe.* However I thought fit to follow the *Record Verbatim* (except in the Marginal Figures and Notes which I have added, with Recommendation of Care for the future.

viz.

viz. the 13. *Car. 2d.* is here *verbatim* transcrib'd. CHAP. II.

CHAP. II.

The Copy of the Parliament Pawn *of the* 13. Car. *2d.*

Anno tertiodecimo Caroli secundi Regis.

CAROLUS secundus Dei gratia Angliæ, Scotiæ, Franciæ, & Hiberniæ Rex, Fidei Defensor, *&c.* Præcharissimo & dilecto Fratri suo Jacobo Duci Ebor'um & Albaniæ magno Admirallo suo Angliæ Salutem. Quia de Advisamento & Assensu Concilii nostri pro quibusdam arduis & urgentibus negotiis nos statum & defensionem Regni nostri Angliæ & Ecclesiæ Anglicanæ concernent' quoddam Parliamentum nostrum apud Civitatem nostram Westm' octavo die Maii prox' futur' teneri ordinavimus & ibidem vobiscum ac cum Magnatibus & Proceribus dicti Regni nostri Colloquium habere & tractatum. Vobis sub fide & Ligeantia quibus nobis tenemini firmiter injungen'd mandamus quod consideratis dictorum Negociorum arduitate & periculis imminentibus ces- I.

CHAP. II. ſante excuſatione quacunq; dictis die & loco perſonaliter interſitis nobiſcum ac cum Magnatibus & Proceribus prædictis, ſuper dictis Negociis tractatur' veſtrumq' Conſilium impenſur' & hoc ſicut nos & honorem noſtrum ac Salvationem & defenſionem Regni & Eccleſiæ prædict' expeditionemq; dictorum negotiorum

Teſte Rege. diligitis nullatenus omittatis T. R. apud Weſtm' decimo octavo die Februarii Anno Regni ſui tertio decimo.

Conſimile. CONSIMILE Breve dirigitur Præcharisſimo Conſanguineo ſuo Ruperto Duci Cumbriæ T. ut ſupra.

II. REX, &c. Archiepiſcopo *Cant'* &c. Conſimilia Archi' Ebor' & Epiſcop'.

III. REX *prædilecto & perquam fideli* Conſiliario ſuo Edro' Dno' Hyde Cancellar ſuo Angliæ ſalutem Quia, &c. Ut ſupra uſq' tractatum & tunc ſic vobis mandamus firmiter injungen'd quod omnibus al' pretermiſſis prædict die & loco perſonaliter interſitis nobiſcum ac cum cæteris de Concilio noſtro ſuper dictis negotiis tractatur' veſtrumq' conſilium impenſur' & hoc nullatenus omittatis T. ut ſupra.

REX

REX *Præcharissimo consanguineo suo* Thomæ Comiti South'ton Thesaurario Angliæ Salt'm Quia, &c. ut supra usq; tractatum & tunc sic Vobis sub fide & Ligeancia quibus nobis tenemini, &c. ut supra. T. ut supra. CAP. II. IV.

CONSIMILIA Brevia diriguntur Personis subscript' sub eodem dat' Videlt' Præcharissimo Consanguineo suo. *Consimilia.*

GEorgio Duci Bucks.
Carolo Duci Richmond.
Georgio Duci Albermarl Exercituum suorum Generali. *Dukes &c.*

JOhanni Marchioni Winton'.
Edro' Marchioni Wigorn'.
Will'o Marchioni Novi Castri.
Henr' Marchioni Dorcestr'. *Marquesses Four.*

CHarissimo Consanguineo suo Montague Comiti Lindsey magno Camerario suo Angliæ. *Earls Fiftyfive.*
Jacobo Comiti Brecon' Senescallo Hospitii.
Edro' Comiti Manchester Camerario Hospitii.
Alberico Comiti Oxon'.
Algernon' Comiti Northumbr'.
Francisco Comiti Salop.

Ca-

CHAP. II.

Carolo Comiti Derb'.
Johanni Comiti Rotel'.
Will'o Comiti Bedford'.
Philippo Comiti Pembr' & Montgomeri.
Theophilo Comiti Lincoln'.
Carolo Comiti Nott'.
Jacobo Comiti Suff'.
Ric'o Comiti Dors'.
Will'o Comiti Sarum.
Joh'i Comiti Exon'.
Joh'i Comiti Bridgewater.
Rob'to Comiti Leic'.
Jacobo Comiti North'ton.
Carolo Comiti Warr'.
Will'o Comiti Devon'.
Baſil' Comiti Denbigh'.
Georgio Comiti Briſtol'.
Lionell' Comiti Midd'.
Henrico Comiti Holland.
Joh'i Comiti Clare.
Olivero Comiti Bullingbrooke.
Mildmay Comiti Weſtmerland.
Thomæ Comiti Berks.
Thomæ Comiti Cleveland.
Edr'o Comiti Mulgrave.
Henr' Comiti Monmouth.
Jacobo Comiti Marlborough
Thomæ Comiti Rivers.
Henrico Comiti Dover.
Henrico Comiti Stamford.

Henr'

Henr' Comiti Peterborough.
Henr' Comiti Winchelsea.
Carolo Comiti Carnarvan.
Mountjoy Comiti Newport.
Philippo Comiti Chesterfield.
Joh'i Comiti Thanett.
Jeronimo Comiti Portland.
Will'o Comiti Strafford.
Rob'to Comiti Sunderland.
Georgio Comiti Norwic'.
Nich'o Comiti Scarsdale.
Henrico Comiti sc'ti Albani.
Edr'o Comiti Sandwici.
Edr'o Comiti Clarendon Canc' Angliæ T. vicesimo nono Aprilis Anno prædicto.
Arthuro Comiti Essex.
Thomæ Comiti Cardigan.
Arthuro Comiti Anglesey.
Joh'i Comiti Bathon'.
Carolo Comiti Carliol' T. vicesimo nono Aprilis Anno prædicto.

Viscounts Eight.

Leicestr' Vicecomiti Hereford.
Francisco Vicecomiti Montague.
Will'o Vicecomiti Say & Seale.
Edr'o Vicecomiti Conway.
Baptist' Vicecomiti Campden.
Will'o Vicecomiti Stafford.
Thomæ Vicecomiti Falconberg'.
Joh'i Vicecomiti Mordant.

Præ-

CHAP. II.

Barons Chevaliers Sixty eight.

PRædilecto & fideli ſuo Joh'i Nevile de Aburgavenny Chr'.
Jacobo Tutchell de Awdley Chr'.
Carolo Weſt de la Warr Chr'.
Georgio Berkley de Berkley Chr'.
Thomæ Parker de Morley & Mont-egle Chr'.
Franciſco Dacres Chr'.
Conyers Darcy de Darcy Chr'.
Will'o Stourton de Stourton Chr'.
Will'o Sandys de la Vyne Chr'.
Edr'o Vaux de Harrowdon Chr'.
Thomæ Windſor Chr'.
Thomæ Wentworth Chr'.
Wingfeild Cromwell Chr'.
Georgio Eure Chr'.
Phil' Wharton de Wharton Chr'.
Franciſco Willoughby de Parham Chr'.
Will'o Pagit de Beau deſert Chr'.
Dudlee North Chr'.
Will'o Shandos de Shudely Chr'.
Joh'i Cary de Hunſdon Chr'.
Will'o Petre Chr'.
Dutton Gerrard de Gerrard Bromley Chr'.
Carolo Stanhope de Harrington Chr'.
Henr' Arundell de Wardour Chr'.
Chriſtophero Roper de Tenham Chr'.
Rob'to Brooke Chr'.
Edr'o Mountague de Boughton Chr'.

Carolo

Carolo Howard de Charlton Chr'. CHAP II.
Will'o Grey de Wark Chr'.
Joh'i Roberts de Truro Chr'.
Will'o Craven Chr'.
Joh'i Lovelace Chr'.
Joh'i Pawlet de Hinton St. George Chr'.
Will'o Maynard Chr'.
Thomæ Coventry de Alesborough Chr'.
Edr'o Howard de Eſcrick Chr'.
Warwic' Mohun Chr'.
Percy Herbert de Powis Chr'.
Edr'o Herbert de Cherbury Chr'.
Fran'co Seymour de Trowbridge C. D. Lanc' Chr'.
Thomæ Bruce de Wharlton Chr'.
Fran'co Newport de Higharcall Chr'.
Thomæ Leigh Chr'.
Chriſtophero Hatton Chr'.
Henr' Haſting de Loughborough Chr'.
Ri'co Byron Chr'.
Ri'co Vaughan Chr'.
Carolo Smith de Carrington Chr'.
Will'o Widdrington Chr'.
Humble Ward Chr'.
Thomæ Culpepper de Thoreſway Chr'.
Iſaaco Aſtley Chr'.
Ri'do Boyle de Clifford Chr'.
Joh'i Lucas Chr'.
Joh'i Bellaſis Chr'.
Lodovico Watſon de Rockingham Chr'.

CHAP. II. Carolo Gerrard de Brandon Chr'.
Rob'to Sutton de Lexington Chr'.
Carolo Kirkhoven de Wotton Chr'.
Marmaduco Langdale de Holme Chr',
Will'o Crafts Chr'.
Joh'i Berkley Chr'.
Denzil Hollis de Ifeild Chr'.
Frederic' Cornwallis de Eye Chr'.
Georgio Delamere de Dunham Massey Chr'.
Horratio Townesend de Lynn Regis Chr'.
29 April, 1661. Antonio Ashley Cooper de Winborne Sancti Egidij Chr'.
Johanni Crew de Stene Chr'.

V. REX Dilecto & fideli suo Rob'to Foster mil' Capitali Justic' nostro ad pl'ita coram nobis tenend' assign' salt'm Quia de Advisamento & assensu Consilij nostri pro quibusdam arduis & urgentibus negocijs Nos statum & defensionem Regni nostri Angliæ & Ecclesiæ Anglicanæ concernen' quoddam Parliamentum nostrum apud Civitatem nostram Westm' octavo die Maij prox' futur' teneri ordinavimus & ib'm vobiscum ac cum Magnatibus & Proceribus dicti Regni nostri colloquium habere & tractatum Vobis mandamus firmiter injungend' quod omnibus alijs pretermissis prædictis die & loco personalit' intersitis nobiscum

nobiſcum ac cum cæteris de Concilio noſtro ſuper dictis negocijs tractatur' veſtrumq; conſilium impenſur' Et hoc nullatenus omittatis Teſte Rege apud Weſtm' decimo octavo die Februarij Anno prædicto. CHAP II.

CONSIMILIA Brevia diriguntur perſonis ſubſcript' ſub eodem dat' Videlt'.

HArbottel Grimſton Baronet' Mag'ro Rotulorum Cancellar' ſuæ.

Orlando Bridgeman Mil' Capitali Juſtic' de Banco ſuo.

Mattheo Hale Capital' Baron' de ſcc'io ſuo.

Thomæ Mallett Mil' un' Juſtic' ſuorum ad pl'ita coram ipſo Rege, *&c.*

Thomæ Twiſden Mil' al' Juſtic' ſuorum ad pl'ita coram ipſo Rege, *&c.*

Wadham Windham Mil' al' Juſtic' ſuorum ad pl'ita coram ipſo Rege, *&c.*

Rob'to Hyde Mil' un' Juſtic' ſuorum de Banco.

Thomæ Terryl Mil' un' Juſtic' ſuorum de Banco.

Samueli Browne Mil' al' Juſtic' ſuorum de Banco.

Edr'o Atkins Militi.

Chriſtophero Turner Mil' Baronibus de ſcc'io.

Gal-

CHAP. II. Galfrido Palmer Mil' Attorn' ſuo Generali.

Johanni Glynn Militi.

Johanni Maynard Militi Servien' d'ni Regis ad legem.

Edr'o Nicholas Militi un' Principal' Secretar'.

VI. I. CAROLUS ſecundus Dei gratia Angliæ Scotiæ Franciæ & Hiberniæ Rex fidei defenſor, *&c.* Vic' Cornub' ſalutem Quia de Adviſamento & aſſenſu Concilij noſtri pro quibuſdam arduis & urgentibus negocijs Nos ſtatum & Defenſionem Regni noſtri Angliæ & Eccleſiæ Anglicanæ concernen' quoddam Parliamentum noſtrum apud Civitatem noſtram Weſtm' octavo die Maij prox' futur' teneri ordinavimus & ibidem cum Magnatibus & Proceribus dc'i Regni n'ri colloquium habere & tractatum. Tibi præcipimus firmit' injungend' quod facta Proclamatione in prox' Com' tuo poſt reception' hujus Brevis noſtri tenend' de die & loco prædict' duos Milites Gladijs cinctos magis idoneos & diſcretos Com' prædict' de qualibet Civitate Com' illius duos Cives & de quolibet Burgo duos Burgenſes de diſcretioribus & magis ſufficien' libere & indifferenter ſuper illos qui Proclamatione hu'mo'i interfuerunt juxta for-

formam ſtatutorum inde edit' & provis' Et nomina eorundem Militum Civium & Burgens' ſic eligend' in quibuſdam Indentur' inter te & illos qui hu'modi Electioni interfuerint inde conficiend' licet hu'modi eligend' preſentes fuerint vel abſentes inſeri eoſq; ad dictos diem & locum venire fac' Ita quod iidem Milites plenam & ſufficien' poteſtat' pro ſe & Communitate Com' illius ac dicti Cives & Burgens' pro ſe & Comitat' Civitat' & Burgorum prædict' diviſim ab ipſis habeant ad faciend' & conſentiend' hiis quæ tunc ib'm de Communi Concilio dicti Regni noſtri favente Domino contigerint ordinari ſuper negocijs antedictis Ita quod pro defectu poteſtat' hu'modi ſeu propter improvidam Electionem Militum Civium aut Burgen' præditorum dicta negocia infecta non remaneant quoviſmodo' Nolumus autem quod tu nec aliquis al' Vic' dicti Regni noſtri aliqualit' ſit electus & Electionem illam in pleno Com' tuo factam diſtincte & aperte ſub ſigillo tuo & ſigillis eorum qui Electioni interfuerint nobis in Cancellariam noſtram ad dictos diem & locum certifices indilate remitten' nobis alteram partem Indentur' prædict' præſentibus conſut' unacum hoc brevi T. R. apud Weſtm' decimo octavo die Februarii Anno Supradicto.

CHAP II.

CHAP. II.

Conſimilia Brevia diriguntur Vicecomitibus ſeparat' Com' ſequen' ſub dat' prædict' Videlt'.

Kant'.
Midd'.
Surr'.
Suſſex.
Southt'.
Lincon'.
Staff'.
Suff'.
Derb'.
Norff'.
Nott'.
Salop.
Northumbr'.

Weſtmerl'.
Eborum.
Wigorn'.
Eſſex.
Heref'.
Devon.
Hertf'.
Wilts.
Northt'.
Somers'.
Glouc'.
Leic'.
Dors'.

Warr'.
Rotes'.
Bucks.
Cumbr.
Berks.
Bedd'.
Hunt'.
Monmouth de duobus Militibus & uno Burgens, in Burgo de Monmouth.

REX *Vic'* Cantabr' Salutem Quia *&c.* ut ſupra uſq; tractatum & tunc ſic Tibi præcipimus firmiter injungend' quod facta Proclamatione in prox' Com' tuo poſt receptionem hujus brevis noſtri tenend' de die & loco prædictis duos Milites Gladiis cinctos magis idoneos & diſcretos Com' prædicti ac de UniverſitateCantabr' duosBurgenſes & de qual't Civitate Com' illius duos Cives & de quol't Burgo duos Burgenſes de diſcretioribus & Magis ſufficien' libere & indifferent

different' per illos qui Proclamationi hu'modi interfuerint juxta formam Statutorum inde edit' & provi' eligi & nomina eorundem Militum Civium & Burgens' prædictorum sic eligend' in quibusdam Indentur' inter te & illos qui hu'modi Electioni interfuerint inde conficien'd licet hu'modi eligend' presentes fuerint vel absentes inseri eosq; ad dictos diem & locum venire fac' Ita quod iidem Milites plenam & sufficien' potestatem pro se & Coi'tate Com' illius ac dicti Cives & Burgens' pro se & Comitat' Universitat' Civitat' & Burgorum prædict' divisim ab ipsis habeant ad faciend' & consentiend' hiis quæ tunc ib'm de Comun' Concilio dicti Regni nostri favente Domino Contigerint ordinari super negociis antedictis. Ita quod pro defectu potestat' hu'modi seu propter improvidam Electionem Militum Civium aut Burgens' prædict' dicta negocia infecta non remaneant quovismodo. Nolumus autem quod tu nec aliquis alius Vic' dicti Regni nostri aliqualit' sit electus & Electionem illam in pleno Com' tuo factam distincte & aperte sub sigillo tuo & sigillis eorum qui electioni illi interfuerint nobis in Cancellar' nostram ad dictos diem & locum certifices indilate remitten' nobis alteram partem Indentur'

CHAP. I.

CHAP. II. prædict' preſentibus conſut' unacum hoc brevi Teſte ut ſupra.

Conſimile Breve dirigitur Vic' Oxon' ſub dat' prædict.

VIII. III. REX Vicecomitibus London Salutem Quia *&c.* ut ſupra uſq; tractatum & tunc Vobis præcipimus firmiter injungentes quod facta proclamatione in prox' Huſtengo noſtro poſt receptionem hujus Brevis noſtri tenend' de die & loco prædict' quatuor Cives de diſcretioribus & magis ſufficien' Civitat' prædict' libere & indifferent' per illos qui proclamationi hu'modi interfuerint juxta formam Statutorum inde edit' & provis' eligi & nomina eorundem Civium ſic eligend' in quibuſdam Indentur' inter vos & illos qui hu'modi Electioni interfuerint inde conficiend' licet hu'modi eligend' preſentes fuerint vel abſentes inſeri eoſq; ad dictos diem & locum venire fac' Ita quod prædict' Cives plenam & ſufficien' poteſtat' pro ſe & Co'itate Civitatis prædict' diviſim ab ipſis habeant, *&c.* ut ſupra mutatis mutandis, *&c.* & in qual't Civitate ſequen' facta proclamatione infra Com' Civitat' prædict, *&c.* ut ſupra & in Villis ſequen' infra Com' Villæ prædict, *&c.* T. ut ſupra.

Consimilia Brevia diriguntur Vicecomitibus seperal' Civitat' & Vill' sequen' sub eodem dat' Videlt'. CHAP. II.

Vicecomitibus Civitatis suæ.	Eborum Norwici Lincoln' Coventr' Glouc'	de duobus Civibus eligend'.

Vicecomitibus Civitatis suæ Bristol, Vic' Civitat' suæ Cantuar' Vic' Civitat' suæ Exon' Vic' Civitat' suæ Lich' Vic' Civitat' suæ Wigorn'	de duobus Civibus eligend'.

Vicecomitibus Villæ suæ Nott' Vic' Villæ de Kingston super Hull Vic' Villæ suæ Southt' Vic' Villæ suæ Novi Castri super Tinam Vic' Villæ suæ de Poole	de duobus Burgens' eligend'.

Vicecomitibus Villæ suæ Haverford-west Vic' suæ Carmarthen'	de uno Burgens' eligend'.

 Majori

CHAP. II. Majori & Ballivis Villæ Berwici ſuper Twedam } de duobus Burgens' eligend'.

IX. 4. REX Conſtabular' Caſtri ſui Dover ac Cuſtod' Quinq; Portuum vel ejus locum tenenti ib'm Sal'tem, Quia, *&c.* uſq; tractatum Et tunc Vobis in fide & Ligeancia quibus nobis tenemini firmit' injungend' mandamus Quod in quolibet Portu Portuum prædict' duos Barones de Melioribus & diſcretoribus eligi & eos ad dictos diem & locum venire fac' Ita quod dicti Barones plenam & ſufficien' poteſtatem pro ſe & Co'itate Port' ſuorum habeant ad conſentiend' hijs quæ tunc ib'm communi de Concilio dicti Regni noſtri Angliæ favente Domino contigerint ordinari ſuper negotijs antedictis Ita quod pro defectu poteſtatis hu'modi ſeu propter improvidam Election' Baronum prædict' dicta negotia infecta non remaneant quoviſmodo Et habeatis ibi nomina prædict' Baronum & hoc breve T. ut ſupra.

X. 5. REX Cancellar' ſuo in Com' Palatino Lancaſtr' vel ejus locum tenenti ib'm ſal'tem Quia, *&c.* ut ſupra uſq; tractatum Et tunc ſic Vobis mandamus

mus firmiter injungentes quod per breve nostrum sub sigillo nostro Com' prædict' detis in mandatis Vic' nostro ejusdem Com' quod idem Vic' facta proclamatione in prox' Com' suo post receptionem dicti brevis nostri &c. in quibusdam Indentur' int' ipsum Vic' & illos &c. Nolumus autem quod idem Vic' &c. Et Electionem illam in pleno Com' prædict' sic factam distincte aperte sub sigillo Com' prædict' & sigillis eorum qui electioni illi interfuerint nobis in Cancellar' nostram Angliæ ad dictos diem & locum certificetis indilate remitten' nobis &c. ut supra. Cap. II

REX Camerario suo Com' Palatini sui Cestriæ vel ejus locum tenenti ib'm salutem Quia, &c. usq; tractatum Vobis mandamus firmiter injungend' quod per seperalia brevia nostra sub sigillo nostro Com' prædict' debite conficiend' detis in mandatis tam Vic' nostro ejusdem Com' Cestr' quam Vic' nostris Civitat' Cestr' quod facta proclamatione in prox' Com' suis post receptionem eorundem brevium nostrorum tenend' de die & loco præd' dictus Vic' dc'i Com' Cestr' duos Milites gladio cinctos magis idoneos & discretos Com' præd' & præd' Vic' dc'æ Civit' Cestr' duos Cives dc'æ XI. 6.

CHAP. II. Civit' de diſcretioribus, *&c.* Et nomina eorundem Milit' ſic eligend' in quibuſdam Indentur' int' ipſum Vic' Civitat' & illos qui hujuſmo'i Electioni interfuerint Ac nomina præd' Civium ſic eligend' in quibuſdam Indentur' int' ipſos Vic' Civitat' & illos qui, *&c.* Nolumus autem quod idem Vic' dc'i Com' Ceſtr' nec præd' Vic' Civitat' præd' nec aliquis, *&c.* Et Electiones illas in plenis Com' & Civitat' præd' ſic fact' diſtincte & aperte ſub ſigillo Com' Palatini præd' & ſigillis eorum qui Electionibus illis interfuerint nobis in Cancellariam noſtram Angliæ ad dictos diem & locum certifices indilate remitten' nobis alteras partes ſeperal' Indentur' præd' preſentibus conſut' unacum hoc brevi T. ut ſupra.

XII. REX Vic' Carnarvon ſalutem Quia,
&c. uſq; tractatum Tibi præcipimus
7. firmiter injungend' quod facta proclamatione in prox' Com' tuo poſt receptionem hujus brevis noſtri tenend' de die & loco prædictis unum Militem Gladio cinctum magis idoneum & diſcretum Com' prædict' & de quolibet Burgo vocat' le *ſhire Town* ejuſdem Com' unum Burgenſem de diſcretioribus, *&c.* ut ſupra in Com' Cornub' mutatis mutandis T. ut ſupra.

Conſimilia

Consimilia Brevia diriguntur Viceco- mitibus seperal' Com' sequen' sub dat' præd' videlt', CHAP II.

Radnor.	*Glamorgan.*	*Anglesey* de
Brecon.	*Pembroke.*	uno Milite
Carmarthen.	*Flint.*	tantum eli-
Mountgomery	*Merioneth.*	gend'.
Cardigan.	*Denbigh.*	

SECT. II.

Observations on this Pawn.

THis is the full Transcript of the *Pawn* or Record of the Writs which were issued for the Summoning this Parliament; and that my Method in managing of them may be the clearer understood, I shall set down some Observations pursuant to it. *Obs.*

I. In the Original of this *Pawn*, or Record, there are no Figures placed in the Margents of the respective Paragraphs of it (but I have thought fit, in respect of the several occasions referring to it, to add the Figures of I. II. III. IV. V. (being Paragraphs particularly relating to the *House of Lords*;) and then the Figures of VI. VII. VIII. IX. X. XI. XII. being

CHAP. II. being Paragraphs particularly relating to the *Houſe of Commons*,) for of all theſe I ſhall ſpeak diſtinctly in this, and the Second Part of this Treatiſe.

II. All the Exemplar Writs are dated the 18th of *Feb.* 13 *Car.* 2. but there being ſeveral Creations of Lords (or at leaſt their Patents not perfect) after the 18th, all the ſubſequent Writs for ſuch Lords were dated the 29th of *April* following, and that is the reaſon of the different Dates of Writs in the *Pawn*, but all were before the Parliament ſat.

III. The firſt Exemplars in this *Pawn* for the *Lords Houſe* do begin with the words, CAROLUS *Secundus Dei Gratia Angliæ Scotiæ Franciæ & Hiberniæ Rex Fidei Defenſor.* And ſo the firſt Exemplar in the *Houſe of Commons*, Fig. 6. begins in the like words; yet all the other Exemplars in the *Pawn* do begin only with the word *Rex*, omitting the other words, which muſt be underſtood that the ſingle word *Rex*, *&c.* is ſo entred only for brevity, not that the Form of the other Examplar or Conſimilar Writs are ſo conciſe, either in the preamble or body of the Writs (for the ſame reaſon.)

IV. In reſpect I do make uſe of the words Exemplar Writs, and Conſimilar Writs, it it is fit I ſhould ſpeak of the Nature of Writs in general. CHAP II.

The Common and Civil Law calls a Writ in *Latin*, *Breve*, *quia brevibus & paucis verbis intentionem Legis exponit.* And of theſe in the Common Law ſome are call'd Original, and others Judicial; the Original (if I do not miſcount them, from the Regiſter of Writs) are 727 in Number: and theſe are us'd in the reſpective Courts in *Weſtminſter* before any appearance had, or other Proceſs iſſued in all matters both real and perſonal, and are always in the King's Name, atteſted by the Chief Juſtice of the Court from whence they iſſue; the other, call'd Judicial Writs,) if I miſcount not the number of them from the ſame Regiſter) are 371, which are ſent out by order of thoſe Courts where the original Writ is recorded, and the Caſe depending; and theſe latter do alſo iſſue in the King's Name, and atteſted by the chief Juſtice of the reſpective Courts from whence they proceed,and ſeal'd with green Wax, with the Seals of the reſpective Courts.

But the Parliament Writs (of which I am to treat) are of another nature and quality, iſſued only by the King's immediate Command and Warrant, and ſeal'd with the great Seal of *England*; and theſe

CHAP. II. theſe have two appellations, *viz. Brevia Clauſa*, (or *operta*,) and *Brevia Patentia*, (or *Aperta*.)

The *Brevia Clauſa* are Writs of Summons clos'd up in yellow Wax, and ſo ſeal'd with the great Seal of *England*, and then (as will be more fully ſhewn, after I have diſcours'd diſtinctly of the Writs) ſent (with *Labells*) to every individual Prince of the Blood, Lords Spiritual, Lords Temporal, and Aſſiſtants, and to every Sheriff of the Kingdom, for Elections of Knights, Citizens, and Burgeſſes for the *Commons Houſe*; and ſo do concern both *Houſe of Lords*, and *Houſe of Commons*, (as alſo the *Convocation Houſes*, dirivatively from the Arch-Biſhops, and Biſhops Writs,) of which laſt I ſhall ſpeak more diſtinctly in this Treatiſe, concerning the *Convocation Houſe*.)

But the *Brevia Patentia* do chiefly concern the *Houſe of Lords*, *viz.* by Patents of *Creations*, (as alſo ſome Officers, as will be ſhewn) and all theſe are call'd *Patentia*, or *Letters Patents*, becauſe they are not inclos'd, but open, with the Impreſſion of the great Seal of *England* at large hanging to them, yet all the Created Patentees have their diſtinct Writs of Summons, but not the Official

Official Patentees, *viz. Clerk of the Crown, Clerk of the Parliament, Clerk to the House of Commons,* &c. CHAP II.

These Patent Writs have no other appellation than Literal, or Letters Patents, as I said. But the Parliamentary close Writs are divided into two Titles, *viz.* Exemplars and Consimilars, and though the word Exemplar is not us'd in the *Pawns*, yet the word Consimile is constantly us'd there, which doth imply an Exemplar. The Exemplars are Writs set down at large in the *Pawns*, and the Consimilars are Writs not inserted in the *Pawns*, and yet are to have a consimilitude with their Exemplars, the Exemplar being so made upon some extraordinary reason, as will be shewn hereafter.

V As for those Writs which concern the *House of Lords* (of which I only treat in this first Part) as they are more in number than any of the other *Houses*, (not including derivative Writs, Precepts, or Citations) so they are of a more nice nature, in respect (as I said) they are personal; for a distinct Writ is to be provided for every individual Lord sitting in the *Lords House*, but not so in the *House of Commons*, or *lower Convocation*, (as will be shewn) and though the main body of the Writs in those concerning

CHAP. II. cerning the *Lords Houſe* do differ but little from the Writs of former Kings, or from thoſe of the *Houſe of Commons*, yet the Titles do very much vary in every Parliament, partly by the new Creation of Barons, partly in their Aſcenſion from Barons to higher degrees, and partly by ſplitting of Titles upon extinction of Families, and for other cauſes they are in few years ſubject to variation in Titles, wherein every Lord is exact in having his due, and therefore ſome of the Heralds, (as I ſaid, according to the ſeveral diſtricts of the Kingdom under their managements) are, or ought to be conſulted with, that the Clerks may commit no miſtakes either in their Titles of Grace and Favour, or in their Titles of Rights and Conceſſions, before the Writs be ſealed, and the not effectual doing this (which ought to be done) might occaſion ſome miſtakes and differences between the Exemplar and Conſimilary Writs in point of Titles, (as will be ſhewn.)

VI. The other parts of the Writs, as well in Exemplars as Conſimilars (which concern not the Titles of the Peers) are the ſame both in the declaratory and mandatory parts, except ſome few words, (of which I ſhall take notice in my proceedings)

ceedings) and herein I ſhall not trouble my ſelf with ſhewing what reaſons were given in ſome Writs for ſummoning a Parliament, or what in others, or the reaſon of thoſe Reaſons, and why in ſome there were no Reaſons given, only a ſhort *Mandamus*. CHAP. II.

VII. All Writs at large recited in this and all former *Pawns*, are the Exemplars of all other Writs of Summons for a Parliament which are not in the reſpective *Pawns*, whereby theſe in this *Pawn* (with the addition of the Biſhops Exemplar Writs, (which are entred in all former *Pawns*) did and do now make 12 Exemplars, but the Writs which are not recited in this and former *Pawns* (which I term *Conſimilars*) at the calling this Parliament, were in all 262.

VIII. Some of the 12 are Exemplars, and other Writs have a conſimilitude to them, yet have no poſitive Conſimilars appointed them, whereof there are but three, *viz.* One to the Lord Chancellor in the *Lords Houſe*, and to the two Palatines in the *Commons*.

IX. All Writs of Summons to the *Houſe of Lords* both Exemplars and Conſimilars are Perſonal and Local, but all Writs of Summons for the *Houſe of Commons* are only Local.

Theſe

CHAP. II.

These 12 *Exemplars* are in this following method ſtated, with their *Conſimilars*, *viz.* thoſe 5 for the *Lords Houſe* are,

		Exemplar.	*Conſimilar*
I.	To the Duke of *York*	1	1
II.	To the Archbiſhop of *Canterbury*	1	25
III.	To the Lord Chancellor	1	0
IV.	To the Earl of *Southhampton*, L. Treaſurer	1 (In this Parliament, 3 Dukes, 4 Marq; 55 Earls, 8 Viſc. 68 Barons.)	138
V.	To the Chief Juſtice of the Kings Bench	1	15

So there was in the *Lords Houſe* 5 *Exemplar Writs*, and 179 *Conſimilars.*——in all 184.

The remaining *Exemplar Writs* relating to the *Houſe of Commons* are 7. (of which I ſhall ſpeak more in the next part of this Treatiſe) *viz.*

VI.	To *Cornwall*	1		4
VII.	To *Cambridge*	1		1
VIII.	To *London*	1		18
IX.	To *Dover*	1	*Cinqports*	7
X.	To *Lancaſter*	1		0
XI.	To *Cheſter*	1		0
XII.	To *Carmarthen*	1	*Wales*	11

So there is for the *Commons Houſe* 7 *Exemplars*, and 73 *Conſimilars*, in all 80 Writs, in both Houſes——264

So

So many Exemplar and Consimilar Writs were issued to Constitute this Parliament *An.* 1661. in the *Lords House*, to Countreys, Shires, and Comitated Cities and Towns, in the *Commons House*, whereof some years after its Sitting, one *Exemplar* and one *Consimilar* was issued for the Bishoprick of *Durham*) all the rest of the Writs for Cities, Towns and Burroughs not Comitated, (of which I shall give an account) do lose their names of Consimilars, when the Exemplar Writs do come to the respective Sheriffs, for then they pass from the respective Sheriffs; under the titles of Precepts, (or Derivative-Writs) as shall be more fully discourst of in the second part, where I treat of the *House of Commons*. CHAP. II.

Now I shall proceed to the Act of *Precedencies*, and give a short description of such as are to be Summon'd for the *Lords-House* only, because I speak more amply of their *Individual-Writs* whereby they are Summon'd

CHAP. III.

Of Precedencies.

HAving ſhewn the Kings Warrant, and the Lord Chancellors, and the Record made up in the Pettibag, call'd the *Parliament Pawn*, and given a touch of the nature of Writs in general, and in particular, of Parliamentary Writs of Summons, conſiſting of Writs Exemplar and Conſimilar, as alſo an hint of Precepts or Derivative-Writs from thoſe Exemplars, (which are to be more fully treated of in the 2*d.* part,) I ſhall proceed to the Act of 31 of *Hen.* the 8*th.* concerning Precedencies in the *Lords Houſe*, occaſion'd from the defect or long diſuſage of *Pawns*, or other State reaſons; for there being no *Pawns* extant but, as I ſaid, from the 21 of *Hen.* the 8*th.* to this time, the other being by *Endorſment* &c. on the *Records* in the *Tower* or *Rolls Chappel*; Our King *Hen.* the 8*th.* did make this *Act of Precedencies*, (which hath its chief Reference to the time when

when a Parliament is Sitting, and so not proper to be inserted in this place, seeing my design in this first part is to treat of matters previous to a Parliament, before I speak of matters *Sedente Parliamento*) yet it may be allow'd in respect I make no other present use of it, than to inlighten the Readers with the Characters of such Persons and Degrees as are to have Writs of Summons to sit there according to that Act, and therefore I shall first shew a Transcript of that Act, then some Observations upon it, and then give some short discourses of the *Noble Degrees* therein mention'd, in order to their Writs which shall distinctly follow. CHAP. III.

The Transcript of the *Act of Precedency*, 31. *Hen.* 8. *Cap.* 10.

The Act of Precedency, 31. *Hen.* 8. *Cap.* 10.

FOrasmuch as in all great Councils and Congregations of men, having sundry Degrees and Offices in the Commonwealth, it is very requisite and convenient that an order should be had, and taken for the placing and sitting of such Persons as been bound to resort to the

CHAP. III. *ſame, To the intent that they knowing their places may uſe the ſame without diſpleaſure or let of the Council. Wherefore the Kings moſt Royal Majeſty (although it appertaineth to his Prerogative Royal to give ſuch Honors, Places, and Reputation to his Counſellors, and other his Subjects as ſhall ſeem beſt to his moſt Excellent Wiſdom.) He is nevertheleſs pleas'd and contented for an Order to be had and taken in this his moſt High Court of Parliament, that it ſhall be Enacted by Authority of the ſame in manner as hereafter followeth.*

Firſt, It is Enacted by Authority aforeſaid, That no Perſon or Perſons of what Eſtate, Degree, or Condition ſoever he or they be of, (except only the Kings Children) ſhall at any time hereafter attempt, or preſume to ſit or have place at any ſide of the Cloth of State in the Parliament-Chamber, neither of the one hand of the Kings Highneſs nor of the other, whether the Kings Majeſty be there Perſonally preſent or abſent.

2. *And foraſmuch as the Kings Majeſty is juſtly and lawfully Supream head in Earth under God of the Church of* Eng-land, *and for the good exerciſe of the ſaid moſt Royal Dignity and Office, hath made* Thomas *Lord* Cromwel *and Lord Privy*

Privy Seal, his Vicegerent, for good and due ministration of Justice to be had in all Causes and Cases touching the Ecclesiastical Jurisdiction, and for the Godly reformation and redress of all Errors, Heresies, and Abuses in the said Church; It is therefore also Enacted by Authority aforesaid, That the said Lord Cromwel *having the said Office of Vicegerent, and all other Persons which hereafter shall have the said Office of the grant of the Kings Highness, his Heirs or Successors, shall Sit and be plac't as well in this present Parliament as in all Parliaments to be holden hereafter, on the right side of the Parliament-Chamber, and on the same Form that the Archbishop of* Canterbury *sitteth on, and above the same Archbishop and his Successors, and shall have Voice in every Parliament to assent or dissent, as other the Lords of the Parliament.* CAP. II

3. *And it is also Enacted, That next to the said Vicegerent, shall sit the Archbishop of* Canterbury, *and then next to him on the same Form and side, shall sit the Archbishop of* York, *and next to him on the same Form and side the Bishop of* London, *and next to him on the same side and Form the Bishop of* Durelme, *and next to him on the same side and Form the Bi-*

CHAP. III. *ſhop of* Wincheſter, *and then all the other Biſhops of both Provinces, of* Canterbury *and* York, *ſhall ſit and be plac't on the ſame ſide after their Ancienties, as it hath been accuſtomed.*

4. *And foraſmuch as ſuch other Perſonages which now have or hereafter ſhall happen to have other great Offices of the Realm, that is to ſay, the Offices of the Lord Chancellor, the Lord Treaſurer, the Lord Preſident of the Kings Council, the Lord Privy Seal, the Great Chamberlain of* England, *the Conſtable of* England, *the Lord Marſhal of* England, *the Lord Admiral, the Grand Maſter or Lord Steward of the Kings moſt Honourable Houſhold, the Kings Chamberlain, and the Kings Secretary, have not heretofore been appointed and ordered for the placing and ſitting in the Kings moſt High Court of Parliament, by reaſon of their Offices: It is therefore now Ordained and Enacted by Authority aforeſaid, That the Lord Chancellor, the Lord Treaſurer, the Lord Preſident of the Kings Council, and the Lord Privy-Seal, being of the Degrees of Barons of the Parliament, or above, ſhall ſit and be placed as well in this preſent Parliament as in all other Parliaments hereafter to be holden, on the left ſide of the ſaid Parliament-Chamber on the higher part of the Form of the ſame ſide, above all*

all Dukes, except only ſuch as ſhall happen to be the Kings Son, the Kings Brother, the Kings Uncle, the Kings Nephew, or the Kings Brothers or Siſters Sons. CHAP. III.

5. *And it is alſo Ordained and Enacted by Authority aforeſaid, That the Great Chamberlain, the Conſtable, the Marſhal, the Lord Admiral, the Great Maſter or Steward, and the Kings Chamberlain, ſhall ſit and be placed after the Lord Privy-Seal, in manner and form following, that is to ſay, every of them ſhall ſit and be placed above all other Perſonages being of the ſame Eſtates or Degrees that they ſhall happen to be of, that is to ſay, the Great Chamberlain firſt, the Conſtable next, the Marſhal third, the Lord Admiral the fourth, the Grand Maſter or Lord Steward the fifth, and the Kings Chamberlain the ſixth.*

6. *And it is alſo Enacted by the Authority aforeſaid, That the* Kings *chief Secretary being of the Degree of a Baron of the Parliament, ſhall ſit and be placed above all Barons not having any of the Offices aforementioned, and if he be a Biſhop, that then he ſhall ſit and be placed above all other Biſhops not having any of the Offices before remembred.*

7. *And it is alſo Ordained and Enacted by Authority aforeſaid, That all Dukes not afore mention'd, Marqueſſes, Earls, Viſ-*

 counts,

CHAP. III. *counts, and Barons, not having any of the Offices aforeſaid, ſhall ſit and be placed after their Ancientry as it hath been accuſtom'd.*

8. *And it is further Enacted, That if any Perſon or Perſons which at any time hereafter ſhall happen to have any of the ſaid Offices, of Lord Chancellor, Lord Treaſurer, Lord Preſident of the Kings Council, Lord Privy-Seal, or chief Secretary, ſhall be under the Degree of a Baron of the Parliament, by reaſon whereof they can have no intereſt to give any aſſent or diſſent in the ſaid Houſe, That then in every ſuch caſe ſuch of them as ſhall happen to be under the ſaid Degree of a Baron, ſhall ſit and be placed at the uppermoſt part of the Sack in the midſt of the ſaid Parliament-Chamber, either there to ſit upon one Form or upon the uppermoſt Sack, the one of them above the other, in order as is above rehearſed.*

9. *Be it alſo Enacted by Authority aforeſaid, That in all Tryals of Treaſon by Peers of this Realm, if any of the Peers that ſhall be called hereafter to be Tryers of ſuch Treaſon ſhall happen to have any of the Offices aforeſaid, that then they having ſuch Offices, ſhall ſit and be placed according to their Offices above all the other Peers that ſhall be call'd to ſuch Tryals, in manner and form as is above mention'd and rehears'd.*

10. *And it is alſo Enacted by Authority aforeſaid, That as well in all Parliaments as in the Star Chamber, and in all other Aſſemblies and Conferencies of Councils, the Lord Chancellor, the Lord Treaſurer, the Lord Preſident, the Lord Privy Seal, the Great Chamberlain, the Conſtable, the Marſhal, the Lord Admiral, the Grand Maſter or Lord Steward, the Kings Chamberlain, and the Kings chief Secretary ſhall ſit and be placed in ſuch order and faſhion as is before rehearſed, and not in any other place, by Authority of this Act.* CHAP. II.

SECT. I.

Obſervations.

1. THis Act is obſervable, being Enacted as it were by the King's ſingle Authority, yet by the Preamble it ſeems to be only an Order, or Ordinance at moſt, and this upon Record in that Houſe, for it doth not concern the *Commons.* C

2. The *Lords Houſe* is here call'd the *High Court of Parliament*, *i. e.* the higheſt Court of Judicature in Parliament, and ſo it is an Act by authority of the ſame, including the Kings.

3. It

CHAP. III. 3. It is alſo (*Parag.* 2.) call'd the *Parliament Chamber*; and (*Parag.* 8.) the ſaid Houſe, not the *Houſe of Lords*, or *Houſe of Peers*, as it is now call'd.

4. Though this Act doth contain the Rules for Places, as the ſeveral degrees do ſit in their diſtinct degrees, yet it doth not contain the intermixt Precedencies of the ſeveral Degrees, both in calling over the *Houſe*, and at other Solemnities, as will be more exactly ſhewn in the local part.

5. In the 8*th Paragraph* the *Lord great Chamberlain*, *Conſtable*, *Marſhal*, *Admiral*, *Steward*, and *King's Chamberlain* are omitted, becauſe it is preſum'd, that thoſe Titles were never given to any under the degree of a noble Baron.

6. Here the Seat for the *State-Officers* (being not Barons) is call'd a *Sack*, but in all Records, where thoſe Seats are mention'd, they are call'd *Wool-Sacks*, being ſtuff'd with Wool, to mind them of the Staple Commodity of the Kingdom.

7. The uſe which I make of this Act is to ſhew the ſeveral Titles of the Degrees of ſuch as are mention'd therein, 2*dly*, the ordering of thoſe Degrees, and 3*dly*, how this Act doth agree or diſagree with the *Pawns* before, and ſubſequent to it.

Firſt, The Degrees mention'd therein are four, *viz.* firſt, *Princes of the Blood*, 2dly,

2dly, *Lords Spiritual*, 3dly, *Miniſters* and *Officers of State*, 4thly, *Lords Temporal.* CHAP. III.

1*ſt*. The *Princes of the Blood* are ſaid therein (*Parag.* 4.) to be, firſt, the King's Son, 2*dly*, the King's Brother, 3*dly*, the King's Uncle, 4*thly*, the King's Nephew, 5*thly*, the King's Brother's Son, 6*thly*, the King's Siſter's Son, as in *Paragraph* the 1*ſt* and 4*th*.

2*dly*. The *Lords Spiritual* are ſaid therein to be the Arch-Biſhop of *Canterbury* and *York*, the Biſhop of *London*, *Dureſm*, and *Wincheſter*, and all the Biſhops of both Provinces according to their Ancientries, *Paragraph* 2, & 3.

3*dly*. The *Miniſters* and *Officers of State Eccleſiaſtical* and *Civil*, are (in the 2*d* and 4*th Paragraphs*) ſaid to be the Vice-Gerent, and eleven more therein mention'd, of which I ſhall ſpeak diſtinctly, *Paragraphs* 2, 4, 5, 6, 8, 9, 10.

4*thly*. The *Lords Temporal* are ſaid to be thoſe five Degrees mention'd in the ſeventh *Paragraph*, *viz. Dukes*, *Marqueſſes*, *Earls*, *Viſcounts*, and *Barons*, of which I ſhall alſo ſpeak more fully, and lower than to theſe Degrees the Act doth not extend.

5*thly*. This Act doth agree with the Method of the *Pawns*, in the placing of the

CHAP. II. the Princes of the Blood, as alſo of the Biſhops, but the *Pawns* do differ from the Act concerning the Miniſters and Officers of State, for they meddle with them no otherwiſe than they are annext to ſome Spiritual or Temporal Degrees, but if they are under the Degree of thoſe Degrees they have then only particular Writs of Aſſiſtance, as ſhall be ſhewn.

6. The Act doth not take notice of the ſeveral Aſſiſtants of the *Long Robe*, *viz.* the Lords Chief Juſtices, *&c.* But the *Pawn* makes a Record of them alſo, and of their Writs, and of their Precedencies, in relation to each other, of whom I ſhall ſpeak more particularly in the Thirteenth Chapter.

7. This Act was made upon the diſſolution of the Abbots and Priors, and that there might be no more room for them in the *Houſe of Lords*, whereas the two preceeding *Pawns* remaining ſtill in the *Pettibag*, (*viz.* of the 22 and 31 *Hen.* 8.) did place them next the Biſhops, now (their Abbies, Monaſteries, and Priories being diſſolved) they in this Act were excluded, as in all future *Pawns* (only Queen *Mary* did venture to ſummon the Abbot of *Weſtminſter*, and the Prior of St. *John*'s of *Jeruſalem*) but that being turn'd into a Deanry, and this diſſolved, they were as uſeleſs, as all the

the others, the Ecclesiastical and Civil Estate of this Kingdom being thereby restor'd to its Primitive Constitution, as will be shewn.

CHAP. IV.

A Discription of the Degrees *concern'd in this* Act of Precedency.

HAving spoken of the *Pawns* (or *Digest of Writs*) of *Summons* in general) as also of the *Act of Precedency*, this having respect only to the *House of Lords* and other great Councils; those both to the *House of Lords* and *House of Commons*, this only to the Dignity of the Nobles, those not only to the Dignity and Degrees of Nobles, but also of the form and order of the Writs constantly enabling the Nobles to make a noble use of their distinct Degrees, that to the Places and Precedencies of such persons (whenever they meet in Parliament) (as by the King's favour may be summon'd) those to the persons actually summon'd, wherein these *Pawns* (much ancienter than the Act) were doubtless a good Guide to the framing of this Act, I think it convenient, before I proceed to particularize their Writs (for the Titles must

be

CHAP. IV. be fix'd before the Writs can be perfected) to take a view of the order of ſuch Degrees as are mention'd in the *Pawns*, but better methodiz'd in the Act) *viz.* 1*ſt*, of the King's Counſellors, (comprehending all the following degrees and others) 2*dly*, of the Princes of the Blood (conſiſting of ſeven Degrees) 3*dly*, of the grand Officers and Miniſters of Church and State, (conſiſting alſo of ſeven Degrees) ſome of them being of a mixt nature, *viz.* Spiritual, Eccleſiaſtical, and Civil,) and 4*thly*, of the Temporal and Hereditary Nobility, (conſiſting of five intire Degrees,) and this I ſhall do by a diſtinct account of them, for the clearer underſtanding of the Writs and Perſons concern'd in them.

And this I do to entertain the Readers time, whilſt the Clerk and others are buſied in Drawing, Writing, and Ingroſſing the Writs, and carrying them to be Seal'd, and then diſpoſing them to the ſeveral perſons and places to whom and where they are to be deliver'd, which will admit of as much or more time than may be ſpent in reading theſe following Diſcourſes, intended for the reviving of the memory of ſome, and improving the knowledge of others, concerning the Perſons to be imploy'd in the *Houſe of Lords*, as alſo concerning the Writs for the *Houſe*

of

of Commons, and herein (in this First Part, as to the *House of Lords*) I shall be guided by the ancient Method of the King's Warrant, the *Pawns*, and the *Act of Precedency*; And first of the King's Counsellors. CHAP V.

SECT. II.

Of the Kings Privy-Counsellor.

AS to the Original of this Officer and of the reason of its different Orthography: sometimes beginning the second Syllable with C. or S. and of its affinitry to the old *Roman Comites Consiliarij*, I shall refer them to my annotations, and here only shew how that by the words in the Kings Warrant, by the *Pawns*, and by the said Act of 31. *Hen.* 8. (all which I have recited at large) we may clearly see that the word *Council*, doth consist of the Persons of the best Quality and Abilities, to give Counsel and Advice to the King. And when such a number as the King thinks fit to select for that purpose do meet in a Body Conjunctively, *Obs.* I.

This

CHAP. V. 2. This Council is called the *Kings Council*, and alſo the Perſons therein are called the *Kings Council*, (yet more properly Counſellors) and to confirm this, the Kings Warrant ſaith: *To Our Right Truſty and well beloved Counſellor Sir* Edward Hyde *Knight Chancellor of* England, (here 'tis Perſonal) then follows, *Whereas We by Our Council*, this intimates a Body of Perſons or Counſellors Congregated.

3. The Writs in the *Pawns* ſometimes do add to the Perſon to whom the Writ is ſent (*Conciliario ſuo*) and ſometimes not, but theſe following words are conſtantly in every Writ, (*Quia de advizamento & aſſenſu Concilij noſtri*, which is more large than what is in the Kings Warrant by inſerting the words (*Advice and Conſent*) *of Our Council.*

4. The ſaid Act ſaith in the Preamble, *Foraſmuch as in all great Councils and Congregations of men* (which explains Councils) *and then, that there may be no diſpleaſure or let of the Council*) (*in reſpect of Precedency*) *therefore* (*for the better reputation of his Counſellors and other Subjects, doth Enact*, &c. And in the 3*d.* Paragraph, the Preſident of the Kings Council is there alſo named, by which we underſtand the Kings Privy-Council (of which he is Preſident) to be a Council

cil diſtinct from other Councils where there are Preſidents; 2*ly*. And from Parliaments (where there are Speakers inſtead of Preſidents) anciently called the Great Council, and ſo it is ſtill, though the name is alter'd to Parliament) and 3*ly*. From other Aſſemblies and Conferences of Councils, (which are the words in the laſt Paragraph of that Act.) CHAP. IV.

5. And therefore this Council here meant in this *Warrant*, *Pawn*, and *Act*, is that which we now call the Kings Privy Council. Tis true the King hath ſeveral other Councils, (as that of *Wales*, and in the North, and others both here and in Foraign Plantations) but this *Privy-Council* is the Supream ſtanding Council, out of which ſometimes the King thinks fit to ſelect ſome few for the more ſafe, ſecret and eaſie diſpatch of Affairs.)

6. Which by the *Jews* were called *Cabala*, but by us properly Comitties. However this *Privy Council* is the ſtanding Council of the Kingdom, giving Forms and Being to all other Councils, eſpecially what concerns the Beginning, Continuing, and Ending of any Parliament, and yet this *Council* or *Parliament* is a greater Council than that, and of greater Authority when it is in being, and therefore anciently, as I ſaid, call'd *Magnum & Publi-*

CHAP. IV. *cum Concilium*, and this *Privatum Concilium*.

7. This Great and publick Council conſiſts of the King, Lords Spiritual, Lords Temporal, (*viz.* of ſuch to whom the King ſends Writs of Summons) and of Commons (*viz.* of ſuch as the People think fit to Elect by vertue of the Kings Writs.) But this *Privatum* or *Privy Council* are of ſuch only as the King Elects out of the Degrees next mentioned, or out of other Degrees, as he ſhall beſt judge of their Abilities for it. Yet very often Parliaments have perſuaded Kings to make Alterations in *Privy Councils*, both as to Perſons and Number.

8. The number of the Perſons of this *Privy Council* are in a manner indefinite, becauſe it depends upon the Kings pleaſure. But anciently it conſiſted only of 12. ſince that they have increaſed and varied, and in the beginning of this Parliament they were 29. but before the end of it above 40. The number of the *Great Council* or *Parliament* is partly indefinite, (in the *Lords Houſe*) and partly circumſcrib'd, (and ſo in the *Commons Houſe* (as will be ſhewn,) for theſe anciently had not above 2. or 300. but this Parliament had in both Houſes above 700. (as will be ſhewn.)

9. This

9. This very name of *Council* and *Counsellors*, (as they are or ought to be) is much more ancient than the *Consuls* of *Rome*, which had their name *a Consulendo*, for their abilities in giving Counsel, and possibly borrow'd from the name of *Neptune* the God of the Sea, who was call'd also *Consiliorum Deus*, so as probably of their two yearly Consuls, one was chosen for the Affairs of the Sea, (as Admiral) the other for the Affairs of the Land, as General, however it is observable that the Title of *Consul* or *Counsellor* did continue 1046. years in that Empire, deducting three years interposition of the *Decemviri* (or 10 Governors,) and 4 years of *Tribunes* (or 3 Governors,) and 12 years of *Tribunes* consisting of 4 Governors, and 30 years by *Tribunes* consisting of six Governors, and 5 years under an *Anarchy*, and 2 years wherein *Tribunes* had a Consulary power, and then the Government again slid into *Consuls*, so as deducting these 56 years, they continued intire under that *Consulary Tutelage* 990 years: and as that way of Government was useful to *Rome* whilst it was a Common-wealth, so we see when *Julius Cæsar* took on him the *Roman* Empire, and turn'd it to a Monarchy, he did not discard the Consulary way of managing Affairs, nor did his

CHAP. IV. Succeſſors; ſo as they continued full 540. years after *Julius Cæſar* in proſecution of that Monarchical Empire, till the Papal Intereſts had ſupplanted the Weſtern Empire, and made General Councils, tending rather to the diſ-uniting of Princes, than for uniting Religion, as was pretended, and inſtead of Conſuls, erected a Conſiſtory and Conclave, the laſt being only new names for a Council.

10. This is certain, that Councils or Counſellors or Conſuls are of that nature, that no Government can ſubſiſt without them, though by different Appellations; and I read of few or none in all the *Roman* Stories, who had the Title of Conſul conferr'd on him, but thoſe who either by their Wiſdom had given ſuch good Counſel as prov'd proſperous to the Empire, or had done ſuch eminent Services, that from ſuch Heroick actions the Emperors and Senators derived Arguments of their Abilities to Counſel, as having actually done, and from that experience might Counſel what was fit to be done, and thereupon formerly call'd Conſul, and now Counſel or Counſellor, and fit to ſit both in *Privy Council* or *publick Parliament*.

11. This Honour was ſtill founded in merit; by the eſtimation of Judgment, Experience, or Reſolution; for what they had Adviſed,

Advised, Counsell'd, or Successfully acted, and therefore they were seldom made *Viri Consulares* till they were 43. years of age, and for such as had been thus Serviceable to the Empire, if a Consulship were not void, yet they had always some Offices or Rewards in store which they conferr'd proportionably to their Services; and such Rewards were purposely reserv'd for such as had either given good Counsel, or followed it, by venturing their Lives and Fortunes for preservation of the Empire, and some such Orders were made in our *Edw.* the *3ds.* time, and confirmed by many Successive Councils, as may be read in Sir *Edw. Coke*, and Judge *Dodridge*. CHAP. IV.

12. There are also other lesser Councils, (besides what I mentioned before) as the Common Council of *London*, (and the like though not for number in other Cities) (which relate only to the Government of those Cities and Counsellors at Law, and the meeting (of such degrees as are qualified for that purpose) are called in some of the Inns of Court, Parliaments, which relate only to matters of Law and Government of their Societies, and Councils of War and Trade, and many of these are great Assistants and often imploy'd both in the Privy and publick Council of the Kingdom.

CHAP. IV.

13. I have been the longer on this ſubject becauſe all the Degrees hereafter mentioned are Members either of the Kings *Privy Council* or the *Parliament*, or both, yet their Writs of Summons are not ſingly *Conciliario*, but by annexation to thoſe Degrees which are capacitated to be Counſellors, but the Degrees mentioned in the Act (of whom I treat next) are conſtantly of the *Privy Council* or *Parliament*; but there are only ſome of the *Parliament* which are of the *Privy Council*, by which means matters are more eaſily manag'd between the *King*, the *Privy Council*, and the *Parliament*, the one conſtantly Sitting, the other Summon'd only upon Emergencies of State, which latter being thus Conſtituted, it may well be call'd *Magnum Concilium Animarum*, or a Council of Souls rather than Bodies, ſo as the King may ſay with *Cicero*, *Conſcientia conciliorum meorum me Conſolatur*, *i. e.* The knowledge and Conſcientious concurrence of minds or Souls, (for ſo *Conſcientia* ſometimes ſignifies) *and integrity of my Counſellors are my Conſolation.*

14. In the firſt Chapter I have ſhewn the Liſt of the *Privy Council*, who gave their Advice (as tis ſaid in the Warrant) for Summoning the Parliament to begin the 8*th.* of *May*, 1661. and all but one of them had Summons, and did ſit in the

Lords

Lords House, or were Elected for the *Commons House*, yet it may be observed that *Prince Rupert* was Summon'd as Duke of *Cumberland*: The Duke of *Laderdale* (being a *Scotch* Lord) was not Summon'd till he was made Earl of *Gilford* some years after: The Duke of *Ormond* was Summon'd as Earl of *Brecknock* in *Wales*, the Lord *Anthony Ashly Cooper* was chosen a Burgess of *Dorsetshire* for the *House* of *Commons*, but his Writ was time enough to sit in the *Lords House*, Sir *Charles Berkley* Knt. was chosen a Burgess in *Somersetshire*, and soon after made Lord *Fitz Harding*, (an *Irish* Title) and so continued in the *House of Commons* to his death, Sir *George Cartret* Knt. and Bar. was chosen Burgess for *Portsmouth*, and continued in the *Commons House* to the end of that Parliament, Sir *Edward Nicholas* Knt. was Summon'd to the *Lords House*, but Sir *William Morrice* was chosen Burgess for *Plymouth*, and continued with the *Commons* to his death. Now I proceed with the chief of such as are for the most part of the Kings *Privy Council*, (mention'd in the Act) and do with others of lesser Degreees Constitute both the *Privatum* and *Magnum concilium* or Parliament.

SECT. III.

Of the Princes of the Bloud.

Obſ. I. IN this Act the King by vertue of his Kingly Office (for ſo is the word in the Act) and Prerogative, having power to give ſuch Honors, Places, and Reputation to his Counſellors, and other his Subjects as ſhall ſeem beſt to his moſt Excellent Wiſdom, (eſpecially to his Council or Parliament) gives the Priority of all Places and Precedings to theſe following ſeven Degrees of the Bloud-Royal, *viz.* (1.) to the Kings Son, (firſt entituled Prince of *Wales* in the 11. *Edw.* the 3*d.*) (2.) to the Kings Children, (3.) to the Kings Brother, (4.) to the Kings Uncle, (5.) to the Kings Nephew, (6.) to the Kings Brothers Son, (7.) to the Kings Siſters Son, (all of theſe have Title of Earls or Dukes) and any one of theſe (where others in priority are wanting) are to be accounted the firſt in their own ſeven Degrees, and are Prior to the 5 following Degrees, which comprehend all the Lords Temporal, and theſe, as they happen to be more or leſs, have their diſtinct Writs, as alſo their proceedings to

all

all or any other Degrees, either Spiritual or Temporal, Official or Hereditary, of whom I ſhall ſpeak more in the following Sections and Chapters; but if there be a failour of any of theſe, or that they are abſent from Parliaments in reſpect of Minority or otherwiſe, then ſome of the Lords Spiritual have precedency to the Lords Temporal, (as will be ſhewn,) CHAP. IV.

All that were Summon'd of this Degree to this Parliament, were only the Duke of *York*, the Kings Brother, and Prince *Rupert* his Siſters Son, *Sect. Cap.* 2. *Fig.* 1. and 2.

SECT. IIII.

Of the Kings Vice-Gerent *or* Vicar-General.

THe words of the Act are, *That foraſmuch as the Kings Majeſty is juſtly and lawfully Supream Head on Earth under God of the Church of* England, *and for the good Exerciſe of that moſt Royal Dignity and Office* (*viz.* of Supream Head of the Church) *hath made* Thomas *Lord* Cromwel (*who was not only Lord Privy Seal* (as in the Act is expreſt) *but Maſter of the Kings Jewel-Houſe, Baron of* Okham, *Obſ.*

CHAP. IV. ham, *Knight of the Garter, Earl of* Eſſex, *and Lord Great Chamberlain,*)

2. His *Vice-Gerent*, (for the good and due adminiſtration of Juſtice to be had in all Cauſes and Caſes touching the Eccleſiaſtical Juriſdiction, and for the Godly Reformation of all Errors, Hereſies, and Abuſes in the ſaid Church, ſo as he injoy'd Dignities and Offices of a mixt nature, Eccleſiaſtical and Civil, and thereby was placed above all the Lords Spiritual, and above all the Lords Temporal of the following Degrees, and not only in reſpect of his Temporal Dignities, but as *Vice-Gerent* in Eccleſiaſticals) had power given him, and to his Succeſſors in that Office, to ſit above thoſe Degrees in Parliament, and to have a Voice and Liberty to aſſent or diſſent as other Lords.

3. But there hath been none imploy'd in this Office ſince that time, (as needleſs I conceive) for the Archbiſhops of *Canterbury* and *York* in their Provinces, and the Biſhops in their Dioceſſes have ever ſince in a manner ſuppli'd the Duty of that Office under their own Titles and by their own Juriſdictions, eſpecially the Archbiſhop of *Canterbury*, who is rankt in the next place in this Act, and in all *Pawns* (except this) where ſome of the Bloud Royal are not exemplars.

SECT.

CHAP. IV.

SECT. V.

Of the Arch-Bishops *and* Bishops.

THE Title of *Bishop* is more ancient *Obs.*
than the Title of *Christian*, as I I.
shall shew in the seventh Chapter; however it became more general after Christianity spread it self.

The word comes from the *Greek*, Ἐπίσκοπος, II.
i. e. one who is, *in Doctrinam & mores sa-
cros gregis Inspector*, and when Bishops
grew numerous it was thought fit to place
one to look after them, and he had the
addition of *Archos*, *i. e. principalis*, and so
call'd *Archi-Episcopus*, or Arch-Bishop, having a certain number of Bishops and their
Diocesses reduced to his Province or Care, III.
so that the Arch-Bishop of *Canterbury* (with
his own Diocess) hath twenty two Diocesses, or Bishopricks (of the twenty six)
within his Province, and the Arch-Bishop
of *York* hath with his own (four) which
makes in all twenty six, (besides the Bishop of *Man*, who hath no Writ of Summons.) Anciently these Arch-Bishops and
Bishops, with Abbots, Priors, Deans, IV.
Arch-Deacons and Proctors (making the
two Convocation-houses) were summoned
to appear two days before the Temporal
Lords,

CHAP. IV. Lords, but ſince *Henry* the Eighth's time, (when Abbots and Priors were excluded) the Biſhops are ſummon'd to meet the ſame day that the Parliament begins, but as Convocation-houſes, they are not ſummon'd to meet at Parliament till two or three days after the Lords Spiritual and Temporal are met and ſitting in Parliament, and thoſe two Convocation-houſes are ſeldom Adjourn'd, Prorogu'd, or Diſſolv'd in three or four days, and ſometimes longer, after the two *Houſes of Lords* and *Commons* are Adjourn'd, Prorogu'd, or Diſſolv'd.

V. Theſe Arch-Biſhops and Biſhops (conſidering them upon a Baronial account diſtinct from the Convocations) are entred in all *Clauſe Rolls* and *Pawns* next the Blood Royal (except when there was a caſual interpoſition (as this laſt of *Vice-gerent*) and their places diſtinctly ſet down, as in this Act: *viz.* the Arch-Biſhop of *Canterbury*, then the Arch-Biſhop of *York*, and the other according to Seniority, or *Antientry* (as the word of the Act is) till the Biſhops of *London*, *Durham*, and *Wincheſter*, were (as by this Act) fix'd in their Precedencies to the other twenty one, and yet there is another method of Precedencies, us'd in the *Lords Houſe*, and in all Solemnities, by way of counter-changing

changing of Precedencies between the Lords Spiritual and Temporal, (as will be ſhewn.) CHAP. IV.

VI. Theſe twenty ſix injoy their Offices of Biſhops upon a Spiritual and Eccleſiaſtical account, and therefore are call'd *Lords Spiritual*, their *Eccleſiaſtical* ſerving *in ordine ad piritualia.*

VII. Theſe, for many Ages did manage the Offices of *Chancellor* and *Keeper* of the *Great Seal*, alſo of *Treaſurer*, *Preſident*, *Privy-Seal*, and *Secretary*, (of which I ſhall ſpeak more) but ſince *Henry* the Eighth's time theſe five Offices have been diſtinctly manag'd by *Laicks*, of the chiefeſt quality and merit, and the Biſhops in a manner circumſcrib'd to the Juriſdiction of their reſpective Dioceſſes, which are of a kind of mixt nature, conſiſting of Spiritualities and Temporalities.

VIII. In the *Lords Houſe* they have almoſt equal Prividledges with the Lords Temporal, except in matters of Blood, when in reſpect of their *Canons*, they commonly withdraw themſelves, appointing *Proxies* and entring *Proteſtation*, but theſe Priviledges are not Hereditary, (like the Temporal Lords) but meerly Succeſſive, and their Writs are ſomewhat of a different Nature from thoſe to the Lords Temporal, (in point of extent concerning the Convoca-

tion-

CHAP. IV. tion-houſes) which do make a kind of a Parliament annext to a Parliament, (of which I ſhall ſpeak more at large.) But how the Biſhops were Summon'd may be read in the ſeventh Chapter.

SECT. VI.

Of the Lord Chancellor, *or* Lord Keeper.

Obſ. THis great Officer being not only recited in this Act, but having a peculiar Writ of Aſſiſtance in this and other *Pawns*? which the next Ten Officers following have not (in reſpect of their Offices) I ſhall diſcourſe more fully of him ſo ſoon as I have given a ſhort view of the Ten remaining to be ſpoken of.

Edward Hyde, Baron *Hyde*, and Lord Chancellor, was Summon'd by Writ, *Feb.* 18. 1661. See Chap. II.

SECT. VII.

Of the Lord Treaſurer *of* England.

Obſ. THis Officer being joyn'd alſo in this *Pawn* to the Earl of *Southampton* (then Lord Treaſurer) and in former *Pawns* to other Degrees, and being intended to be diſcours'd of in the fourth *Exemplar*,

plar, and in the fifth *Section* of the Barons of the *Exchequer*, I ſhall defer its inlargement to thoſe Chapters. CHAP IV.

Thomas, Earl of *Southampton*, Lord Treaſurer of *England*, was Summon'd by Writ, *Feb.* 18. 1661. See Chap. II.

SECT. VIII.

Of the Lord Preſident *of the* King's Council.

THis Officer from the time of King *John* was call'd *Principalis* and *Capitalis Conſiliarius*, and ſo continu'd till Queen *Elizabeth*'s time, and after not us'd, till once in King *Charles* the firſts time, and ever ſince, to the end of this Parliament, the Lord Chancellor or Lord Keeper hath ſupply'd the duty of that Place, though not the Title; the difference of granting them was, that one was always by Patent, and the other only by delivery of the Great Seal. *Obſ.* I.

2. There are alſo other Lord Preſidents which ſit in the *Lords Houſe*, *viz.* the Preſident of *Wales*, and Preſident of the *North*, but being not mention'd in this Act, and the latter not ſitting in this Parliament, I refer them to my *Annotations*, as alſo other Preſidents of lower Degrees, as of Colleges, &c.

SECT.

CHAP. IV.

SECT. IX.

Of the Lord Privy-Seal.

Obſ. IN *Edward* the Third's time, and long after, this Office was call'd Keeper of the Privy or Private Seal, diſtinguiſhing him from the other, call'd the Keeper of the Great Seal; afterward he was call'd Clerk of the Privy-Seal, (Clerk being then a Title of Eminency) and *Gardien del Privy-Seal*, and in 34 *H.* 8. Lord Privy-Seal.

2. He hath his Office by Patent, but the Keeper of the Great Seal (as I ſaid) only by delivery of that Seal, and 'tis very probable that this Office was in imitation of that which was us'd by the *Romans*, the Officer whereof was call'd *Comes privatorum*, and as *Caſſiodore* calls him, the Governour of the King's private Affairs.

3. Whilſt the *Court of Requeſts* was in uſe he was alſo call'd the Maſter of it, being Maſter or Superiour to the Four Maſters of *Requeſts*, who were to receive, peruſe, and preſent all Petitions to the King, or to the Parliament in time of Parliament, and direct the Petitioners in the right way of proceeding in their buſineſs, and for want of this direction many men are ruin'd

by

by crafty and unskilful directors, and the Parliament troubled with needless applications; for I conceive this Court was plac'd (as will be shewn) between the *House of Lords* and *House of Commons* for the Masters to sit there in time of Parliament, as Tryers of Petitions to either House, and were to judge, whether the matter was proper for either House, or any other Court, which doubtless did take off a great expence of time from both Houses, and from intangling them in matters which were properly relievable in other places.

CHAP. IV.

4. There are three sorts of Seals which are chiefly us'd for publick Affairs; two of them pass under the names of Privy or Private, the other, the Great or Broad-Seal: yet for a clearer distinction, one of the two is call'd the Privy Signet, and hath four Clerks to attend its Office, the other the Privy-Seal and hath also four Clerks to attend its Office; and the third is call'd, (as I said) the Great Seal, and hath properly six Clerks to attend it, but increas'd to many more. The Privy Signet is under the Custody of the Chief Secretary of State; the Privy Seal, under the Custody of the Lord Privy Seal; and the Broad Seal under the Custody of the Lord Chancellor, or Lord Keeper, so as most matters which concern a declaration of the King's pleasure in writing, do

CHAP. IV. take their rise from the Privy Signet, and from thence transmitted to the Privy Seal, and from thence to the Great Seal, to receive its determination.

5. But to pass by all private or publick Matters about which these three Officers are concern'd, this is certain, that the Clerks of these three Offices (excluding none) in some form or other are concern'd in the Warrants and Writs, &c. for the Summoning every Parliament.

6. When the chief Officer of this Office did pass under the Title of Keeper, or Clerk of the Privy Seal, most of them were Ecclesiasticks, yet having this Office, he had his Writ of Summons and Place in the Lords House, as may be collected from the Rolls of 15 *Edw.* 3. when Sir *William Keldsly* was Keeper of the Privy Seal, and 20 *Edw.* 3. when Mr. *Jo. Thoresby* was call'd Clerk of the Privy Seal, and from 28 *Edw.* 3. when Sir *Michael of Northumberland* was Keeper of the Privy Seal, (*Sir* being an Epithite given in those days to the *Clergy*) and still in use in the Universities for Batchelors of Arts) and from 11 *R.* 2. and 1 & 2 *H.*4. when Sir *Richard Clifford* was Keeper of the Privy Seal, and these had Writs, and from 3, & 4 *H.* 6. a Writ was expresly sent *Magistro Willielmo Alrevill Custodi privati sigilli*, and

and from that time (the *Rolls* and *Pawns* which ſpeak of them are dormant or wanting) to the *Pawn* of 30 *H.* 8. when the Writ to *John*, Earl of *Bedford*, is there entred *Custos privati ſigilli*, and he being ſo in 31 *H.* 8. (when the Act was made) his Precedency was ſetled (as is therein ſhewn) and there firſt intituled Lord Privy Seal, and ſo this Officer hath continued in that additional Title of Lord to this time. However in the *Latin* Writs he is ſtyled only *Custos privati ſigilli*, without the addition of *Dominus*, and ſo in the very *Pawn* of that year, and in 36 *H.* 8. and is no more mention'd in any of the *Pawns*, till 6 and 7 *Edw.* 6. when *John*, Earl of *Bedford*, was ſtill *Custos privati ſigilli*, and from that time thoſe *Pawns* which are extant do not mention that Officer, till 1 *Car.* 1. when *Edward*, Earl of *Worceſter*, was entred *Custos privati ſigilli*; and 15 *Car.* 1. when *Henry*, Earl of *Mancheſter*, was *Custos privati ſigilli*, and had their Writs; but in this *Pawn* of 13 *Car.* 2. none is mention'd, and yet the Lord *Roberts* was then Lord Privy Seal, ſo as it was an omiſſion of the Clerks, as I conceive.

CHAP IV.

7. Moſt of the Keepers of the Privy Seal (as I have obſerv'd) were Eccleſiaſticks before 30 *H.* 8. but ſince that time this Office hath been conferr'd only upon ſuch

CHAP. IV. as were Temporal Lords, above the degree of Barons, and not under.

8. This great Officer hath alſo an appartment near the Lords Houſe, for his accomodations, and ſometimes us'd for the Lords Committees, as will be ſhewn.

9. Theſe four laſt mention'd are plac'd in this order in the *Lords Houſe*, whether or not they be of any of the Noble Degrees. *John*, Lord *Roberts*, of *Truro*, Lord Privy Seal, was Summon'd by Writ of *Feb.* 1661. See Chap. 2.

SECT. X.

Of the Lord Great Chamberlain *of* England.

THE five foregoing Officers of State, *viz. Vice-Gerent*, *Chancellor*, *Treaſurer*, *Preſident*, and *Privy Seal*, were anciently choſen out of Eccleſiaſtick Degrees, but thoſe which I am now to ſpeak of (except the Secretaries, being for the moſt part alſo Clergy-men) were choſen out of Laicks, perſons of the greateſt Merit, Fortunes, or Families, and had their Places as they were annext to the Degrees of the Nobility.

2. The learned *Inſtitutor* ſaith, that if the King gave Lands to a man, to hold of him

to

to be Chancellor of *England*, Chamberlain of *England*, Conſtable of *England*, Marſhal of *England*, or High Steward of *England*, &c. theſe Tenures were call'd *Grand Sergeanties*, and theſe and ſuch like *Grand Sergeanties* were of great and high Juriſdictions, ſome of them concerned matters Military in time of Wars, and ſome ſervices of Honour in time of Peace. CHAP IV.

3. This Officer ever was, and ſtill is in great Veneration and Uſe, and I conceive, though now moſt of his Imployments are about the King's Court, yet the word *Camerarius*, which we call Chamberlain, was like to that among the *Romans*, call'd *Comes Ærarij*, and had ſuch relation to the Treaſury of the Kingdom, as the Chamberlains of *London*, and the Chamberlains of the Palatines of *Lancaſter* and *Cheſter* have to their diſtinct Treaſuries (of which I ſhall ſpeak more fully in order (as alſo in my Annotations) and I apprehend that theſe great Officers need not Writs, becauſe it is requiſite theſe ſhould be always attending on the Kings Perſon; but when they are otherwiſe commanded to his Imployments in their Offices, and there is ſcarce any of them, eſpecially this, but are ſo glutinated to ſome Noble Perſon, that it cannot be ſaid whether the Writ be more in reſpect of the Office, or

CHAP. IV. Perſon that Manageth that Office.

4. This Office was injoy'd for many Succeſſions by the Earls of Oxford (till *Richard* the Second by violence took it away) the *Houſe of Commons*, 1 *H.* 4. pray'd the King, that it might be reſtored to *Richard*, then Earl of *Oxford*, being (as it was then alledged) his due Inheritance, yet in 1 *H.* 6. that King granted it to the Duke of *Glocester*, the 36th of *Hen.* 8. the Writ was to *Edward*, Earl of *Hertford*, *Magno Camerario Angliæ*, and 1 *Edw.* 6. to *John*, Earl of *Warwick*, *Magno Camerario Angliæ.* Afterwards, by a Match, it was hereditated to the Family of the *Berties*, who, after ſome diſputes about the Title, did ſit in Parliament, in the time of *Charles* the Firſt and this Parliament, as Earl of *Lindſey*, and Lord great Chamberlain of *England*, whereby one part which his Lordſhip is to act (as his Predeceſſors had done) is to take care, that all things be provided in the *Houſe of Lords* that may ſuit with the Grandeur and Conveniencies of the Perſons who are there to be imploy'd, and for that and other purpoſes he hath alſo an Appartment near the Lords Houſe, as will be ſhewn.

5. *Montague* (*Bertie*) Earl of *Lindſey*, Lord Great Chamberlain of *England*, was ſummon'd by Writ, *Feb.* 18. 1661. See *Cap.* 2.

SECT.

CHAP IV.

SECT. XI.

Of the High Conſtable *of* England.

IT may be well ſuppos'd, that *Conſtabularius Angliæ*, was inſtead of *Comes ſtabuli* amongſt the old *Romans*, which was commonly taken for the Maſter of the Horſe to the *Emperour*, and is a Place ſtill of great Honour in moſt parts of *Europe*; but I conceive he was rather call'd *Comes ſtabuli*, as an Officer or Office of refuge, for ſo *ſtabulum* alſo ſignifies. However for many Ages this Office was held in *Grand Sergeanty* by thoſe perſons hereafter nam'd, but in 12 *H.* 8. it became forfeited to the Crown, and ſince that never granted to any Subject, but *pro hac vice*, at ſome Solemnities, as at the Coronation of King *Charles* the Second, in *April* 1661, a little before this Parliament, *Algernoone Piercy*, Earl of *Northumberland*, was made High Conſtable of *England*, *pro hac vice*, for with the Ceremony of that day his Office ended; and *Henry* the Eighth, I conceive, did enter it in the Act of 31 of his Reign, that in caſe there ſhould be any uſe of this Officer, when any ſuch Solemnity happen'd, in time of Parliament, his place might be known without diſpute.

CHAP. IV.

3. Before the 13*th.* of *Henry* the 8*th.* in ſome reſpects it had a greater power than the *Earl Marſhal*, and in others equal to it, and ſo the extravagant parts being taken away, the reſt fixt in the *Earl Marſhal*, (of whom I ſhall ſpeak next) however it hath left a name of great honor and uſe; thoſe of Honor are the Conſtable of *Dover*, &c. thoſe of Uſe are the high Conſtables and Conſtables diſperſt in all parts of *England.*

4. Whilſt this great Officer was of conſtant uſe, he was conſtantly ſummon'd to Parliaments, *viz.* 50. E. 3. *Thomas de Woodſtock*, *Comes de Buck*, *Conſtabularius Angliæ*, and ſo that 1. 3. and 4. *Ric.* 2. & *Thomas Dux Gloſtriæ*, *Conſtabularius Angliæ*, 17. *R.* 2. and the 1*ſt.* of *Hen.* the 4*th* *Henry Percy* Earl of *Northumberland* Conſtab. *Angliæ*, and the 2*d.* of *Hen.* the 5*th.* and 1. *H* 6. Summons to *Humphrey* Duke of *Gloſter* Conſt. *Angliæ*, and to *John* Duke of *Bedford* Conſt. *Angliæ*, 2. *H.* 6. and from thence again to the Duke of *Buckingham* Conſt. *Angliæ*, but from thence to the 20. of *Hen.* the 8. there are no *Pawns*, as I ſaid, to guide us to the knowledge of ſuch as were ſummon'd to the intervening Parliaments, but it appears by other Records that in the 13*th.* of *Hen.* the 8. this Office of

Con-

Conſtable of *England* was turn'd into an *hac vice*, and ſo only granted upon the Solemnity of *Coronation*, and thereupon is not mention'd in any following *Pawns* to this time, or was of any uſe in this Parliament. CHAP. IV.

SECT. XII.

Of the Earle Marſhal of England.

THis great Officer hath not ſo great a Latitude of power as the Conſtable of *England* had, yet he hath under his Juriſdiction the Care of the Common Peace of the Land, in deeds of Ams and matters of War, (when it happens in Forraign or Domeſtick parts) in moſt of which he is guided by the Civil Laws, and yet not to do any thing repugnant to the Common Laws. In times of War he is more abſolute, in times of Peace leſs: this mane of Marſhal ('tis very probable) had its Original from *Mars* the *Romans* God of War, and was the ſame which they call'd *Comes Militum*.

2. However with us this Great Officer had and hath ſeveral Courts under his Juriſdiction, *viz.* the Court of *Chevalry* (now almoſt forgotten) and the Court of Honor

CHAP. IV. Honor (now quiet layd aſide) but the *Sedes Mariſcalli* or Court of *Marſhalſee* is ſtill in being (where he may ſit in Judgment againſt *Criminals* offending within the verge of the Kings Court) and the chief Officer under him is call'd the *Knight Marſhal.*

3. As alſo the Herauld Office or Colledge, where when doubts ariſe, concerning Deſcents, Pedegrees, Eſcuchteons, &c. he determins them; this was Incorporated by *Ric.* the 3*d.* and many priveledges added by *Philip,* and *Mary,* 4. and 5.

4. Heraulds amongſt the old *Romans* were a certain Order of Prieſts, (call'd *Fæciales*) and ſo term'd becauſe *Bello paceq; faciendo apud eos jus erat pronuntiare,* &c. they were alſo call'd *Caduceatores,* (from a little wand, which they carried) whereon was fixt two wings to repreſent *Mercury,* (the nimble Meſſenger of War) & *quod Contentionem & Bella Cadere facerent.*)

5. This Office or Colledge conſiſts of 3 Regulators of Arms, Ceremonies, Pedegrees, and Deſcents of Nobility and Gentry; the firſt is call'd *Garter Rex Armorum Principalis,* chief King at Arms, and is alſo an Officer to the Soveraign, and Knights Companions of the moſt noble order of the *Garter* : the 2*d.* call'd *Clarentius* alſo King of Arms, but his Juriſdiction is only on the Southſide of *Trent*; The 3*d.* call'd *Norray,* alſo

also King of Arms for the Northside of *Trent*; these two being confin'd, but *Garter* not confin'd. CHAP. IV.

6. Besides these, there are 6 more properly call'd Heraulds, *quasi Honorem tenentes, Hæredes Aulæ dicentes*, such as are able to give an account to the Court, of *Heyres* to *Families*, and these have distinct Titles distinguishing their Imployments, *viz.* 1. *York*, 2. *Lancaster*, 3. *Somerset*, 4. *Richmond*, 5. *Chester*, 6. *Windlesour*.

7. And there are also 4 Under Graduats call'd *Pursevants*, or such who with readiness do pursue the Commands of their Superior Officers, (properly in Marshal Causes) and therefore call'd *Pursevants* at Arms, to distinguish them from other *Pursevants* or Messengers from other Courts, and these 4 have also 4 distinct Titles. *viz.* *Bleumantle*, 2. *Rougecross*, 3. *Rouge-Dragon*, 4. *Portcullis*; but of the *Earl Marshal*, and *Heraulds*, I shall speak more as they are imployed in Parliamentary Ceremonies.

8. There is no doubt but these Earls Marshals have for many ages sat in Parliaments, *viz.* the Duke of *Norfolk*, Marshal of *England*, was summon'd 15 *Ed.* 2. But 11 *R.* 2. the Title of Earl Marshal of *England* being by Patent granted to *Thomas de Mowbray*, Earl of *Nottingham*, and entail'd on the Heirs Males of his Body, which failing, yet

CHAP. IV. yet the Title of *Mowbray* deſcending on *Thomas Earl* of *Arundel*, *King James* did by *Pattent* make him *Earl Marſhal* for life, and he was Summon'd to *Parliament* by both Titles, but he dying, *Thomas Earl* of *Arundel* and *Mowbray* Grandſon and Heir to the ſaid *Thomas* had no *Writ* provided for him, in *Feb.* 1660 when this *Pawn* was made, being then ſuppos'd to be a *Lunatick*, and upon that account kept cloſe at *Padua* in *Italy* ; but ſoon after by the Solicitation of *Henry Howard* (next *Brother* and Heir to the ſaid ſuppos'd *Lunatick*) the Dukedom of *Norfolk* was reſtor'd after a long Attainder, and by Act of Parliament ſettled on the ſaid *Thomas* the Grandſon, and the ſaid *Henry* being ſoon after created *Earl* of *Norwick*, did manage the Office of *Earl Marſhal*, and had a *Patent* for the ſame from this preſent *King Charles*, therein ſetling this Office upon him and the Heirs Males of his Body, with a large Intaile for want of ſuch Iſſue to the next Heir Male of that *Noble Family*. So *Henry* was Summond about the middle of this *Parliament* as *Earl* of *Norwich*, with the Title alſo of *Earl Marſhal*, and *Duke Thomas*, dying at *Padua* about the end of this *Parliament*, *Henry* the Brother ſucceeded in the *Dukedom*, and ſat as *Duke* of *Norfolk*, and *Henry* the *Eldeſt Son* of the ſaid

ſaid *Duke Henry*, being then intituled *Earl* of *Arundel*, did ſit as *Earl* of *Arundel* and *Lord Mowbray*, ſo as that Title of *Earl Marſhal* is in *Duke Henry*, and the Title of *Mowbray* in the *Earl* of *Arundel*, and that Title of *Earl Marſhal* only inpoſſibility to come again into *Mowbray*. And this may be added, that during *Duke Thomas* his Life *James Earl* of *Suffolk* by Deputation did execute that Office for reaſons which I leave to other Writers. CHAP IV.

SECT. XIII.

Of the Lord Admiral *of* England.

THE Kings of *England* do conſtantly make Admirals of Squadrons of Ships, but the Admiral which I am here to ſpeak of, is the higheſt of all, intituled the Lord Admiral of *England*, and may be well call'd Admirals, from their ſeeing and knowing the *mirabilia*, or Wonders of the Deep. The *Greeks* call'd this Officer *Thalaſſiarcha*, from *Thalaſſa*, the Sea, and *Archos*, the Chief at Sea, and from thence the *Romans* (according to the *Latin* Idiom) call'd him *Thalaſſiarchus*, and of later days *Admirallus* (which is no *Latin* word) and in *Engliſh* Admiral. *Obſ.* I.

2. To

CHAP. IV. 2. To him is committed the Government of the King of *England*'s Navy, and Power to decide all cauſes *Maritim*, as well Civil as Criminal, and of all things done on, or beyond the Seas in any part of the World, and many other Juriſdictions on the Coaſts, and in Ports, Havens, and Rivers, and of ſuch Wrecks and Prizes as are call'd by the Lawyers, *Lagon*, *Jetſon*, and *Flotſon*, that is, Goods lying in the Sea, floting on the Sea, or caſt by the Sea on the ſhore (admitting ſome few exceptions and Royalties granted to other Lords of Mannors.) And theſe and all other Caſes dependant on this Juriſdiction are determin'd in his Courts of *Admiralty*, by ſuch Rules of the Civil Law as do not invade the Common Laws of *England*.

3. And of theſe Civil Laws which concern Sea affairs there are two moſt eminent Guiders to *Civilians*, *viz.* Thoſe made at *Rhodes* (in the *Mediterranean*) by the *Grecians*, and augmented by the *Romans*, call'd *Lex Rhodia*, or the *Rhodian Law*. The other made at *Oleron* (an Iſland anciently belonging to *England*, but lying on the borders of *France*) by our King *Richard* the Firſt, both of which are ſtill in great veneration.

4. So as well for the Laws by which he

go-

governs the Maritim concerns, as for his great Jurisdiction, being as vast as the Ocean, he may be said to have *alterum Imperium, extra & intra Imperium*, and therefore this Honour and Care is intrusted to the hands of some one of the Blood Royal, or some one or more joyntly of the most eminent of the Nobility.

CHAP. IV.

5. And in respect of this Power there is a constant Converse and Commerce with all parts of the World, especially where the Civil Laws are practis'd, and therefore it hath been the prudence of our former Kings (even to this day) to allot him a place in the Lords House, as to the Marshal of *England*, (for both of their concerns are chiefly manag'd (as I have shewn) by the Civil Laws) so as the Lord Marshal and Lord Admiral may be look'd on as the two Supporters to the learned Professors of those Laws, as the other Lords are to the Professors of the Common Laws, and possibly the greatest number of the Masters of *Chancery* (of whom I shall speak in order) (who sit in the Lords House) were originally contrived to be Doctors of the Civil Laws, upon this ground, That if there were at any time just occasion in that House to make use of any points in that Profession, they might give their advices or opinions therein.

6. This

CHAP. IV.

6. This Dignity, as I ſaid, was ever conferr'd upon ſome of the chief Nobility, by vertue whereof they had their Writs of Summons, and their Place in the Lords Houſe, and this long before the *Act of Precedency*, for we find the Earl of *Arundel*, in 13 *Edw.* 3. and the Earl of *Northumberland*, in 7 *R.* 2. the Earl of *Devon*, and Marqueſs of *Dorſet* in the ſame Kings time, and ſo the Earls of *Salisbury*, *Shrewſbury*, *Worceſter*, and *Wiltſhire*, and others of the like Degrees recited in the *Clauſe Rolls*, (needleſs to renumerate) being Admirals were ſummon'd, and in our extant *Pawns*, in 36 *H.* 8. *Johanni Dudley, Vicecomiti Liſle, Magno Admirallo*, and in 1 *E.* 6. *Tho. Dom. Seymer, Magno Admirallo*, and in 7 *Edw.* 6. *Edv. Fenys, Domino Clinton, Magno Admirallo*, and in 1, 2, 3, 4, *Mariæ*, & *Phil.* & *Mar. Gulielmo Howard de Effingham, Magno Admirallo*, and in 4 & 5 *Phil.* & *Mar. Edw. Fenys* (again) and *Charles*, Earl of *Nottingham*, in Queen *Elizabeth*'s time, and *George*, Duke of *Buckingham*, in King *James*'s time and King *Charles* the Firſt's time, were ſtill ſummon'd to Parliament with the Title of Admiral added to their hereditary Titles in their Writs, and to this Parliament, *Jacobo, Duci Ebor. Magno Admirallo*, &c. And all theſe had their places in the Lords Houſe according to

to the *Act of Precedency*, as those before the Act was made.

This Office was conferr'd on the Duke of *York* for this Parliament. *Vid. Cap.* 2.

SECT. XIV.

Of the Lord Steward *of the* King's House.

Obs. I. AS for the Orthography and Etymology and Antiquity of this Title *Steward*, I shall refer them to my *Annotations*. However as it is sometimes writ with a *T*, and sometimes a *D*, it is under four Considerations; the first, as it represents a Royal Name and Family, and therefore for distinction, this is writ Stewart with a *T*, and hath the superintendence, chief interest and influence in all Parliaments since that Name was of that use in *England*.

2. The other three are Titles official, and written *Steward* with a *D*: and as a further distinction from the first, in *Latin* they are call'd *Seneschalli*, and this, the chief of the three, is call'd *Seneschallus Angliæ*, or Lord High Steward of *England*, of whom I shall give a full account in the Chapter of the *Trials per Pares*, and shew how this great Officer is imploy'd either in or out of Parliaments.

CHAP. IV.

3. The laſt and leaſt Degree of the 3 is call'd alſo *Seneſcallus*, ſuch as are the Stewards of Corporate Towns, or Mannors which are not concern'd in the Summons, or of uſe in Parliaments, otherwiſe than as conſiderable Aſſiſtants in Elections of Members to ſerve in Parliaments; But the Lord Steward of whom I now ſpeak was call'd in *H.* the 8*th.* time, *Magnus Magiſter Hoſpitij Regis*, or the Great Maſter of the Kings Houſhold, and ever ſince *Magnus Seneſcallus Hoſpitij Regis*, or the Lord high Steward of the Kings Houſe, and he hath not only an eminent Employment, Truſt, and Authority, in ordering the Kings Houſhold, but an Authority above all Officers of that Houſe, except the Chappel, Chamber, and Stables, but in all Parliaments is obliged to attend the Kings Perſon, to adjuſt their Parliamentary expences, (*Weſtminſter* being anciently the Kings Court, and ſtill within its Verge and his Lordſhips Juriſdiction.)

4. His place is appointed by the Act of *Precedency* in this order; not but that he was Summon'd to Parliaments before that Act, as may be ſeen in ſeveral Clauſe-Rolls of *Rich.* the 2*d.* &c. but after the ſaid Act, *viz.* 36. *H.* 8. *Charles* Duke of *Suffolk* was Summon'd, and his Writs directed *Magno Magiſtro Hoſpitij ſui*, but after

after that, as in this very Parliament 1661. the Writ to the Duke of *Ormond* was *Jacobo D'no Brecon*, (being his *English* Title by which he sits in Parliament) *Vid. Cap.* 2. *Senescallo Hospitij*, (*Magnus Magister* & *Senescallus*, being still the same Officer, though varying in Title. CHAP. IV.

SECT. XV.

Of the Lord Chamberlain of the Kings Houshold.

THat High-Chamberlain before mentioned is called *Magnus Camerarius*, but this hath not that Epethite of *Magnus*, and yet his authority is very great within the Verge of the Kings Court; so that though there is some Subordination, yet in many great *Regalios* he hath an intire command, and even in some things which concern the conveniency of a Parliament, (and its places of Addresses to the King) that the furniture of the Rooms may be sutable to the Majesty and Grandure of such as are imployed there. *Obs.* I.

2. He hath been anciently summon'd to sit there, as may be seen in the *Clause-Rolls* of the 25. and 27. and 28. of *Edw.* the 3*d.* in the Summons of Sir *Bartholomew*

CHAP. IV. *Bergehurst Camerario Hospitij*, he being also Guarden of the *Cinqueports*, and in 1. *H.* 4. to Sir *Tho. Erpingham, Baneret, Camerario Hospitij*, he being also Guarden of the *Cinqueports*, and so the 10. *H.* 6. to *Radulpho Cromwel Chevalier* or *Baron, Camerario Hospitij*, I might instance many others, but I shall skip as the Records do to the Act of *Precedency*, 31. *H.* 8. where he is call'd the Kings Chamberlain, and in the Pawns of the 36. *H.* 8. the Writ was *Carolo Duci Suff. Magno Magistro Hospitij sui & Præsidenti Consilii sui*, (and in the same *Pawn* which may be observable, the Office of great Chamberlain of *England* was supplied by *Edward* Earl of *Hereford*, of a lesser Degree than a Duke) in the 6. and 7. *Edw.* 6. the Writ was *Tho. D'no Darcy Chevaleer Camerario Hospitij sui*, and in the 43. *Eliz.* to *Tho. Cary* Lord *Hunsden, Camerario Hospitij*, and continues in the same Office, he was Summon'd again *primo. Jacobi*, and in the 15. *Car.* 1. *Philip* Earl of *Penbrook* was Summon'd, *Camerario Hospiti sui*, and to this Parliament, first *Edward* Earl of *Manchester, Camerario Hospitij*, then *Henry* Earl of St. *Albans Camerario Hospitij*, and after him *Hen.* Earl of *Arlington, Camerario Hospitij*, who continued his place and precedency in this Parliament to the Dissolution of it.

Edward

3. *Edward* Earl of *Manchester* Lord Chamberlain of the Kings Houshold was Summon'd so by Writ 18. *Feb.* 1661. *Vid. Cap.* 2. CHAP. V.

SECT. XVI.

Of the Principal Secretary of State.

HE brings up the Honourable Rere to all the 12. Officers of State, both in this *Act of Precedency* and in the *Pawns*, and therefore I may the more justifiably defer my Discourse of him, till I come to his Writ of Summons, and past the method of the *Pawn*, as I have done the method us'd in the *Act of Precedency*, and so conclude these Sections with some few Observations.

Observations.

WHen the Act of 31. *H.* 8. was made, the State Officers (though now but 9 in use, were then 12. a Number (as I shall shew) agreeable to the 12 Judges, 12 Masters of Chancery, 12 Constituting a Jury, and much more of the efficacy of that number, (cited by the Learned Institutor and *Petrus Bongus de Sacris Numeris*) and this number is thus used by us, as tis thought, in veneration, either *Obs.* I.

CHAP. IV. to the 12 Tribes of the *Jews*, or 12 Tables Sacred among the Old *Romans*, or to the 12 Apoſtles of the Chriſtian Religion, or 12 Signs in the *Zodiack* reverenct in *Aſtrology*

2. That if the Writs to any of theſe Officers, be to any of the Lords Spiritual, or ſuch Officers as have uſually conſiſted of the Clergy, as the Lord Chancellor or Lord Keeper, the Lord Treaſurer, Lord Privy Seal, then the Writs were like the Aſſiſtants Writs to the Judges, (of which I ſhall ſpeak in order) but if any of theſe Offices be executed by any of the Temporal Lords, then the Writ is the ſame as to that noble Perſon to whom the Office is anext, or if any be Summon'd meerly *virtute Officij* without annexation, to the Degree of ſome Lord Spiritual or Temporal Lord, then the Writ is only as an Aſſiſtant Writ, and they ſit in the *Lords Houſe* but as Aſſiſtants without Vote, *&c.* as will be ſhewn.

3. Sir *Edward Nicholas* Knight was ſummon'd by Writ dat. 18. *Feb.* 1661. *Vid. Cap.* 2. and now I proceed to the fixt Nobility, call'd Lords Temporal.

CHAP.

Chap. V.

Sect. I.

Of the Degrees of Nobles.

I Have given a ſhort Character of the Grand Officers and Miniſters of State, and now according to the *Act of Precedency*, I ſhall ſpeak of the fixt Nobility, as they are conſider'd in Diſtinct Degrees; and theſe are not mention'd diſtinctly in the Kings Warrant for Summoning a Parliament, but referr'd therein to the Lord Chancellor to diſtinguiſh them by their Writs. *Obſ.*

1. As for the Nobility in general, moſt Authors derive the word *Nobiles* or *Nobles* in the Plural, from *Noſcibiles*, viz. *Viri Nobiles* or Perſons indu'd with great knowledge than other men, and ſo conceive it may admit of another *Etymology*, viz. *Nobilis*, *quaſi Non-bilis*, *i. e.* men of ſuch debonair and complacent tempers, and ſo much Maſters of their paſſions, that they are not (in reſpect of their better Education) ſubject to choler, wrath, or fierceneſs, (for ſo the word *Bilis* is *Engliſht*) but of even and ſerene tempers, which diſpoſitions are

CHAP. V. fitteſt for Affairs relating to Government: but to paſs theſe niceties, the Queſtion is amongſt ſome.

2. How far the Degrees of Nobility do extend? which is partly reſolv'd by Sir *Tho. Smith* in his *Republica*, who ſaith there be two ſorts of Nobles, *viz. Majores* and *Minores*, (and this was according to the Old *Romans*,) the *Majores* he calls the fixt Hereditary Nobles diverſifide into 6 Degrees, *viz.* Princes of the Bloud, (of whom I have ſpoken in *Cap.* the *4th.*) Dukes, Marqueſſes, Earls, Viſcounts and Barons, (not of the Bloud) and deſcend no lower, and theſe are capacitated by ſuch Creations and Writs to ſit in the *Lords Houſe*. The *Minores* he begins at Knights, (for he wrote before Baronets were known) Eſquires, and Gentlemen, and deſcended no lower; and out of theſe, the Knights, Citizens, and Burgeſſes for Parliaments are Elected and Compos'd, and thereby capacitated to ſit therein, as the *Repreſentatives* of the *Commons* of *England*: but of theſe *Nobiles Minores* I ſhall ſpeak more in the ſecond part of this Treatiſe; but of the *Majores* now in their Order, which conſiſt of 5 Degrees, beſides thoſe of the Stem Royal, (of which I have ſpoke) and firſt of Dukes.

SECT.

SECT. II.

Of Dukes.

Obs. I.

BEfore I proceed to the Writs of Summons to the Individuals of these Degrees, I shall give a brief description of the nature of them; and first as for the word Duke, it is the same with *Dux* in *Latin*, (from *Duco* to lead) for they were antiently Leaders of Armies, and thereby gain'd that Title, (as might be shewn from Histories) and were it not for hindering my other intentions, I might recite most of the Learned *Seldens* Authorities, (which he hath rendred from other Authors concerning Dukes) but in short he tels us that *Comes i. e.* a Count or Earl was esteemed of an higher quality than Duke, and that Earl was chief in Matters Civil, and Duke in Matters Military; but in process of time the Sword got the upper hand, and prioritie of Earl; and further saith that both Dukes and Earls from Substitutes to their Princes, (in certain dependent Territories) became afterwards Soveraigns, (as the great Duke of *Tuscany*, &c. and the Earl of *Flanders*, &c. (still owning the Titles of Dukes or Earls, though they had

CHAP. V. had gain'd an intire and independent Soveraignty.)

2. The diverſity of Names attributed to Dukes, both in ſacred, prophane, and modern ſtories, were according to the humour of the region where they ſway'd; for in ſome Nations he was call'd *Princeps*, *Magnus*, *Illuſtriſſimus*, *Robuſtus*, *Millenarius*, (that is a Duke, or Leader of a Thouſand Men) in other Countries, *Grave*, *Waiward*, and *Deſpot*, and ſtill the words Duke and Earl, promiſcuouſly us'd to one and the ſame Perſon: but whatever they were or are in foreign parts, Dukes are now in *England* accounted the chief and moſt honourable Subjects, and firſt Degree of Nobility (except Princes or Dukes of the Blood-Royal) and, as a diſtinction from the reſt, is call'd *Grace*) given to no other Spiritual Lord, but the Arch-Biſhops of *Canterbury* and *York*, and to no other Temporal Lord, (except to the Lord High Steward, *pro hac vice*, upon tryal of Peers) for the Princes and Dukes of the Blood, are intituled *Highneſs*, and all the other Temporal Lords, *Right Honourable*, but any of thoſe being Admiral or General, *Excellence*.

3. The Title of Duke was very probably us'd here in *England* before *Edward* the Third's time; for Hiſtory tells us of *Aſclepio-*

piodolus, Duke of *Cornwal*, in *Anno Christi*, 232. (which was in the time of our old *Britains*) and well might he be call'd Duke, for disgarrisoning of all the *Roman* Holds, and for his quick Marches to *London*, and killing the Governour thereof, and for many other Heroick Actions, in freeing his Country from their Servitude. However, there were many Dukes Created in *Germany* about that time. But our History tells us, That none was Created a Duke in *England*, till 11 *Edw*. 3. *An. Christi*, 1344. when the King in Parliament Created his eldest Son, *Edward*, (being first made Earl of *Chester*) then Duke of *Cornwal*, and from thence that County was erected to a Dutchy or Dukedom, and many more Dukes, both in that King's time, and almost in every Kings Reign since that time, have been Created to that Title.

CHAP. V.

Prideaux Introduct. to Hist.

Selden. *Speed's* Acts.

4. The Dukes of *England* are of two sorts, first, those of the Blood Royal, *i. e.* such as have a possibility to inherit the Crown upon a legal succession. 2*dly*, Those not of the Blood Royal, *i. e.* such as are not related to the Succession of the Crown, or at least so remote, that it is not visible to meer probability; and these two sorts have sat in former and in this Parliament, as will be shewn.

As

CHAP. V.

5. As they are diſtinguiſh'd in their Titles, ſo they are alſo in their Coronets, Robes, and Habits, &c. with which they are inveſted before they enter the *Houſe of Lords*, (which will be in the third Part of this Treatiſe repreſented in Figures.)

6. Here I muſt not paſs over one obſervable, That to this Parliament of 13 *Car.* 2. there were three Dukes ſummon'd by Writ, *viz. George*, Duke of *Buckingham*, *Charles*, Duke of *Richmond*, and *George*, Duke of *Albemarle*; the Duke of *Buckingham* was then Maſter of the Horſe, the Duke of *Richmond* of the Blood Royal, by the *Scotiſh* Line, yet neither of thoſe two appendant Titles were mention'd in their Writs; but *George*, Duke of *Albemarle*, in his Writ is intituled, *Generalis exercituum ſuorum*, and is plac'd the third in that Record, and the reaſon may be, becauſe there was no proviſion for that great Office in the *Act of Precedency*, whereby to preceed all of the ſame degree (as other degrees do) (being a Title not mention'd in the Act, though on ſome occaſions he preceeds by vertue of his Office the other grand Officers) and ſo being not in the Act he is named in this *Pawn* the laſt of the three Dukes, without reſpect to his Office of Generalſhip. Nor do I find in any *Clauſe Roll*, or *Pawn*, the Title of General

neral annext in any Parliament Writ to any one of the Degrees (except this) though History does plentifully furnish us with several persons of those several Degrees who were Generals when Parliaments were summon'd; and yet, as I said, there is no provision in this Act, for the Place or Precedency of this great Officer, as there is for the Marshal, Admiral, &c. although his great merits might well have deserv'd an additional Clause to that Act for his precedency. CHAP. V.

7. Three Dukes were summon'd 18 *Feb.* 1661. as in the *Pawn*, *vide cap.* 2. The next Degree to Dukes are Marquesses.

SECT. III.

Of Marquesses.

THE third Degree of the Hereditary and fixt Nobility, is intituled, *Marquio*, (and *Marquess* in *English*) which began in *Germany*, *Anno Christi*, 925. when *Henry*, (Emperour of *Germany*) and the first of that Name in that Empire) Created *Sigefred* (then Earl of *Kinglesheim*) Marquess of *Brandenburgh*; who after, in the Year 1525. having the addition of Duke of *Prussia*, did exchange the Title of *Obs.* I.

CHAP. V. of Marquess, to be call'd Duke of *Brandenburgh*: However, he was the first Marquess of that Empire, and probably the Emperour did fix this Title between the Dukes and Earls, that there might be no more disputes concerning them; for the two Titles of Duke and Earl were promiscuously us'd till this Title of Marquess was interpos'd; and the same reason might also occasion *Philip* the Fair, King of *France*, 425 years after, *viz. Anno Christi*, 1350. to insert into *John*, Duke of *Britain's* Patent: *Ut ne posset* (saith the Patent) *in dubium revocari Ducem ipsum* (*qui Comes fuit aliquando, &c.*) *ut Ducem in posterum deberet vocari, &c.* and the reason is therein given, *Quod Comitatus ejus potius debet duci & esse Ducatus, quam Comitatus, quoniam sub se habet decem & ultra Comitatus*, and 56 years after, *viz. Anno Christi*, 1386. This might occasion also our *Richard* the Second, to make *Robert d' Vere* the first Marquess of *England* by Creation, and hereby the dispute between the two Titles of Duke and Earl, or *Comes*, was setled both in the *Empire*, in *France*, and in *England*, by the interpos'd Title of Marquess.

Selden.

2. From whence this Title is derived, there are several conjectures, but most agree, That it comes from *Marken*, or *Mark*, or *March*,

March, (*High Dutch* words) ſignifying with them as with us, a *Mark* or *Limit*, and from thence he that was deputed Governour of that Limit or Mark which he was to take care of, and preſerve, was call'd a *Marches*, or Marqueſs, and the Territory under his Juriſdiction, a *Marquiſate*, and to this day the Marquiſate of *Brandenburgh* is divided into three Marks, or Marches, *viz.* *Alte-Mark*, or old March, the middle Mark, and the new Mark, or March: and we in *England* do ſtill call ſuch kind of Limits by the name of *Marks*, or *Marches*, *viz.* the *Marches of Wales*, and the *Marches of Scotland*, which were Frontiers to be defended againſt the *Scots* and *Welch*; and ſome would derive Marqueſs from *Mare*, the *Sea*, becauſe their Marken or Limits were *juxta Mare poſita*, and the learned *Selden* (in his Titles of Honour) likes it well enough, that Marqueſs ſhould be derived from *Marken*, but not *Marken* from *Mare*.

CHAP. V.

Heylin's Coſm.

3. But I muſt not ravil into Diſputes of this Nature, and therefore ſhall refer them to his Book, and my Annotations, and conclude this *Section* with this, That as moſt *Sir-Names* are deriv'd from ſome ſignificant word or words, ſo theſe noble Titles (without derogation to their other Titles) are from ſome ſignal Action,

CHAP. V. Action, as a Duke from leading an Army; a Marqueſs from *Maris acquiſitio*, (a gaining ſomething from the Sea, or preſerving ſomething againſt the Sea) and ſo of the other Titles (as will be ſhewn) and thereupon had condignal Honours conferr'd on them, to teſtifie their Imployments, which are ſince (as Memorials of their Merits) therein become hereditary.

4. Four Marqueſſes were ſummon'd, 18 *Feb.* 1661. as in the *Pawn*, *vide Cap.* 2.

SECT. IV.

Of Earls.

Obſ. I. THe learned *Selden* tells us, (as I have ſhewn) That the Titles of Dukes, and Counts, or Earls, were promiſcuouſly us'd as well in foreign parts as in *England*, till the Title of Marqueſs was interpos'd; and it is agreed, that *Comes* is the *Latin* word for Count, (in whatever Territory that word is us'd) and that Count is deriv'd from *Comitatus*, or County; and *Comitatus* from *Committo*, (denoting the particular County committed to his Care) and *vice verſa*, *Committo* begets *Comitatus*, or County, and *Comitatus*, *Comes*, a Count, *i. e.* Earl.

Of

Of these *Counts* the learned *Selden* reckons but 6 Sorts, *viz.* the *Single Count*, (who hath no addition but his Christian name) 2*d. Count Palatine* (from *Palatium* or some Palace in it,) 3*d. Count* of the *Empire*, 4*th. Count* of *Frontiers*, where the Title of *Marquess* is also us'd instead of *Count*, 5*th. Count* of *Provinces*, (or Counties joyn'd) which in Foraign parts are call'd *Landgraves*, (the word *Grave* and *Comes* signifying the same Title) and 6*th. Count* of Cities or Towns, and these latter, as in *England*, are call'd *Comites Castrenses* or *Burgraves*, or *Counts* of Castles or Burroughs, (all which are more fully describ'd in his second Book.) But I find that *Cassiodorus* in his 6*th.* Book mentions 22 Sorts more than Mr. *Selden*, of which 6 of Mr. *Seldens*, or 28 of *Cassiodorus*, we in *England* retain but few, *viz.* a *Count* of a County, (as *Algernonus*, *Comes Northumbriæ*; A *Count* of a City, (as *Albericus* or *Awbry*, *Comes Oxoniæ* (or *Oxford*,) and *Guilelmus*, *Comes Novi Castri* or *New Castle* upon *Tine*, (being both a Castle and Burrough.)

CHAP. V.

3. All the curiosity lies in finding out how *Comes* or *Count* happens to be transmutted into the word *Earl*, so much different in Pronuntiation and Orthography from each other, and yet, as we say, are the same in Substance.

4. Now

CHAP. IV. 4. Now it being no hard matter to believe (as I have ſhewn) that Duke is deriv'd from *Duco*, and Marqueſs from *Mare*, but Earl from *Comes* or *Count*, is not ſo intelligible; but this may be ſaid, that the *Saxons* from whom we borrow this word Earl, did uſe it as a word of Honour, and in the ſame ſence with *Comes*, for they did call their chiefeſt Governors of Shires, (of which many of our Counties ſtill retain that name, as will be ſhewn) and of Cities and Burroughs, by the name of *Earldermen*, and for a more eaſie pronounciation *Ealderman*, and after *Alderman*, and for brevity *Earl*, and the *Danes* after them *Earlan*; and commonly the *Earlan* or *Earl* had a Shire or more for his *Earldom*, and the number of *Earls* increaſing, ſome had part of a Shire, others ſome chief Town, of which he was made *Earl* or *Earldermanus*; and whatever other Etymologers ſay, (of which I can ſpeak more freely in my Annotations) I conceive the Dominion of thoſe *Earls* were allotted near ſome ſpreading Rivers, (in Fenny-Countries) which are to this day call'd *Eas*, and thoſe *Inland Iſles* (which we now write *Iſland*, and ſome corruptly calls *Eyes*) were anciently writ *Ealands*, as *Rumen-ea*, (now *Rumney-Marſhes* in *Kent*) and *Ely* an

Sir William Dugdale.

an *Island* in *Cambridgeshire* is anciently writ *Ealand*, and so *Worrel Island*, (near *Chester*) sometimes call'd *Ealand*, and sometimes *Island*, and I could reckon up what I have seen in *Cambridgeshire*, and *Lincolnshire*, at least 40 antient Cuts and Sewers of Water, which still are call'd and writ by the name of *Ea*, *viz.* *Boston Ea* in *Lincolnshire*, *Popham Ea* in *Northhamptonshire*, (signifying great Waters in those places) and many more might be instanced to prove that as Marquess may safely be deriv'd from *Mare*, (as denoting one that had the guard of the inundations from Saltwaters) so *Earl* may as safely be deriv'd from *Ea*, (or one that had the guard and care against the *Inland* innundations of fresh waters) and some observe that this word *Ea* is still retain'd in most of those Counties which are intituled Shires, or bordering on those Shires (Shire being (a *Saxon* word) as will be shewn) but in other Counties which are not call'd Shires, the word *Ea* is scarce known, so as *Comes* or *Count* was us'd in such places as were call'd Counties, and *Earl* in such as were call'd Shires.

CHAP. IV.

5. This Tutelage of grounds gain'd or preserv'd from waters, was so great an honour, that *Caius Marius*, (who was made seven times *Consul* or *Comes*, (for

CHAP. V. as *Selden* faith, *Comites dici poſſunt Conſules a Conſulendo*) which was render'd *Earl*, did by a Cut or Drain fo fecure the Inundation of Salt waters often overflowing a large Fenny County near *Arles* in *France*, that in memory of fo benificial a Work, it was called *Foſſa Mariana*, (or the *Conſul Marius* his Drain) and in *Pompeys* time the fecuring of the inundations of *Freſhes* about 40 Miles from *Rome* was efteem'd to be fo good Service, that one of the two Confuls were ufually appointed to attend the *Gallick Enemy*, the other had the care of the *Ea* or *Watry Enemy*; and it is no fmall honour now to the Earl of *Bedford* to be Governour of 365000 Acres of Fenny Grounds, intituled by his name of *Bedford Level* fubject to inundations, but by his vigilance prefervs it.

6. And when this Title of Earl was firft given in *England*, (as tis faid) by *William* the firft, to *Hugo de Aurank* or *de Ibrinks*, making him Earl of *Cheſter*, it was doubtlefs from fome eminent Service done in preferving the Banks or Brinks of that County againft the inundations of the River *Dee* upon the South-fide of *Worrel Ealand* aforefaid, reaching from the Town of *Cheſter* to the *Hebrea*, for fhortnefs call'd *Heber*, and fo round that *Hundred*, (befides the Banks in other parts of that County.) Some

Some do queſtion whether this *d' Aurank* or *d' Ibrink* was the firſt Earl, but tis likely he was ſo Titularly, and other the like Earls before him: but that which is agreed on is, that *Albericus* or *Aubry d' Vere*, was the firſt that was by Charter (or Patent) created Earl by *Henry* the 2*d*. who had the additional Title of Earl of *Oxford* or *Oxenford* in *Oxfordſhire*, and continues in that Family to this day; but I cannot paſs the word *Ford*, which doth imply a paſſable Ea or Water, which was neceſſarily to be preſerved from the overflowing of at leaſt 7 ſeveral Rivers in that little County, for the more ſafe paſſage of Men and Oxen.

CHAP. V.

7. To conclude, I hope I may be allow'd ſo much of the Art of Tachygraphy or ſhort writing, as may render my application of this word more plauſible, by writing *Earl* for *Ea Regalia*, ſo as whether *Ea* be conſider'd as a *Saxon* word, or the plural of the pronoun *Ea*, it confirms my notion, and may ſerve as well to explain the word Earl, as *S P Q R* the Senate and People of *Rome*, or *D N S* to ſignifie a Baron of the Realm or Chr. *Chevaleer*.

8. I have ſaid ſufficiently of the word; now as to the antiquity of it in *England*, it is Authentick from Hiſtory and Record, that the word *Earl* and Honour of it, was

CHAP. V. in uſe in the *Saxons*, and *Danes* time, and continued with the *Normans*, and Earls had the like extenſive power in Shires and Counties as they have had ſince their formal creation by Charter, which it ſeems was a mode and form not us'd till this to the Earl of *Oxford*, ſince which there hath been ſome variations in the Form, but eſpecially in the time of *Henry* the eighth and King *James*, as will be ſeen when I come to recite ſo much of their Charters of Creation as relate to their intereſts in Parliament.

9. The learned *Selden* divides this Title into two ſorts, a Local and a Perſonal Earl; by Local he means ſuch Counties, Cities, Caſtles, Towns, or Burroughs, as are fix'd to the Title of Earl, (or *Comes*) as Earl of *Oxford*, Earl of *Kent*, &c. (being not County Palatines) or of ſuch as are County Palatines, whereof there are five, *viz. Cheſhire*, *Lancaſhire*, (which are in the Crown) *Pembrokeſhire* (in the preſent Earl of *Pembroke*) *Durham* and *Ely*, (which two are County Palatines, belonging to the Biſhops of thoſe Counties, never granted to any Temporal Earls) ſo as the Biſhops of *Ely* and *Durham* do ſit in Parliament *Virtute Tenuræ*, and not *Virtute Comitatus Palatinæ*.

As

As for Perſonal Earls, there are but three remaining at this day, *viz.* the Earl or Lord Great Chamberlain, granted to *Berty*, Earl of *Lindſey*, with a large intale to that Family, 2*ly*. the Title of Earl Marſhal granted to *Hen. Howard* Earl of *Norwich*, and after Duke of *Norfolk*, with a large intale as I have ſhewn, 3*ly*. granted by Patent to *Savage* Earl *Rivers* being made a Baron in 5 *Edw.* 6. and alſo Viſcount of *Colcheſter* in 19 *Jacobi*, and in the 2*d*. of *Charles* the firſt was made Viſcount *Savage* of *Rock Savage* in *Cheſhire*, whereby he is a double Viſcount, and Earl *Rivers*, which is the Name of an illuſtrious Family, and not of a Place, but all the other Earls are intituled from ſome noted Place.

CHAP. V.

10. Forty nine Earls Summon'd the 18*th*. *February*, 1661. and ſix more Summon'd the 29*th*. of *Aprill*, 1661. See the *Pawn. Cap.* 2.

The next I am to treat of is the *Vicecomes*, *Vice* Earl, or Viſcount.

CHAP. V.

SECT. V

Of a Viſcount.

Obſ. I. WHat hath been ſaid of a Duke or a Count, whilſt their Titles were interchangeably us'd, may be alſo appli'd to a Viſcount; for when Dukes and Counts increas'd in their number, there was a kind of neceſſity to take in others to their aſſiſtance, who afterwards by merit and the favour of their Prince, arrived to an Intereſt of their own, and therefore the word *Vicecomes*, or Viſcount, may properly here intend a Companion, (for the word *Comes* doth as well ſignifie a Companion or Aſſociate, as a Count or Earl) and the addition of *Vice* (which ſignifies inſtead, or by courſe or turns (of which word *Turn* I ſhall ſpeak more) did intimate, thar when the Turn of this *Comes* came to Govern, he was for that time called *Vicecomes*, all other times *Comes* only, or, as I conceive, as the one was call'd *Comes*, becauſe he commanded a County, the other was called *Vicecomes*, from the *Latin* word *Vicus*, becauſe he commanded a Village, Street, or Structure, or ſome leſſer Command than that of a County.

2. The

2. The dignal Title of *Vicecomes* is also ancienter in foreign parts, than in *England*, and is the same with *Vidame*, or *Vicedominus* (which are properly the foreign Titles of a Substitute to a Bishop) but as we take the Title in an officiall sence, it signifies the King's Deputy or Sheriff in every County, and so is as ancient as the *Saxons*, who made *Comes* to signifie Earl, and *Vicecomes*, or Viscount, to signifie the Office of *Shereeve*, or Sheriff, for we had the words Earl and Sheriff from the *Saxons*, and the Count and Viscount from the *Romans*, *Comes* and *Vicecomes*: and probably for the same reason, that Marquess was interpos'd to Duke and Earl in *Richard* the Second's time, so it was thought fit in *Henry* the Sixth's time (though some say in *Henry* the Fifth's time) to interpose the Title of Viscount to *Comes*, or Earl, and the Noble Baron, there having been the like promiscuous use of the Titles of *Comes*, or Earl, and Baron, as had been of Duke and *Comes*, and thereupon I conceive *John d' Beaumont* was Created the first Viscount of this interposing Dignity, it being, as Mr. *Cambden* saith, an old Name of Office, but a new Name of Dignity, or a *Vicecomes*, or Sheriff, turn'd from an annual Office into a Dignity hereditary.

CHAP. V.

Yet

CHAP. V. 3. Yet this Office of *Vicecomes*, or *Shereeve*, or Sheriff, was, and ſtill is an Office of dignity; only the difference is, that the *Vicecomes* dignified, (as I ſaid by *Hen.* the *6th.* is a Parliamentary and Nobilitated Dignity and Place, (both in their Patent of Creation, and in the *Act of Precedency*) fixt between Earl and Baron, &c. made Hereditary, but the other *Viſcountſhip* or *Sherifdom* is Official and Annual and not Hereditary, and hath no place in the *Lords Houſe*; and particularly excepted to be choſen into the *Houſe of Commons*, by the Writs of Elections, (as will be ſhewn) and the reaſon is, becauſe the Official *Viſcountſhip* is in the King, who gives only an annual Deputation to the Perſon who executes that Office in ſuch County, of which he is made *Vicecomes* or *Deputy* to the King, and ſo is not the Noble *Viſcount*, (who cannot be made Sheriff or return'd of a Jury) but hath his conſtant Writ of Summons to every Parliament, (as will be ſhewn;)

4. Seven Viſcounts Summon'd by Writ 18. *Feb.* 1661. and One Viſcount Summon'd by Writ 20*th.* *Ap.* 1661.

And now I come to the Barons, the laſt Degree of the Nobility, but anciently the Firſt or Second.

SECT.

SECT. VI.

Of Barons.

I Shall refer the Etymology of this word Baron to my Annotations, (becauſe the learned *Cambden*, *Selden*, and others have taken pains about it) but for many ages, as at preſent, it comprehends all ſuch Prelates and Biſhops as are Summon'd by vertue of their Baronies or Tenures to ſit in the *Houſe of Lords*.

As alſo all ſuch Dukes, Marqueſſes, Earls and Viſcounts, as did anciently mount to any of thoſe 4 Degrees, by the proportion of their Baronies, which they obtain'd by gift from the King, or other acquiſitions, ſo differing from the other 4 in Nominal gradations, rather than Eſſential. And though there were Nominal differences antiently in the Tenures of Dukes, Marqueſſes, Earls, Viſcounts, and Barons, yet they were all ſubject to a general Contribution to the Kings affairs, according to their certain number of Knights Fees; for as Baronies made the other 4 Superior Degrees, ſo the increment of Knights Fees (whereupon I conceive Sir *Thomas Smith* made that Degree of *Nobiles Minores*) did capacitate a Baron to be made a Ba-

CHAP. V. a Baron, and ſo a certain number of Baronies to be a Viſcount and Earl, and of *Earledoms* to be a Duke, as may be read in Sir *Edward Coke*, (and others more ancient by him cited) and Mr. *Selden* (forgiving the Knight) ſaith that *Iſtud verbum Baro eſt caput & ſcala dignitatum Regalium, i. e. Majoris Nobilitatis.*)

2. In former times theſe proportions were obſerv'd amongſt the Temporal Lords, but not with the Spiritual, for Mr. *Selden* tells us of a Biſhop (*pag.* 580. Tit. Hon.) that had 220 Baronies, and did ſit in Parliament by vertue of his Baronies, yet was neither Duke nor Earl) ſo thoſe were the computations of Honour and Contributions, till the method of Creations were us'd, and at laſt by the late Act of Parliament all *Tenures* in *Capite* were Diſſolved, and thereby the *Tenurial* Contributions, but not the Titles of Honour: yet for a little variety I may inform ſome, that in former times the Spiritual Barons had ſome exemptions from Contributions, unleſs there was (as the learned *Selden* calls it) *Trinoda neceſſitas*, *viz.* of War, of Repairs of Caſtles, or Bridges, but they were generally exempted from Perſonal Aſſiſtance in War; for though (as he ſaith) that in the 4*th.* year of *William* the Firſt, that King made the Biſhops, *&c.* ſubject to Knights Service

vice in chief, by creation of their Tenures, and so was the first King that turn'd their possessions by *Frankalmoine* a *French* word signifying charitable Gifts, for so began their temporalities) into Baronies, and thereby made them Barons of the Kingdom by Tenure, yet when it was pray'd by them in the 5*th*. *Hen*. the 3*d*. *Ut omnes Clerici tenentes Baronias, &c. personaliter procederent contra Regis adversarios, &c.* it was answer'd by the Bishops (and their Answer allow'd) *Quod non debent pugnare cum gladio materiali sed Spirituali, scilicet cum Lachrymis & orationibus humilibus & devotis, & quod propter beneficia sua manutenere debent pacem non bellum, & Quod Baroniæ eorum ab Eleemosynis puris stabiliuntur, &c.* So as (he conceives that) the Baronies of the Clergy were made of such Lands as formerly were, as I said, held in *Franckalmoine*. CHAP. V.

3. But what ever exemptions the Spiritual Barons had, the Temporal Barons were oblig'd by their Baronial Tenures (of several natures) to all defensive and offensive duties for the King and Kingdoms preservation, according to the proportion of their dependent tenures or territories; and so are yet in honour oblig'd to perform, and they all had and have equal

CHAP. V. equal Votes in Parliament by vertue of their Baronial Intereſt; for as to matters Parliamentary, the Title of Baron is more ancient, copious, and comprehenſive, than any of the other Titles of Lords in Parliament.

4. This word Baron we ſee is appilicable, not only to the two degrees of Lords Spiritual, *viz.* Archbiſhops and Biſhops, but to the 5 degrees of Lords Temporal, ſo as the noble Barons and all the Degrees above them do ſet in the *Lords Houſe*, *virtute Baroniæ*, and by Writs of Summons, the Superior Titles to the Barons differing rather upon ſome *extrinſick order*, than any real *intrinſick diſtinction*.

5. As for thoſe Titles of Barons which are given to Degrees equal or under the noble Barons, they are of ſeveral ſorts; *1ſt.* Some noble Barrons by Ancienty never Summon'd to a Parliament, yet capable of Summons; *2ly.* The Barons of the Exchequer, (which are 4 in number, who are Summon'd by Writ *ad conſulendum*, or to be Aſſiſtants in the *Lords Houſe*, (as will be ſhewn;) *3ly.* Barons of the Cinqueports (out of whoſe number 16 are uſually Elected) to ſit in the *Houſe of Commons*, (as will be ſhewn;) *4ly.* Barons

rons of Court-Barons, who are alſo capable of being Elected to ſit in the *Houſe of Commons*; 5*th*. Barons in the Law-*French* call'd Baron, *i. e.* and Husband, (and *Feme* the Wife) but I here only ſpeak of the *Nobiles Barones* diſtinct from theſe Titular Barons, though ſuch of them as ſit in the *Lords Houſe* are in ſome ſort thereby Nobilitated, of whom I ſhall ſpeak more when I come to the Aſſiſtants; and ſuch as ſit in the *Commons Houſe* are thereby Dignified though not Nobilitated, (of whom I ſhall ſpeak when I come to the *Houſe of Commons.*) CHAP V.

6. Now it may here be obſerved, that ſome Perſons of merit have been Summon'd to ſit in the *Lords Houſe* as Barons, which were not Barons, or any otherwiſe capacitated to ſit there but by Writs of Summons; upon this occaſion Sir *Edward Coke* cites a Caſe where one Summond by Writ to ſit in the *Lords Houſe*, died before he ſat there, and it was adjudged that if he had ſat there, he had been Nobilitated thereby, but having not ſat there, whereby that writ was not executed for want of his Perſonal attendance, it was adjudg'd that the direction or delivery of the Writ barely to the Perſon to whom the Writ was directed, (without Perſonal appearance and inveſtiture of Robes and a poſſeſſion

CHAP. V. ſeſſion of place) was not ſufficient to enoble him, without a conjunction of thoſe Circumſtances and Ceremonies.

7. But Barons created by Letters Patents, (and made to them and their Heirs) are thereby *Nobilitated*, and to be eſteem'd *Nobles* though they do not Sit, in reſpect of the power given them by Patent to Sit without reſtrictions or ceremonial qualifications; and therefore Sir *Edward Coke* ſaith, that though the Creation by Writ be ancienter than by Patent, yet the Creation by Patent is the ſurer way, for that one may be ſufficiently Created by Patent and made Noble, though he never ſit in Parliament, and he gives this reaſon; *That if iſſue be joyn'd whether one be a Baron or not, that point ſhall not be tried by a Jury of 12 men, but by the Records of the Parliament, and if he did not ſit there, there can be no Record, but a Patent is a Record.*

8. So there were 62 Barons Summon'd by Writs of the 18. of *Feb.* 1661. and 6 more by Writs of the 29. of *Ap.* 1661. whereby the number of Temporal Lords Summon'd to this Parliament began the 8*th.* of *May* 1661. were—140. *viz.*

1. Two Dukes of the Bloud.
2. Three Dukes not of the Bloud.

3. Four

CHAP. V.

3. Four Marquesses.
4. Fifty five Earls.
5. Eight Viscounts.
6. Sixty eight Barons.

In all of the 6 Degrees 140. as in the *Pawn Cap.* 2. which we may compare with former times, *viz.*

Regno.		Anno.	Num.Maj. (*The highest Number Summon'd in these Years.*)	Anno.	Num.Mi. (*The lowest Number Summon'd in these Years.*)
Edwar.	3.	25°	62	4°	18
Richar.	2.	8°	63	18°	36
Henry	4.	1°	50	11°	39
Henry	5.	2°	44	3°	29
Henry	6.	38°	55	1°	23
Edwar.	4.	7°	47	12°	37
Henry	8.	37°	45	28°	44
Edwar.	6.	6°	59	1°	47
Mariæ		2°	56	1°	42
Elizabeth.		30°	60	43°	52
Jacobi		21°	98	1°	84
Caroli	1.	15°	109	1°	97
Caroli	2.	13°	140		

I do insert this observation, That the Ingenious Historian may see, whether the greater or lesser number of the Nobility in Parliament hath been most advantageous to its Constitution; and the like may be observed concerning the number of the

K *House*

CHAP. V. *Houfe of Commons*, (of which I fhall fpeak in the next part.)

By which we may fee that the higheft Number was in 12. and 13. of *Car. 2d.* and the Loweft in the *4th.* of *Edw.* the *3d.* not troubling the Reader with the Numbers Summon'd to Intervening Parliaments.

Thus having given fome fhort Illuftrations of thofe Titles of Honour which are mentioned in the Parliamentary Writs and the *Act of Precedency*, for the clearer fatisfaction of fuch as are not verft in matters of that nature; I may now with the more content to them and my felf proceed to the particular Writs of Summons to thofe noble Degrees which I have regularly mention'd, according to their prefcrib'd Order, both from the method of the Writs in the *Pawns* and Act; and thefe Writs of which I am particularly to fpeak (others falling in collaterally) are;

Sect. 1. The form of the Writs to any of the Bloud Royal.

2. The form of the Writs to Archbifhops and Bifhops.

3. The form of Writs to the Lord Chancellor or Lord Keeper.

4. The form of Writs to Dukes not of the Bloud, Marqueffes, Earls, Vifcounts, and Barons, wherein the Grand Official Titles beforementioned are inferted.

CHAP.

CHAP. VI.

CHAP. VI.

Of Writs of Summons, and first of the Exemplar Writs for Summoning Princes, Dukes, and Earls of the Bloud-Royal to the Parliament.

SECT. I.

I Have shewn in Chap.2. how Parliament Writs are sorted into Close Writs, and Open Writs or Patents, and those into Exemplars and Consimilars. I need not inlarge more therein, but proceed to the first Exemplar Writ of Summons, and so to other such Writs of Summons to other Degrees as concern the *Lords House*; for I shall speak of other Parliament-Writs of another nature, when I have dispatcht the Summoning Writs and Patents of Creation, according to the method of *Pawns* and *Clause-Rolls* made before the *Act of Precedency*, as also in all *Pawns* since that Act. Those of the Bloud-Royal are placed in the first Rank of those Records, and were still Exemplar to the rest, and therefore the Writ which I am now to speak of, *viz.* To the Duke of *York* (Brother to King *Charles* the 2d.) is

CHAP. VI. is the Exemplar of the Conſimilar Writ to Prince *Rupert* Duke of *Cumberland*, (being Son to the Siſter of King *Charles* the Firſt) and ſo perſuant not only to the ſaid Act, but to the moſt ancient methods of Writs of Summons, (as will be more fully ſhewn in the following Chapters.)

But before I recite this Writ, methinks I hear ſome ſay, *Nolumus conſuetudines Angliæ mutare*, therefore let us know what Writs of this nature were iſſued in former Ages by former Kings, which is a Queſtion ſo pertinent to my own ſcruples, that (I hope) the ſame eaſe I gave to my ſelf (after my inquiry) will ſerve to ſatisfie others; for having gone backward with as much ſafety (to the avouching of Records as I could,) and being not ſatisfied with what was delivered to us, concerning the Parliament Writs in the *Brittiſh*, *Romans*, *Danes*, *Saxons*, or *Norman* times, or by ſome of the *Plantagenets*, or thoſe of *Hen. 3ds.* time, from whence moſt Writers of our *Engliſh* Parliaments take their Original; I fixt upon and took my Riſe from the Writs in the *15th.* of *Edw. 2d.* which are clear and ſtill extant in the Records of the Tower, which the other are not.

By theſe Records it is evident, that in 97. Parliaments, as I account them, which were Summon'd from that *15th.* year to this

this Parliament, there is no material dif- CHAP
ference in this Exemplar Writ from those VI.
Antecedent; and therefore that this Writ to the Duke of *York* may be compar'd with that of *Edw.* 2*d.* I have here set them both down *verbatim*, so that upon 339. years experience, *viz.* from the year 1322. to the year 1661. Inclusive, we may acquiesce, that we in this Age have not much trespass't or varied from the ancient and wise Form prescribed to us by so many former Kings, and continued to this time.

The Form of the Exemplar Writ to the Princes of the Bloud.

Tempore Edw. 2. 15.

E*Dwardus Dei Gratia Rex Angliæ Dominus Hiberniæ & Dux Aquitaniæ, Edwardo Comiti Cestriæ filio suo Charissimo*

Salutem, Super diversis & arduis negotiis nos & statum Regni nostri specialiter tangentibus Parliamentum nostrum apud Eboracum a die Paschæ prox' futuro in tres septi'anas teneri & vobiscum & cum ceteris Prelatis Magnatibus & Proceribus dicti Regni habere proponimus colloquium & tractatum.

CHAP. VI. *Vobis Mandamus* in fide & dilectione quibus nobis tenemini firmiter injungentes. Dictis die & loco omnibus aliis pretermiſſis perſonaliter interſitis ibidem nobiscum & cum ceteris prelatis magnatibus & proceribus ſupradictis negotiis tractatur veſtrumq; Conſilium impenſur' Et hoc Nullatenus omittat' Teſte me ipſo apud Weſtm' decimo quarto die Martii Anno Regni noſtri decimo quinto.

Caroli 2. 13

CArolus Secundus Dei Gratia Angliæ Scotiæ Franciæ & Hiberniæ Rex fidei defenſor, &c. Præchariſſimo & dilecto fratri Jacobo Duci Eborum & Albaniæ magno Admirallo ſuo Angliæ Salt'm Quia de

Adviſamento & aſſenſu Conſilii noſtri pro quibuſdam arduis & urgentibus negotiis nos ſtatum & defenſionem Regni noſtri Angliæ & Eccleſiæ noſtræ concernentibus Quoddam Parliamentum noſtrum apud Civitatem noſtram Weſtm' octavo die Maii prox' futur' teneri ordinavimus & ibidem nobiſcum ac cum magnatibus & proceribus dicti Regni noſtri colloquium habere & tractatum.

Vobis Mandamus in fide & ligeantia quibus nobis

nobis tenemini firmiter injungentes quod consideratis dictorum negotiorum arduitate & periculis imminentibus cessante excusatione quacunque CHAP VI.

Dictis die & loco personaliter intersitis nobiscum ac cum magnatibus & proceribus predictis super predictis negotiis tractatur' vestrumque consilium impensur' Et hoc Sicut nos & honorem nostrum ac Salvationem & defensionem Regni & Ecclesiæ predictæ expeditionemque dictorum negotiorum diligitis nullatenus omittatis Testeme ipso apud Westm' decimo octavo die Februarii Anno Regni nostri Decimo tertio.

SECT. II.

Observations.

IN *An.* 12. *Hen.* 8. the words *fidei Defensor*, were then added before *Salutem*, instead of *Super diversis causis.* The latter Writs are *Quia de advisamento & assensu concilii nostri pro quibusdam causis*, yet I find the word *Quia* us'd in the great Councils or Parliament Writs, before *Edw.* 2*ds*. time, and probably the words *assensu Concilii nostri* is added to shew the distinction of his *Privy-Council* and his *Publick Council* or *Parliament*.

CHAP. VI. 2. Inſtead of *Specialiter tangentibus*, the latter Writs are *concernentibus quoddam.*

3 Inſtead of *habere proponimus*, the latter Writ is *teneri ordinavimus*, and *habere* is put in between *Colloquium* and *Tractatum.*

4. *Ligeantia* is put in the latter Writs inſtead of *Dilectione*, this word *Dilectione* being for many Ages particularly apply'd to the Epiſcopal Writs.

5. The latter Writs do contain all that are in the more Ancient, (except the Inſertions of ſome Cauſes of Summons, and ſome inlargements added upon Emergent occaſions) *viz. quod conſideratis dictorum negotiorum arduitate & periculis imminentibus ceſſante Excuſatione quacunque.*

6. And alſo thoſe words are added near the end of the latter Writ, *viz. Sicut nos & honorem noſtrum ac Salvationem & Defenſionem Regni & Eccleſiæ predicte expeditionemque dictorum negotiorum diligitis*, which additions are only more full Expreſſions to oblige the Attendances of the Grandees.

Thus having ſhewn the Exemplar Writs to the Bloud Royal, Ancient and Modern, I ſhall ſet down ſuch Earls, Dukes, or Princes of the Bloud Royal to whom this Exemplar Writ was directed, even to this time, according as they are either in the Clauſe Rolls in the Tower, or in the *Pawns* in the Pettibag-Office, which I ſhall recite in *English*, though the Writs are in *Latin*. CHAP. VI.

SECT III.

THe Exemplar Writ was then to *Edward* Earl of *Chester*, Eldest Son to King *Edw. 2d.* and by vertue of this Writ, this Prince had his Exemplar Writ but for this one Parliament, and was soon after King *Edw. 3d.* *Obs.* I. *Exemplar.* 15 *Edw.* 2.

2. To *Edward* Prince of *Wales* and Earl of *Chester*, Eldest Son to *Edw. 3d.* and this Prince had Exemplar Writs for 9 Parliaments, *viz.* 3 *Edw.* 3. 4. *Edw.* 3. and 4. *Edw.* 3. 5. *Edw.* 3. 25. *Edw.* 3. 27. *Edw.* 3. 28. *Edw.* 3. 29. *Edw.* 3. 42. *Edw.* 3. 3 *Edw.* 3.

3. To *Thomas* Earl of *Norfolk*, soon after created Duke (Marshal of *England*, great Uncle to *Edw.* 3. who had his Exemplar Writ but for this one Parliament. 4 *Edw.* 3.

4. To *Henry* Earl of *Lancaster*, (soon after created Duke, (Son to *John* the 4. Son of *Edw.* 3.) who had Exemplar Writs in this Kings and *Richard* 2. and *H.* 4*ths.* time, for 7 Parliaments, *viz.* 14. *Edw.* 3. 17. *Edw.* 3. 18. *Edw.* 3. 22. *Edw.* 3. 25. *Edw.* 3. 23. *Rich.* 2. 1 *Hen.* 4. as Duke of *Lancaster.* 14 *Edw.* 3.

5. To *John* Duke of *Lancaster*, (who then was 37 *Edw.* 3

CHAP. VI. was King of *Caſtile* and Duke of *Acquitane*) the 4*th*. Son to *Edw*. the 3. as aforeſaid, and Uncle to *Rich*. the 2.) who had Exemplar Writs for 17. Parliaments in this and *Rich*. the 2*ds*. time, *viz*.

37 *Edw*. 3. 38 *Edw*. 3. 1 *R*. 2. 3 *R*. 2. 4 *R*. 2. 7 *R*. 2. & 7 *R*. 2. & 8 *R*. 2. and 8 *R*. 2. 9 *R*. 2. 13 *R*. 2. 14 *R*. 2. 15 *R*. 2.
Exemplar. 17 *R*. 2. 20 *R*. 2. and 20 *R*. 2. 21 *R*. 2.

50 *Edw*. 3. 6. To *Richard* Prince of *Wales*, (Duke of *Cornwall* and Earl of *Cheſter*, Grand-child to *Edw*. the 3*d*. and Son to *Edw*. the former Prince of *Wales*, and afterwards King *Richard* the 2*d*.) who had an Exemplar Writ but for this Parliament, and at the opening thereof he did ſit in the Kings Chair.

10 *Ric*. 2. 7. To *Edmund* Earl of *Cambridge*, Duke of *Clarence*, and firſt Duke of *York*, (the 5. Son of *Edw*. the 3*d*.) who had Exemplar Writs for 3 Parliaments, *viz*. the 10. 11. 12. of *Rich*. 2. as Duke of *York*.

11 *Ric*. 2. 8. To *Thomas* Duke of *Gloceſter* Uncle to the King, who had one Exemplar for one Parliament.

1 *Hen*. 4. 9. To *Henry* Prince of *Wales* and Duke of *Cornwall*, who had his Exemplar Writs for 9. Parliaments in his Fathers life time, and was after King *Hen*. the 5*th*. *viz*. 1 *H*. 4. 2 *H*. 4. 3 *H*. 4. 6 *H*. 4. 7 *H*. 4. and 7 *H*. 4. 9 *H*. 4. 11 *H*. 4. and 13 *H*. 4.

To

10. To *Thomas* the 2*d.* Son of *Hen.* the 4*th.* Duke of *Clarence* and Earl of *Albemarl*, had Exemplar Writs for 7 Parliaments, in this and *Hen.* 6*ths.* Reign, *viz.* 1 *H.* 5. 3. 4. 5. of *Hen.* the 5*th.* and in the 1*st.* and 6. and 3 *H.* 6. CHAP. VI. *Exemplar.* 1 *Hen.* 5.

11. To *John* Duke of *Bedford* 3. Son to *Hen.* 4*th.* who had Exemplar Writs for 5 Parliaments in this and *Hen.* 6*th.* Reign, *viz.* 8 *H.* 5. 4. and 4. 11. 14 *H.* 6. 8 *Hen.* 5.

12. To *Humphrey* Duke of *Glocester*, (the 4*th.* Son of *Hen.* 4.) he had Exemplar Writs for 10 Successive Parliaments, *viz.* 4. 6. 9. 10. 15. 18. 20. 21. 25. and 25 *H.* 6. 2 *Hen.* 6.

13. To *Rich.* Duke of *York*, (Grand-child to *Hen.* 4. and Eldest Son to *Edw.* the 4. when Duke of *York*) who had Exemplar Writs for 4 Parliaments, *viz.* 27. 29. 31. 33 *H.* 6. 27 *Hen.* 6.

14. To *George* Duke of *Clarence*, (3*d.* Brother to *Edward* the 4*th.*) who had Exemplar Writs for 3 Parliaments, *viz.* 7. 9. 12. *Edw.* 4. 7 *Edw.* 4.

15. To *Edward* Prince of *Wales*, (Eldest Son to *Edward* the 4*th.*) who had Exemplar Writs for Two Parliaments, and after was King *Edward* the 5*th.*) *viz.* 22. and 23. *Edw.* 4. 22 *Edw.* 4

CHAP. VI. Note, That from this time to the 21. of *Hen.* the 8*th.* we are diſappointed of the knowledge of any Exemplars, and from thence to the 21. of King *James* there are no Exemplar Writs to any of the Bloud Royal, only to other Lords Temporal, as will be ſhewn in its proper place; but in the 21. of King *James*

Exemplar.

21 Jacob. 16. An Exemplar Writ was to *Charles* Prince of *Wales*, Duke of *York*, for that one Parliament, who was afterwards King *Charles* the Firſt.

15 Car. 1. 17. To *Charles* Prince of *Wales*, who had an Exemplar Writ for one Parliament, and after was King *Charles* the Second.

13 Car. 2. 18. To *James* Duke of *York*, who ſat by vertue of the aforementioned Writ in the Parliament begun the 8*th.* of *May*, 1661. to the end thereof.

SECT. IV.

Obſervations on the Title of York.

THere were other Dukes of *York* beſides theſe which are mention'd in this Collection, *viz. Edward* the Son of *Edmund* Duke of *York*, and upon *Edwards* Death his Brother *Richard* was created Duke

Duke of *York*, and *Henry* the ſon of King Henry the 7th. was created Duke of *York*, who after was ſtiled King *Henry* the 8*th*. but theſe 3 Dukes of *York*, being not mention'd in any Clauſe Rolls to have Exemplar Writs, I have omitted them in the Regiſter of Exemplars. CHAP. VI.

2. The City of *York* was dignified with the Title of an Arch-Biſhoprick (in the year 180 as ſome ſay) but all agree that *Taurus* was Arch-Biſhop there in the year 610.) and alſo with the Title of a Dukedom in the 10*th*. year of *Ric.* the 2*d*. whereas *London* the Metropolitan of *England* hath onely a Biſhoprick, but no Dukedom, Earldom or Marqueſate appropriate to it, and in *Anno* the Civil Government of the City was honour'd with the Title of a Lord Mayor,as it was at *London*, but how far the equivalency of that Title extends to thoſe two Cities, will be further diſcourſt when I ſpeak of *London* in its proper place, and in my Annotations.

3. Whilſt the quarrel continued between the Dukes of *York* and *Lancaſter*, which laſted for many Ages, *York* had the Title of *White-roſe*, the *Houſe of Lancaſter* call'd the *Red-roſe*, till both were inoculated into one Stock of *Hen.* 7*th*.

4. The Title of this *James* Duke of *York* and *Albany*, (in *Scotland*) is the ſame which

was

CHAP. VI. was given by King *James* to Prince *Charles* (afterwards call'd King *Charles* the First) being first created Duke of *Albany*, &c. and at 4 Years of age Duke of *York*.

SECT. V.

Of Consimilar Writs to the Royal Exemplars.

NOw I should proceed to the Consimilars of these Exemplars, but in respect that they consist of a very great number, and it were too great a labour to treat of all Consimilars, I shall forbear to recite them. Especially being in hopes that my Learned Friend Sir *William Dugdale* will publish a particular Treatise of them, and ease me of that labour; so as I shall only take notice here of the Writ for this Parliament to Prince *Rupert*, (the Sisters Son to King *Charles* the First) and this is Consimilar in all parts to the Duke of *Yorks* Exemplar, (except in the Title) so I need not set it down at large, but by abbreviation shall thus render it, *viz. Carolus*, &c. *Rex*, &c. *Præcharissimo Consanguineo Duci Cumbriæ Salutem*, and so *Verbatim* with the Dukes Exemplar. Duke of *Cumberland* being his *English* Title.

SECT.

SECT. VI.

Observations on these Consimilars.

1. FIrst in most of the Clause-Rolls and *Pawns* from the 15. of *Edw.* the 2. to this time, after the Exemplar Writs are set down, these words following are in the Clause-Rolls and *Pawns*, *viz.* *Consimilia Brevia diriguntur Subscriptis*, and in some, *Consimiles Literæ* (instead of *Brevia*) *directæ Subscriptis*, and in some, *Consimiles Literæ directæ Conscriptis*, thereby seeming to retain the ancient words of *Patres Conscripti*, which the *Romans* did usually apply to their Elected Senators. But here it is only *Consimile Breve*, in the singular, *Dirigitur præcharissimo*, &c. *Ruperto*, there being no other of the Bloud in *England*.

2. Princes of the Bloud have been Consimilars, when Princes of the Bloud have been Exemplars, as in the 25 *Edw.* 3*d.* *Edward* Prince of *Wales* was Consimilar to *Henry* Earl of *Lancaster* his Uncle, of the Bloud; but not where any were Exemplars who were not of the Bloud: and so many more might be cited, which may be seen in *Cottons* Collections of the Tower Records.

3. In

CHAP. VI. 3. In this Conſimilar Writ, Prince *Ruperts* Foraign Titles are omitted, becauſe none of the Peers do ſit in the *Lords Houſe* but in reſpect of their *Engliſh* Titles; yet in the Proxy-writs which they allow to others, their Foraign Titles are recited without ſcruple, as will be ſhewn in the 10*th*. *Section* of the 12*th*. *Chapter*.

4. I cannot but take notice here, that till the Union with *Scotland*, there was a Chair plac'd in the *Lords Houſe* on the right hand of the Kings Chair, for the King of *Scots*, and call'd the King of *Scots* Chair. Yet I cannot find by any Records of the *Houſe* of *Lords* or elſewhere, that the King of *Scots* did ever ſit there, or was Summon'd, or had any proxy to ſit there for him, by vertue of any Exemplar or Conſimilar Writ.

And now I ſhall proceed to the Exemlar for Biſhops.

THE

CHAP. VII.

The second Exemplar,

viz.

To the Archbishop of Canterbury.

THE Examplar for Bishops (of which I am now to speak) is not entred into this *Pawn* in the Pettibag, (which I have recited *verbatim*) as all the other Exemplars are, but it is entred in the Chancery Crown-Office, (an Office of Record also, as I have shewn) being issued after the Parliament was sitting; nor would I have entred it here (in respect my design in this first part is to write only of such Writs as were previous to the sitting of this Parliament) had not I found that the Exemplar for Bishops is constantly entred in all the Clause-Rolls extant, (from the 15 of *Edw. 2d.*) and in all *Pawns* extant, (from the 21 of *Hen.* 8.) except in this of the 13. *Car. 2d.* which omission (proceeding from the reasons which will *Section* I

CHAP. VII. be given in the following Chapter) was upon the firſt ſitting of this Parliament rectified; and therefore I thought fit rather a little to deviate from my method, than to defer or puzzle the Reader with the diſcourſe of it at too great a diſtance from all the other Writs of Summons, of which I intend to treat according to the order of the *Pawn*; and ſo I crave leave, as moſt ſuiting to all former precedents, to treat of this Exemplar in the ſecond place, eſpecially having the *Act of Precedency* unrepeal'd alſo to juſtifie my proceedings.

2. Before I proceed to diſcourſe of Archbiſhops or Biſhops, it is convenient to look back to the ſeveral Titles which were given to thoſe who were Managers of the Religion practis'd in this Iſland, before the name of Biſhop was here known.

This Religion was by the *Jews* call'd *Paganiſm*, and the Profeſſors thereof *Pagans*, *Panims*, *Ethnicks*, *Gentiles*, *Heathens* and *Infidels*, which Titles are all of the ſame nature. The word *Pagan* comprehending the other five, only the word *Infidel* was not uſed till after Chriſts time; and then thoſe who did not believe the Chriſtian Religion, were by the Chriſtians called Infidels or Unbelievers; but the word in *Hebrew* for *Pagan* was uſed (after the building of *Jeruſalem* by *Melchizedeck*,

zedeck, before call'd King of *Salem*) when those who did live in neighbouring Villages or more remote places, and not coming to partake in the Devotions offer'd to God in *Jerusalem*, were from *Pagus* a Village called *Pagani*, or refusers of that Religion which the *Hebrews* did practice there; and whoever afterwards were not of the *Hebrew* or *Jewish* Religion, were called *Pagans*, &c. (as *Plautus* calls all who were not *Grecians*, *Barbaros*, or *Barbarians*) So that the *Pagan* Religion is to be esteem'd, but as the *Hebrew* or *Jewish* Religion adulterated by the Progeny of *Noah*, who (growing numerous) spread themselves into many parts of the World, and by mixing with other Nations perverted their Primary Religion (which they had from *Noah*, (and afterward more methodically dictated from their High Priest *Melchizedeck*) into *Paganism*.

This mixt Religion was brought into this Island by *Mesech* the 6*th*. Son of *Japhet* the Son of *Noah*, who here call'd himself *Samothes*, and after *Samothes*, *Magus*, *Shanon*, *Druis*, *Bardus*, *Longobardus*, and *Celtes*, succeeded each other; (Seven in all) who being Priests were also call'd Princes of this Island: The *Hebrews* (and *Welsh* (who some say had most of their native Language from the *Hebrew*) using

CHAP. VII. the ſame word for Prince and Prieſt.

These Seven were men of great learning, gain'd partly by tradition from *Noah*, and partly by being contemporary with *Sibylla Samia*, and *Pythagoras*; from one they learned the Prophecies of Chriſts Incarnation and Sufferings; from the other, the high ſpeculations of the Souls immortality and tranſmigration: of which I ſhall ſpeak more in my Annotations.

Of theſe and the Founders of this Religion, and their Doctrines, I ſhall give a more large account in my Annotations, as well for the vindication of that diſcountenanced Book of *Beroſus*, publiſht by *Johannes Annius*, as to free this Iſland from the common imputation of a pitifull illiterate ſort of People, which either the lazineſs of later Writers, (though otherwiſe deſerving) inclin'd them to think it not worth their while to abſtract the notions of what was true, from what was meerly fabulous; or the Malicioufneſs of others, whoſe intereſt it was to ſuppreſs the Records of the Ancient Renown of this Iſland; ſuch as might have demonſtrated their variety of knowledge in all kinds of Literature.

For the preſent I ſhall only ſelect two of thoſe 7 Wiſemen of *Brittain*, as moſt eminent in Philoſophy, Policy, and Matters

ters Divine, *viz. Druis* and *Bardus.* CHAP VII.

Druis is ſet forth in Hiſtory to be Maſter of *Pythagoras*, (from whom tis alſo ſaid that *Timagoras* brought the *Greek* Letters to *Athens*) He took upon him to be Judge in Cauſes Eccleſiaſtical and Civil; and performed all the Rites and Ceremonies of that Religion in *Groves*, (imitating the Idolatrous *Jews*) which *Groves* chiefly conſiſted of Oaks, (as a Tree ſacred to *Jupiter*) and from thence (ſay they) he took his name *Druis*, (Δρῦς ſignifying an Oak) however he was Founder of the Sects called *Druids* in this Iſland.

The other was *Bardus* the Founder of the Sect of the *Bards*, Learned alſo in Magick-Philoſophy, (in the beſt ſence, as Studiers of Wiſdom and Inquirers into the energy and activity of natural Agents) and Politicks; but they were more Famed for their skill in Poetry and Muſick; and thereby did cheerfully Sing Rime, and ſo (like *Orpheus*) charm men into Civil Religion, and Heroick Actions.

From theſe did ſpring (as I ſaid) the two Sects of *Druids* and *Bards*; which our *Brittiſh-Welſh*, *Roman* and *Saxon* Hiſtories do ſo often mention, that there is no doubt concerning them.

CHAP. VII.

The *Bards* continue even to this day in ſome parts of *Wales*, (of which I ſhall ſpeak more) but the *Druids* being afterwards more imployed in the Prieſtly Functions, and growing numerous when the *Romans* were Poſſeſſors of this Iſland, (and had divided its Government into Three Provinces) they alſo committed the charge of the Religious Duties within theſe 3 Provinces, to Three of the chiefeſt *Druids*, (altering their Title from *Druids* into *Archflamins*, and the leſſer *Druids* into the Title of *Flamins*, (for ſo was the Eccleſiaſtical conſtitution among the Old *Romans*) the chief of the Three *Archflamins* being there called *Flamen Dialis*, or *Jupiters Archflamin* or High Prieſt; and as thoſe there, were Subject to the Senate, or Empire of *Rome*; ſo now theſe here, were Subject to the Emperors, Kings, or Governours of this Iſland, not diſputing their power to alter, put in or out, as they ſaw juſt cauſe.

Theſe *Archflamins* and *Flamins* continued till ſome time after the coming of Chriſt; but when they perceived that the Oracles of the *Sibylls* (which they had ſo long adored) were fulfill'd by the coming and paſſion of Chriſt) and that all Oracles were ceaſed, theſe *Flamins*, *Druids* and *Bards*, did give way to the Chriſtian Inſtitutions, (as will be ſhewn.)

But

But to reduce this Section to the subject in hand, it doth appear by our most Ancient Histories, that these *Druids* and *Bards* were consulted with both in Peace and War, both in the *Brittish*, *Romans*, and *Saxons* time, even to the coming of Christ; though the form of their Councils and mixing with the Laicks, do not appear (for reasons before alledged) now. I shall proceed to shew the Institution of Christianity instead of *Paganism*, and then the Titles of such as did manage it in this Island, and how they were still mixt in Civil Councils. CHAP VII.

3. The Religion which succeeded *Paganism* in this Island, was the Christian, which had its denomination from Christ; who may be said to have been before his death in this Island, Prophetically, Personally, and Nominally; but least I should divert the Reader too much from the method intended in this Treatise, I shall refer the discourse of those 3 points to my Annotations.

But concerning the introducing of Christianity into this Island of *Brittain*, what is most credited in our Histories, is, that *Joseph* of *Arimathea*, (the same who beg'd the Body of Christ after his Crucifixion) with 12 Disciples more, are said to plant it here within Thirty Years

 after

Twelve Apoſtles were writ on the 12 Foundations of the Heavenly *Jeruſalem.* CHAP. VII.

After theſe 12. Chriſt did Conſtitute 70. other Diſciples of a leſſer Degree; but the names of theſe 70. are no where certainly to be found; however we have the Scripture to juſtifie the number of Seventy; and there were alſo thoſe who were called *Presbyteri*, alſo Deacons, of which Deacons the Eccleſiaſtical Stories tell us of 7. by name, but no number of the names of the *Presbyteri*; however theſe remaining Apoſtles, Diſciples, Preſbyters and Deacons, were ſoon reduced into the Title of Biſhops, (in all places) not by ordinary Inſtitution, but by an higher and a more extraordinary Function; and theſe Biſhops among themſelves had alſo ſeveral eminent Titles of diſtinction, (within few years after Chriſts death, according as their charge of Souls did extend) *viz. Epiſcopus*, *Patriarcha*, *Archiepiſcopus*, *Papa*, *Presbyter*, *Inſpector*, *Paſtor*, *Curator*, *Obſervator*, *Miniſter*, & *Cuſtos animarum*, which 7 laſt Titles being but deſcriptions of the Office of the 4 chiefeſt, *viz.* Biſhops, Patriarchs, Archbiſhops and Popes: I ſhall ſpeak firſt of theſe 4.

5. It is evident that the firſt eminent Title in the Eccleſiaſtical affairs of Chriſtianity, was

CHAP. VII. after Christs Resurrection; and *Aristobulus* (being, before his coming, Ordained Bishop of *Brittain*) was one of the 12 which were sent with *Joseph* to take care of his charge here: and this is that *Aristobulus* mentioned by St. *Paul* in his Epistle to the *Romans*, *Cap.* 16. *Verse* 10. who was the first Bishop we in these parts hear of, (being 5 years before any was made Bishop of *Rome*) which brings me to the discourse of the several Titles of such as were the first Managers of Christian Religion.

4. The first Titles which were given to the Managers of Christianity, were to Christ himself, who by St. *Paul*, *Matth.* 21. 4. is called the Prophet of *Nazareth*, and by St. *Paul*, *Heb.* 3. 1. High Priest and Apostle, and He by his Divine Authority did constitute 12 Apostles (*Matth.* 10. 1. and *Luk.* 6. 13.) by particular names) who were called both Disciples and Apostles: but the Selected 12. were of an higher nature; for some of them were also called Evangelists, (and none of the Disciples had that Title, except St. *Luke*, one of the 4. nor any call'd an Apostle, (except those 12.) but St. *Paul*, *Gal.* 1. *v.* 1. And these 12 Apostles were of so eminent a Degree, that it is said in the *Revelations Cap.* 21. and 14. that the names of the Twelve

CHAP. VII. was the Title of Biſhop; the *Presbyteri* ſtill ſubmitting to the Biſhop whenever he was placed over them.)

This Title of Biſhop (as I ſaid) was placed on ſome of the Original Apoſtles and Diſciples; as St. *James*, St. *Mark*, &c. for the word *Epiſcopus* doth properly ſignifie one that doth Inſpect or Circumſpect all the concerns of Chriſtian Religion; ſo as thoſe who live under him may be inſtructed to a Good and Pious Life ſutable to the Rules of Chriſtianity, (whoſe duty is more particularly expreſt in St. *Pauls* Firſt Epiſtle to *Tim. Cap.* 3.) ſo that the word *Epiſcopus*, as the Superior Order, was more generally uſed than any other Title wherever Chriſtianity was practiſed; Yet other Titles were alſo uſed in ſeveral parts of the World, as they did agree with the Idiom of their native Language, *viz.* The *Hebrews* called their Biſhop *Princeps*, *Sacerdos*, *Patriarcha*. (*Patriarcha* was alſo apply'd to the Fathers or chief of every one of the 12 Tribes as upon a Civil account, ſo alſo upon the Eccleſiaſtick) The *Syrians*, *Preſbyter*, *Paſtor*, *Miniſter*, and *Curator animarum*: The *Arabians*, *Paſtor*, and *Obſervator animarum*: The *Æthiopians*, *Papa*, *Paſtor*, and *Cuſtos animarum*: The *Græcians*, *Patriarcha*, & *Archiepiſcopus*, &

& *Paſtor animarum*, (all which are thus so rendred into *Latine* by Dr. *Walton's* *Polyglotta* from the Oriental tongues;) ſo as the 4 chief Titles and the others having but one ſignification, and thoſe Titles diſperſed into ſeveral Regions, every one uſing what they thought fit in their own Territories, I ſhall only betake my ſelf to *Epiſcopus* and *Papa*, as having been uſed not only in *Brittain* and *Rome*, but more univerſally in moſt parts of the World, (unleſs we admit *Presbyter* from *Presbyter-Johns* Country to be an Eccleſiaſtical Title) So having ſhewn the meaning of the word Biſhop in general, the Antiquity of it is not to be paſt over. The *Jewiſh Græcians* did uſe it in their Old-Teſtament, for in *Pſal.* the 109. 28. they read *Epiſcopatum ejus accipiet alter*, (which very Text St. *Luke* cites in the Firſt of the *Acts v.* 20. upon the Election of *Matthias* to be an Apoſtle, (inſtead of *Judas*) *viz. Let another take his Biſhoprick*, which ſhew that the word was in uſe among the *Græcians* before Chriſts time, and was no new impoſed word upon the Chriſtians, but a compliance with *Jewiſh* Titles to win the circumciz'd *Jews* in *Greece*; and this may be ſaid, that though *Rome* did change the name from Biſhop to Patriarck, Archbiſhop, and Pope, which ſignifies

CHAP. VII. ſignifies no more than Father or chief Father, yet *Brittain* hath been very conſtant to the name of Biſhop, and did not take upon it Archbiſhop till the Emperor *Conſtantius Chlorus* or the Pope, thought it worthy of that Title.

6. In this Section I place *Brittain* before *Rome*, becauſe our Hiſtories tell us that *Ariſtobulus* was ordained Biſhop of *Brittain*, (and *Joſeph* of *Arimathea* there with him) 5 years before *Linus*, (the firſt Biſhop of *Rome* was made Biſhop of *Rome*) and ſo now I ſhall take a ſhort view of the Priority and Succeſſions in both places, relating to the ſubject of this Treatiſe.

Ariſtobulus is affirmed, as I ſaid, to be the firſt Biſhop of *Brittain*, and ſome few years before any Biſhop was Conſtituted at *Rome*; but what the names were of ſuch Biſhops as ſucceeded him, is uncertain; (for the reaſons before given) but the Story relates, That about an 100. years after Chriſt, one *Lucius* was King of *Brittain*, and was the firſt King of this Iſland who embraced the Chriſtian Religion. Whereupon he ſent *Damianus* and *Fugatius* to *Eleutherius*, then Pope of *Rome*; ſo it is very probable they were Biſhops and Succeſſors to *Ariſtobulus*, and Inſtruments of the Kings Converſion; for none elſe could be ſuppoſed to make attempts on the

the King, but ſuch whoſe eminent Titles and Employments did give them the more opportune admiſſion; and doubtleſs theſe were very conſiderable Perſons, eſpecially *Damianus*, whoſe very name continues at *Rome* even to this day in great renown; for we find that at one time, a Biſhop was of that name, and at another time a Biſhop Cardinal, and a Church is ſtill in *Rome*, (dedicated *Sancto Coſmo*, and *Damiano*) belonging to one of the 14 Deacon-Cardinals. Theſe two Biſhops, or at leaſt eminent Perſons, were ſent to *Eleutherius*, to confer about the ordering of the Church-Affairs, and it ſeems they did acquaint the Pope, (as appears by that Letter) that King *Lucius* had the Old Teſtament, and the Writings of the Apoſtles, called the New Teſtament; ſo that the Chriſtian Doctrine being fixt here, there ſeemed nothing more to be done, than to ſettle the Diſcipline, and the means for its ſupport; wherein it may be juſtly collected, that the King deſired ſuch concurrence with the Pope of *Rome*, as might not diſoblige him or the *Roman* Emperour *Commodus*, to whom he was a Tributary, and with whom in all Civil matters this King ſtood then more fair and quiet than his Predeceſſors had done before him.

I have

CHAP. VII. 7. I have given a brief account of the Managers of the Chriſtian Religion in *Brittain*, from *Ariſtobulus* to *Damianus* and *Fugatius*, in the time of King *Lucius*. I will now ſee what was done at *Rome* in that time, concerning which their Hiſtories tell us that *Linus* was the firſt Biſhop, (who according to computation, was 5 years after *Ariſtobulus* was Biſhop of *Brittain*) but St. *Jerome* is as zealous to have St. *Peter* the firſt Biſhop of *Rome* before *Linus*, as *Ireneus* to have *Linus* the Firſt, (two great Fathers of that Church) ſo that if St. *Peter* be firſt, then we muſt account 13 to *Eleutherius*, (before named) if *Linus*, then *Eleutherius* is the 12*th*. (and with this computation of *Ireneus*, moſt Hiſtories do agree) The firſt Eight of theſe Twelve had no other Title than Biſhop; till *Eugenius* the Ninth of that See, took upon him the name of *Papa* or *Pope*, (and afterwards *Hildebrand* call'd *Gregory* the 7*th*. challenged it as his ſole right to be called Pope) and ſo *Eleutherius* being the 4*th*. Pope from *Eugenius*, and the 9*th*. in Succeſſion from *Linus*, did return a kind Anſwer to King *Lucius*, by two eminent Perſons which the Pope alſo ſent, *viz*. *Helvanus* and *Meduanus*, and with them a Letter, which may be read at large, where-

in

in the Pope takes notice that the Old and New Testament were then in *Brittain*, and in that Letter (leaving the ordering of Ecclesiastical affairs in *Brittain* to the King) declared him to be Christs Vicar in his own Kingdom: which made King *Lucius* go cheerfully on, and (as History tells us) that whereas the *Archflamins* had been the chief Managers of the *Pagan* Religion in this Isle, (each having one Province) the King reduced those Three Provinces to Two, and placed Two Archbishops therein, and instead of the *Flamins* did constitute Bishops, and so there was an amity between the Archbishops and Bishops of *Brittain*, and the Archbishops or Popes of *Rome*, neither of them strugling for Priority, but still carrying on the work of Christianity. CHAP. VII.

But the Emperours of *Rome* declining in their power, and the Pope still taking advantage of their declinations, grew at last so considerable with the Emperours, that they could not safely deny them any thing; so that whereas the Emperors of *Rome* formerly had the disposal of their Popes, and the Kings of *Brittain* of their Bishops, (and so other Princes in their Territories) the Popes by degrees did take the power to themselves, to make what Bishops they pleased, to summon Councils, make Decrees,

CHAP. VII. crees, diſtribute them, and enjoyned obedience to their Univerſal Juriſdiction, that the name of Pope might be the more authentick.

It was uſed in many parts of the World beſides *Rome*; for (it is ſaid) that about 300. years after Chriſt, *Neſtorius* the Heretick had 6000. Biſhops appeared againſt him, which were under the Government of ſeveral Popes, and this was above 300. years before *Boniface* the 3*d.* (Popes increaſing as well as Biſhops) who obtained of *Phocas* then Emperor of *Rome*, that none ſhould be called Pope, but the Pope of *Rome*; and though *Gregory* (the firſt) his immediate Predeceſſor, (but one) declared againſt it, and many Popes before him, yet *Boniface* having obtained this Supremacy (what he did in other Kingdoms I ſhall omit) in *Brittain*, to make ſure that none ſhould be placed there, but ſuch as ſhould be dependent on *Rome*; he confirm'd *Auguſtin* a Monk the Archbiſhop of *Canterbury*, (being made ſo by his ſaid Predeceſſor *Gregory*) and ſoon after, he and 4 ſucceeding *Bonifaces* filled up all the reſt of the Biſhopricks, with ſuch Foraigners or others as had a clear dependance on *Rome*, by *Promotions*, *Stipends*, or Forraign Intereſts, (amongſt the reſt, *Fælix* a *Burgundian* was

was made Biſhop of *Dunwich*, in *Suffolk*, (the fifth Biſhoprick then in rank, of which I ſhall ſpeak more) and ſo in a few years after, all the Biſhopricks which were then, and ſoon after added, were filled up with his dependents, as alſo all Abbies, Priories, Monaſteries, &c. and ſo continued to be ſupplied according to his appointment from *Rome* without any material oppoſition by the Kings of this Iſland, (but ſuch as hereafter mentioned.) And having this Power, it was no hard matter to fix themſelves into all Councils within this Kingdom; for in all Hiſtories we find them as Actors therein, and in reſpect of their Eccleſiaſtical Intereſts, one of the Eſtates; and when the name of Parliament was given to our chief Council, they were methodically fix'd in the ſecond rank of the *Pawns*, and ſo in the *Clauſe Rolls*: and this place in Parliament was never denied them whilſt they continued here. But the Pope's Power and Supremacy over this Iſland was ever diſguſted by our ſucceſſive Kings; yet being back'd by ſo great a Temporal Prince (as the Pope of *Rome*) joyned with the Intereſt which by long continuance they had gained from the Emperours, the Kings of this Iſland had little ſucceſs in their ſtruglings. For we ſee King *John* tried it, to his coſt, by

CHAP VII.

CHAP. VII. ſingle oppoſitions, without the Kingdom's unanimous Conjunctures. Aftewards *Henry* the Third began again, and other ſucceeding Kings did try what Parliamentary or Municipal Laws could effect, and to that end theſe following Laws were Enacted.

H. 3. 7. *Henry* the Third, *Anno* 9. *cap.* 33. (being part of the great Charter) that Parliament did grant, That all Patrons of Abbies which have the Kings Charters of *England* of Advowſon, or have old Tenure, or poſſeſſion of the ſame, ſhall have the cuſtody of them when they fell void, as it hath been accuſtomed, and as it is before declared. See *Coke Inſt.* 2.

Henry the Third, *Anno* 9. *cap.* 36. (being alſo part of the great Charter) the Parliament did grant, That if any Man ſhould hereafter give Lands to a Religious Houſe, the Grant ſhall be void, and the Land forfeit to the Lord of the Fee, and in corroboration and Inlarging of this Statute many other Laws were made 7 *Ed.* 1. and by 18 *Ed.* 3. & 15 *R.* 2. and 23 *H.* 4. called the Statute of *Mortmain.*

Ed. 1. *Edward* the Firſt, *Anno* 35. *cap.* 1. made the Statute *de Aſportatis Religioſorum*, wherein it is declared, That the Monaſteries, Priories and Religious Houſes in this Realm were founded by the King and his Pro-

Progenitors, and by the Noblemen and their Anceſtors; and that no Abbot, *&c.* ſhall lay any Tax on any Religious Houſe, to ſend the ſame beyond Sea, or carry any Goods with them out of the Kingdom; and that no Abbots (being Aliens) ſhall impoſe any Tax, *&c.* CHAP. VII.

Edward the Second, *Anno* 9. Enacted, That the King by his Letters may abſolve Excommunications, where they were made in prejudice of his Liberty or Prerogative; (to ſhew the King's Power above Eccleſiaſtick Cenſures of the Pope; and this may be of great Uſe.) *Edw.* 2.

Edward the Third, *Anno* 25. That the King went on further by Act of Parliament, forbidding (under a *Præmunire*) all applications to *Rome* for obtaining any Eccleſiaſtick Preferments, or in Suing to the Court of *Rome* for Reverſing any Judgments. *Edw.* 3.

Richard the Second did back this Statute with ſeveral other Statutes, *viz.* in *Anno* 3. *cap.* 3. and *Anno* 7. *cap.* 12. *&* 15. and *Anno* 13. *cap.* 2, *&* 3. and *Anno* 16. *cap.* 2, *&* 5. and in theſe ſame Parliaments the Archbiſhop proteſted againſt the Pope's Authority in *England*: And good reaſon for it, as Sir *Richard Baker* in his Hiſtory tells us, That about this time the Abbots, Biſhops, *&c.* which were placed here *Rich.* 2.

CHAP. VII. by the Pope, were ſo numerous, that it was propoſed to him by the *Commons*, that he would pleaſe with their Revenues to make 150 Earls, 1500 Knights, 6200 Eſquires, and Erect 200 Hoſpitals for maintaining of maimed Soldiers, *&c.* But it ſeems he had not that Courage which *Henry* the Eighth did after aſſume, and it was needleſs for one or two to oppoſe his Power.

H. 4. However, *Henry* the Fourth went on, and in the Second and Seventh Years of his Reign, made Acts againſt Purchaſing of Bulls from the Pope, for Exemptions or Benefices.

H. 5. Alſo *Henry* the Fifth, *Anno* 5. *cap.* 4. made Acts againſt Proviſors from the Pope; and all theſe ſubject to a *Præmunire*.

H. 6. In *Henry* the Sixth's time, the Biſhop of *Wincheſter*, being made Cardinal, was admitted of the King's Council, with this Proteſtation, That he ſhould abſent himſelf in all Affairs and Councils wherein the Pope or See of *Rome* were concerned, (which he aſſented to:) and alſo he Enacted, That no Alien ſhould be a Broker.

That Priories and Aliens Lands ſhould be ſeiz'd in time of War.

That no Advowſon, Preſentation, Collation, or Induction, be made to any A-

lien

lien of any Benefice or Ecclesiastick Dignity. CHAP. VII.

That Aliens attending the Queen or King be removed and banished (except those allowed by the Council.)

That Aliens should lodge only in *Englishmens* Houses; and to serve in War, if able.

That no Priors be Collectors of Disms.

He also confirmed the Statutes against Provisions by the See of *Rome*.

In *Edward* the Fourth, *Richard* the Third, and *Henry* the Seventh's time, there was a Calm to that See; none of the Laws repealed, but so slenderly used, that they made no great impression at *Rome*; and though these and former Kings did strive to make their respective Supremacies in Ecclesiastick Matters within their Dominions, and to lessen the Pope's Power and Profit, yet none could substantially effect it, till *Henry* the 8th, who seeing there was no other remedy, and that all Laws against the *Roman* See were evaded, and other Essays fruitless, he fell to't with right down Blows (which is the only way to master a good Fencer) as will appear in this next Section. *Ed. 4. R. 3. H. 7.*

CHAP. VII.

H. 8. 8. *Henry* the Eighth did ſo contrive his matters, that he did firſt ingratiate himſelf with the Pope by writing (in defence of the Church of *Rome*) a Book againſt *Luther*; which ſo affected the Pope, that he immediately ſent him a *Bull*; (which is in the ſame nature of a Patent with us)
Anno 12. and therein gave him the Title of *Defenſor Fidei*; which he accepted, and for three
Anno 21, 22, 23. years, *viz.* in the 21, 22, and 23 years of his Reign went plauſibly on, by making ſeveral Acts about Wills and Teſtaments, Mortuaries, and againſt Pluralities, and Sanctuaries, and Deeds to Churches; but
Anno 24. in the 24*th* he began to diſcover his Opinion, that though he was for the Doctrine of the Church of *Rome*, againſt *Luther*, yet he had no mind to ſuffer his Kingdom to be exhauſted for the Support of the Court of *Rome*: whereupon an Act of Parliament was made againſt all Appeals
Anno 25. to *Rome*; and the next year, *Anno* 25. That no *Firſt Fruits* ſhould be paid (as formerly, out of this Kingdom) to *Rome*: And in another Act, That not any Impoſition ſhould be laid on his Subjects by colour of any Power from the Pope; and then, to ſecure himſelf, and rivet his Subjects to him, an Act was made, declaring his Title and his Succeſſor's to the Crown: That being done, an Act of Parliament

liament was made, *Anno* 26. to intitle him *Supream Head* of the Church of *England*; and in the ſame year a poſitive Act, That no *Firſt Fruits* or *Tenths* ſhould be paid out of any Promotions in *England*, to the Pope of *Rome*. CHAP. VII. *Anno* 26.

In this time the King makes Archbiſhops, Biſhops, and Suffragans; and in the 27*th* year chuſeth ſixteen Spiritual and 16 Temporal Lords to ſettle the Canons for the Church of *England*, and erect an Office of Augmentation: ſo, as having gained the two points of his Supremacy, in oppoſition to the Church and Court of *Rome*, viz. *Defenſor Fidei & Supremum Caput*, one from the Pope himſelf, the other from the Parliament; and ſetled an Office for his purpoſe: In the ſame year all Monaſteries, &c. under 200 *l. per Annum*, and all the Ornaments, Goods and Jewels belonging to thoſe Houſes, were ſetled on him and his Heirs by Acts of Parliament. And four years after, *viz.* 31 *H.* 8. it was Enacted, That the King and his Heirs ſhould have all Monaſteries, Abbies, Priories, and other Religious Houſes diſſolved, or to be diſſolved, with their Mannors, Lands, &c. And yet it is obſervable, That in this very Parliament of 31 *H.* 8. there were twenty *Roman* Biſhops, twenty four Abbots, and two Priors, *Anno* 27. *Anno* 31.

CHAP. VII. in all forty ſix, and but forty four Temporal Lords, the Act for Precedency in the Houſe of Lords made the ſame year, being not (as I conceive) altogether for regulating Precedencies, but for purging the Abbots, &c. by that Act of Parliament; ſo as doubtleſs they loſt their Intereſt more by the King's reſolution for expunging them, than by Vote of Parliament.

9. However, the Abbots, Priors, &c. being thus diſſolved (their Baronies, by which they did formerly there ſit, being diſpoſed of to other perſons,) they had no foundation to ſit in the Lords Houſe, which caus'd the firſt great Alteration in the Method of the following Writs, for ſuch as were to ſit there, (as will be further ſhewn.)

And in this great Alteration, doubtleſs, there was alſo a Divine Hand; for as Pope *Boniface* the Third (before mentioned) did put out all the *Engliſh* Biſhops, and placed Foreigners (his creatures) in their rooms, and made many more Biſhopricks than he found; ſo now, by the *Lex Talionis* (Like for Like) *Henry* the Eighth did put out all the Pope's dependents, and placed ſuch Biſhops in their rooms as would juſtifie the King's Supremacy here, and renounce the Pope's. And accordingly Biſhop *Bonner*,

Cranmer,

Cranmer, *Gardiner*, and others, (who wrote againſt the Pope's Supremacy) were made, one an Archbiſhop, and the others Biſhops. And he alſo did erect ſix new Biſhopricks, *viz. Cheſter*, *Glouceſter*, *Peterborough*, *Briſtol*, *Oxford*, and *Weſtminſter*, (which laſt, (after one Biſhop,) was turned to a Deanary, as now it is) and ſuch of the Nobility and Gentry that ſtuck to his Reſolutions, wanted not Lands and Mannors to gratifie them. CHAP. VII.

So that, now he had the Lords Spiritual and Temporal and Commons in Parliament, and the Kingdom it ſelf on his ſide, and even the Nobility and Gentry of *England*, who formerly were almoſt entire for the Popes Authority, their Judgments were now ſplit in two, ſome for the Court and ſome for the Church of *Rome*; and ſo even the King and many of his Council did live and die in that Perſuaſion. But he did not think himſelf ſafe in carrying on ſo great an oppoſition as was like to be, (well knowing how the Papal Intereſt was diſpers'd in all Kingdoms and States of *Europe*) till he had incouraged the offſpring of the *Waldenſes*, and other oppoſers of *Rome* in *France*, *Germany*, and in other Kingdoms and States, to revive their Doctrines, as alſo to imbrace the *Lutherans Centum Gravamina*, and the *Calvinian Inſti-*

Institutions, and others less remarkable, (yet all serving to his purpose) whereby, in a few years after, almost all *Christendom* was brought into a Papal and Antipapal Ballance, or rather consisted of Professors of the *Roman* Religion, and Protestors against both the Court and Church of *Rome*, as Usurping and Antichristian.

10. But on the other side, the Pope seeing that he could not by forcible ways withstand this almost universal desertion of him, he made his Applications to several Kings and Princes for his assistance; And at last, by a more plausible way, he did obtain a Council of *Trent*, wherein it is observable, That he did not think fit to move in his Point of Supremacy, till after eighteen years, that That Council had been sitting by Adjournments and Prorogations, and then the Question was, That *Episcopus Locum principalem teneret à Pontifice Romano dependentem*; to which the opposers did so far comply, that they allowed, *principalem Locum sub Romano Pontifice*, but not *dependentem*; so, after that Council had sate nineteen years, (in the sixth of Queen *Elizabeth*) it was dissolved by 4 Legats, 20 Cardinals, 3 Patriarchs, 25 Archbishops, 168 Bishops, 7 Abbots, 39 Proctors, and 7 Regulars of General Orders, without Determining that Point (to the

the ſatisfaction either of *England* or other Kingdoms and States) the Diſpute of which begot 7 Civil Wars in *France* (which laſted near 40 years, till within 3 years of Queen *Elizabeths* Death) alſo Inquiſitions in *Spain* and *Flanders*, Tumults and Wars in *Germany*, and near 40 years Wars in the *Netherlands* between them and *Spain*, and for ſome few years, Fire, Fagots and Inſurrections in *England*.

11. In this Hurly Burly about Supremacy, *H.* 8. left his Crown to an Infant, *Edward* the 6*th*; who had the Laws againſt *Rome* corroborated, and his Revenues augmented by Chappels, Chantries, &c. enjoying them but few years; and then the Pope revived freſh experiments by Queen, *Mary* to reverſe all, eſpecially after ſhe was Married to King *Phillip*, compelling a ſubmiſſion to the Popes Supremacy by Fire and Fagots, ſo as, in *H.* 8. time and even till now (upon the ſuddain Changes of Religion it might be ſaid by the Hiſtorian) *Deus bone hic ſuſpenduntur Papiſtæ, illic comburuntur Antipapiſtæ:* but her time being ſhort, the Supremacy was once more reverſt, and taken up by Queen *Elizabeth*, who managed it with ſuch dexterity (conſidering the conjuncture of Affairs in this and other Kingdoms and States) that it was needleſs for the

Ed. 6.

Mary.

Eliz.

CHAP. VII. the Pope to make any open Attempts, but by Mariages, Foreign Negotiations, and the aſſurances given by ſome of the chiefeſt Nobility and Gentry of the *Roman* perſuaſion in this Kingdom (who were, as they pretended, for the Church, and not for the Court of *Romes* Supremacy) of their peaceable reſolutions; the Billows of penal Laws ſeem'd to be calmed, and this Kingdom thought it ſelf as ſecure, as the pretty *Halcion* in her Neſt.

But thoſe who kept to *Calvins* Inſtitutions in *England* and *Scotland*, were finely yoak't together to a diſturbance; for it being inſinuated to them That the Title of *Supream Head of the Church* (given by Act of Parliament) was declined and dwindled into an *&c.* and that the Title of *Defender of the Faith* (given by the Pope) did only remain with an *&c.* made them call to mind what was alledged in the Council of *Trent*, That the original of Church-Government was Ariſtocratical, and Governed by a certain number of the Presbytery, and afterwards it was thought fit to put it into a Monarchical way, *viz.* by a Biſhop (as Superintendent;) and finding that the Popes and Kings of *England* and other Princes, had long diſputed about this Eccleſiaſtical Monarchy, without determination (only in a connivance) they

they thought it convenient to return to the Primitive way of Ariſtocracy, and ſet up Presbytery (that original Government as was pretended,) and thereupon one & all cried againſt Biſhops (which bravely workt for the Papal intereſt;) & the clamour proved ſo geat that the Learned King *James* did what he could by Writing to quiet them,& his unfortunate, though Bleſſed Son, King *Charles* the Firſt tried it by Action, but without Succeſs. For the *Independent*, *Anabaptiſt*, *Fifth Monarchy-Men* and others, coming into the *Presbyters* aſſiſtance, he was neceſſitated after the Wars with *Scotland* upon the ſame grounds, amongſt other condeſcentions to yield (with the Conſent of the Lords Temporal, and Commons) and paſs an Act for Aboliſhing the Biſhops temporal Jurisdiction in this Kingdom.

CHAP. VII.

17. *Car*. 1.

Now ſee what followed; inſtead of making of Earls, Knights and Squires, and maintaining of Hoſpitals, as was propoſed to *Richard* the 2*d*. (as I ſaid) the Biſhops were not only put out of the Houſe of Lords, but the Temporal Lords ſoon after, and the Knights and Squires ſecluded from the Houſe of Commons, and the Hoſpitals, (and all) ruined by an inteſtine Bloody War, the King Sacrificed, and every one of the Machineers diſappointed of their original plauſible intentions;

CHAP. VII. tions; and in conclusion, by most miraculous Turns in Affairs, there was a total submission to a Reestablishment of that Form of Church and State, which they had before so zealously overthrown, and the Bishops again brought into the Lords House.

12. I should now proceed to the Writs, which impowred the Bishops to sit in the Lords House: but first I think it pertinent to shew how these two Titles, of *Fidei Defensor*, & *Caput Ecclesiæ Anglicanæ*, were used, disused, and altered in theirs and other Writs.

Though all the Kings of *England*, at their Coronation, are Sworn to defend the Christian Faith, and the words *defensionem Ecclesiæ Anglicanæ*, having been in most Parliament-Writs since the 11*th* of *Edward* the 3*d.* Yet the Pope (as I said, for the good Service which *Henry* the 8. had done, in Writing against *Luther*) sent him a Bull, and therein intituled him *Defensor Fidei*, with this Caution, that it should be placed next his Title to *France*, and before his Title to *Ireland*; and it may be observed, That in the same year he sent the like Bull to the Emperor *Charles* the 5*th.* intituling him also *Defensor Fidei*; upon which the Emperor took an Oath, not only to be *Defensor Fidei*, but

but *Defensor Pontificiæ dignitatis, & Romanæ Ecclesiæ, i. e.* Defender of the Court and Church of *Rome*. But *Henry* the 8*th*, though he accepted the Title, did not think fit to be bound by an Oath; nor do I find that he ſtiled himſelf in any publick Acts *Defenſor Fidei*, till the 21 of his Reign, and then in a Decree made in the *Star-Chamber* (which is Printed in *Poltons* Abridgment) he is Stiled *Defenſor Fidei, & in terra Eccleſiæ Anglicanæ & Hiberniæ Supremum Caput*, which was 5 years before the *Supremum Caput* was ſettled by Act of Parliament; but as a preparative to it in the 22 of his Reign he is ſtiled *Præpotentiſſimus & Metuendiſſimus Angliæ & Franciæ Rex*, and only *Fidei Defenſor* is added, and no mention of *Supremum Caput*. Then, in the 30 year of his Reign he is Stiled, *Defender of the Faith, and Lord of* Ireland, *and on Earth Supream Head, immediately, under Chriſt, of the Church of* England. In the 32. year he left out the word *immediately*, and the next year the words *under Chriſt*. So that, in the 33 of his Reign the Title was *Hen. by the Grace of God King of* England, France, *and* Ireland, *Defender of the Faith, and of the Church of* England, *and alſo of* Ireland, *on Earth Supream Head.* And thus by making himſelf King of *Ireland*, he diſobeyed

CHAP. VII. beyed the Pope, in placing *Defender* after *Ireland*; and this Title continued thus all his Life, and the Circumſcription on his Great Seal wrot accordingly; and ſo did his Son, *Edward* the ſixth, on His Great Seal, and in Publick Acts. And the like did Queen *Mary* in the firſt year of her Reign; but upon her Marriage with King *Philip*, in the ſecond year of her Reign, (and firſt of both) their Title was *King and Queen of* England *and* France, Naples, Jeruſalem *and* Ireland, *Defenders of the Faith*, *Princes of* Spain *and* Cicily, *Arch-Dukes of* Auſtria, *Duke of* Milan, Burgundy *and* Brabant, *Counteſs of Hasburgh*, *Flanders* and *Tyroll*, quite joſtling out *Supream Head* during their Reigns.

When Queen *Elizabeth* came to the Crown, the Circumſcription of her Great Seal was *Elizabetha Dei gratiâ Angliæ*, *Franciæ & Hiberniæ Regina*, *Fidei Defenſor*, yet ſhe maintained both Titles of *Defenſor* and *Supream* during her Reign.

When King *James* came to the Crown, the Circumſcription of his Broad Seal was alſo *Jacobus Dei gratiâ Angliæ*, *Scotiæ*, *Franciæ & Hiberniæ Rex*, *Fidei Defenſor*, and no more; yet he maintained the other Point both in his Government and Writings, as may be read in his *Præmonition to all*

all Christian Monarchs, and his *Declaration against* Vorstius, and his *Defence of the Right of Kings against Cardinal* Perrone, and in several of his Speeches in Parliament, leaving men at liberty, as Queen *Elizabeth* did, to use the Title of *Supream Head* in their Pulpits and Evidences as they thought fit; so as the learned *Cambden* in his Dedication of his *Britannia* to King *James*, instead of *Defensor*, writes him *Propugnator Fidei*.

When King *Charles* the First came to his Crown, the Circumscription of his Great Seal was *Carolus Dei gratiâ Rex Angliæ, Scotiæ, Franciæ & Hiberniæ, Fidei Defensor*, and no more; yet to justifie both Titles, in the seventeenth year of his Reign he caused the 39 *Articles* (which were agreed on in the fourth of Queen *Elizabeth*) to be reprinted, and in the Front did publish his own Declaration in these words: *Being by God's Ordinance, according to our just Titles, Defender of the Faith, and Supream Governour of the Church within these Our Dominions*, He therein *declares, That the Articles of the Church of* England, *allowed and authorized heretofore, do contain the Doctrine of the Church of* England, *and requires his Subjects to continue in the uniform profession thereof. And* then, as to the Discipline he *further declares himself Su-*

 pream

CHAP. VII. *pream Governor of the Church of* England, and *that if any difference arise about the external Policy concerning Injunctions, Cannons, or other Constitutions whatsoever thereunto belonging, the Clergy in their Convocations is to order and settle them,* (having first obtained leave under his Majesties Broad Seal so to do) and *he approving their said Ordinances and Constitutions.* So here the word *Supream Head* is changed into *Supream Governour.*

When King *Charles* the Second came to the Crown, the Circumscription of his Broad Seal was *Carolus Secundus Dei gratiâ Angliæ, Scotiæ, Franciæ & Hiberniæ Rex, Fidei Defensor,* and no more; yet to justifie both Titles, the very same year of his Return, *Anno* 1660, he publish'd a Declaration to all his loving Subjects (well worth the reading) concerning Ecclesiastical Affairs, which shews both his Christian condescention to his Subjects, and Justifications to those two Titles for which he is styl'd by Writers *Supream Moderator.*

Now though in all Parliament-Writs which have come to my view, and in other publick Acts, and Writings since the first of Queen *Elizabeth* to this time, after the words *Defender of the Faith* (except in their Broad Seals) there is added only

only one *&c.* which I conceive was done for brevity, and must be understood in relation to the Act of 36 *Hen.* 8. never yet repealed, and every man had then and hath still liberty in their Deeds or Pulpits to mention the full Titles, but by degrees, about the year 1640. it began to cease in Pulpits, and soon after in Pens, contenting themselves with the *&c.* CHAP VII.

These and other matters (seeming trivial, though proving dangerous in the consequences) were yielded to as condescentions to gratifie a *dissenting party* in *England*, who, very probably, were incited thereunto, by underworking Papal Contrivers, (being excellent Artists in spurring on the least humour of Schism in this Church) and so dealing in little things till greater were ripen'd, in which latter they often made Attempts, as may be read in Queen *Elizabeth*, King *James*, King *Charles* the First, and this present King's time (yet without success) except in the Assassination of King *Charles* the first, which was manag'd with such dexterity, that it was made difficult to judge whether some of the *English* Dissenters in those times, or the *Romish* Incensors were the chief Actors. And after that it was carried on by a subtil way of redeeming their credits in this King's Preservation at *Worcester*, yet still

CHAP. VII. underhand endeavouring to ſubvert the whole Fabrick of this Kingdom, as was diſcovered about the end of this Parliament, 1678. (which determin'd my publick Employments, and therefore ſhall leave that Subject to other Pens.)

Thus the new Empire of *Rome* and the old Empire of *England* have ſtrugled through many Ages for Supremacy.

It is the Intereſt of *England* to be quiet within its own liquid Arms, and ſo increaſe it ſelf, with other Kingdoms and States, by a real mutual Traffick and Commerce. But it is the Intereſt of *Rome* to be troubleſome, and increaſe it ſelf in all Kingdoms and States, without any real commutation or advantage to any but it ſelf.

Yet it is difficult to make the *Diſſenters* to the Church of *England* believe that the way which they take in oppoſing *Rome* will in time be deſtructive to their own Deſigns and Opinions. Some of the *Diſſenters* to the Church of *England* ſee and know this, yet are ſo inveigled by ſuch *Diſſenters* to the Court of *Rome* (who pretend to be for that Church, but not for that Court) under a plauſible notion of Liberty, as may deſtroy that which they ought to maintain, *viz.* to prevent the Inundation of *Rome*, whereby they bring it to this Queſtion, Whether they had better com-

comply with a Foreign Intereſt, which they pretend to hate, or their Native Intereſt, which they pretend to love; and whether they are not like (by concurring with thoſe pretended half *Romaniſts*, which they do in effect, by oppoſing the *Engliſh* Conſtitutions) to fall into that which they pretend to avoid. For theſe admitting one Error, are ſubject by thoſe deluſions to ſtrike upon greater, becauſe they who now are only for the Church of *Rome* againſt the Court, will undoubtedly (when they have gain'd their Proſelytes) be both for the Church and Court of *Rome*, when they have once the Diſſenters of the Church of *England* to be its Oppoſers; for Diſſention mounts as naturally to violent Oppoſition, as Conſpiracies to Rebellion.

And now, craving pardon for this long digreſſion, I ſhall proceed to the Writs by which the Biſhops have been anciently and ſtill are Summon'd to ſit in Parliament *Cum Prælatis Magnatibus & Proceribus*, giving this Hint, That their Summons to Parliament were ſtill in relation to their Baronies, and their advancements to other Dignities as well Eccleſiaſtical as Civil, was and is in reſpect of their great Learning, Knowledge, Fidelity and Experience in Affairs.

And now I ſhall ſet down the Form of their Writs of Summons both Ancient and Modern.

SECT. XIII.

The Form of the Exemplar Writ *to the Arch-Biſhop of* Canterbury, 15 *Edw.* 2.

EDwardus Dei gratiâ Rex Angliæ, Dominus Hiberniæ, & Dux Aquitaniæ, venerabili in Chriſto Patri Waltero eadem gratiâ Cantuarii Archiepiſcopo, totius Angliæ Primati, Salutem. Quia ſuper diverſis arduis negotiis nos, ſtatum Regni noſtri ſpecialiter tangentibus, Parliamentum noſtrum apud Eborum à die Paſchæ proximo futuro in tres ſeptimanas teneri, & vobiſcum & cum cæteris Prælatis magnatibus & proceribus dicti Regni habere proponimus Colloquium tractatum Vobis Mandamus in fide & dilectione quibus nobis tenemeni firmiter injungentes, quod dictis die & loco omnibus aliis prætermiſſis perſonaliter interſitis ibidem nobiſcum & cum cæteris Prælatis Magnatibus & Proceribus ſupra dictis negotiis tractaturi veſtrumq; Conſilium impenſuri, Præmonentes Priorem & Capellanum Eccleſiæ veſtræ Cantuariæ Archidiaconos totumq; Clerum

Clerum vestræ Diocesæ quod iidem Prior & Archidiaconus in propriis personis suis dictum Capellanum per unum idemq; clerum per duos procuratores idoneos plenam & sufficientem potestatem ab ipsis Capellano & Clero habentes una vobiscum intersitis modis omnibus tunc & ibidem ad faciendum & consentiendum hiis quæ tunc & ibidem de communi consilio (favente deo) ordinari contigerint super negotiis antedictis. Et hoc nullatenus omittatis. Teste meipso apud *Derby* 10 Martii Anno Regni nostri quintodecimo.

Observations.

THe same reasons which guided me in the 3*d.* Chapter, to begin with a Writ in *Ed.* 2*d.* time to a Prince of the Blood, induced me here also to begin with a Writ of the same Date, from the same King to the Bishops; and here it may be observ'd, that this is the first Writ in the Tower-Record, wherein the *Præmonentes* are added to the Writ, for before this Writ (in respect of the Bishops Baronies) their Writs were in the same Form, as to the Temporal Barons (of which some are Cited by Mr. *Pryn* and others) but here such of the Clergy as are therein mentioned, *viz.* Priors, Archdeacons, &c. were to be Forwarn'd, Cited, or Summon'd by the Biſhops; and yet this Clauſe of the *Præmonentes* in their Writs was not conſtantly us'd in after-times; for in ſome ſubſequent Kings Reigns ſince this of *Ed.* 2. it is omitted; but very rarely. And ſo in ſome Clauſe Rolls there are Exemplars to the Archbiſhop, but no Conſimilars mentioned; and likewiſe an Exemplar to ſome Temporal Lord, but no Conſimilars named, which doubtleſs was the Error of Clerks, for there are Seal'd Writs of both ſorts, extant at ſuch times as they were omitted in the Rolls. But from *Hen.* 8. to this time, there is no material alteration from this Ancient Form; Except in ſome few particulars, which will be ſhewn in the following Writs.

SECT. XV.

The Firſt Writ in the Pettibag amongſt the Pawns 21. Hen. 8. *is to Cardinal* Wolſey *Archbiſhop of* York, viz.

HEnricus octavus Dei gratiâ Angliæ & Franciæ Rex Fidei Defenſor & Dominus Hiberniæ. Reverendiſſimo in Chriſto Patri Thomæ miſeratione divina tituli ſanctæ Cicilliæ Trans-Tyburinæ Sacroſanctæ

crosanctæ Romanæ Ecclesiæ Presbytero Cardinali Archiepiscopo Eborum, Angliæ Primati & Apostolicæ ac etiam de Latere Episcopo Wintoniensi nec non exempti Monasterii Sancti Albani Commendatorio perpetuo Salutem. Quia de advisamento & assensu Concilii nostri pro quibusdam arduis & urgentibus negotiis nos statum & defensionem Regni nostri Angliæ & Ecclesiæ Anglicanæ concernentibus quoddam Parliamentum nostrum apud Civitatem nostrum Londini tertio die Novembris proximo futuro teneri ordinavimus; ac ibidem vobiscum ac cum cæteris Prelatis Magnatibus & Proceribus dicti Regni nostri Colloquium habere & tractatum. Vobis sub fide & dilectione quibus nobis tenemini firmiter injungendo mandamus quod consideratis dictorum negotiorum arduitate & periculis imminentibus cessante excusatione quacunque, dictis die & loco personaliter intersitis nobiscum & cum Prælatis Magnatibus & Proceribus prædictis super dictis negotiis tractaturum vestrumque Concilium impensur' & hoc sicut nos & honorem nostrum & salvationem & defensionem Regni & Ecclesiæ supra prædictorum expeditionemque dictorum negotiorum diligitis nullatenus omittatis Præmonentes tam Decanum & Capitulum Ecclesiæ vestræ

CHAP. VII. Ebor' quam Prior' & Capit' Eccleſiæ veſtræ Wintoniæ nec non Archidiaconum totumq; Clerum veſtrarum dioceſium prædictarum quod iidem Diaconus & Prior nec non Archidiaconi in propriis perſonis ſuis ac utrumque Capitulorum prædictorum per unum idemque Clerum per duos procuratores Idoneos plenam & ſufficien' poteſtatem ab ipſis Capitulis & Clero diviſim habentes prædicto die & loco perſonaliter interſerint ad conſentiendum hijs quæ tunc ibidem de Communi Concilio dicti Regni noſtri (divina favente Clementia) contigerint ordinari. Teſte meipſo apud Weſtm' nono die Auguſti Anno Regni noſtri viceſimo primo.

Conſimilia brevia dirigenda Archiepiſcopo Canturienſi & Epiſcopis ſubſcriptis ſub eadem dat' *viz.*

Reverendiſſimo in Chriſto Patri Gulielmo eadem gratiâ Archiepiſcopo Canturienſi totius Angliæ Primati.

Cutberto Epiſcopo *Londin.* D.
Johanni Epiſcopo *Exon.* D.
Nicolao Epiſcopo *Elien.* D.
Johanni Epiſcopo *Lincoln.* D.
Laurentio Epiſcopo *Sarum.* D.
Johanni Epiſcopo *Carlilin.* P.
Johanni Epiſcopo *Roffenſi.* P.

Roulan-

Roulando Epiſcopo *Coventry* & *Lichffeldiæ*. CHAP. VII.

Henrico Epiſcopo *Aſſavenſis*. D.
Georgio Epiſcopo *Landavenſis*. D.
Thomæ Epiſcopo *Bangorenſis*. P.
Gulielmo Epiſcopo *Norwicæ*. P.
Johanni Epiſcopo *Herefordiæ*. D.
Roberto Epiſcopo *Wintonienſis*. D.
Gulielmo Epiſcopo *Bathon*. & *Wellen*.
Roberto Epiſcopo *Ceceſtriæ*. D.
Cuſtodi Spiritualitatis Epiſcopatûs *Wigorn*. ipſo Epiſcopo in Remotis agente.
Cuſtodi Spiritualitatis Epiſcopatûs *Dunelmenſis* ipſa ſede vacante.
XX. in all.

SECT. XVI.

Obſervations on this Writ to Cardinal Wolſey.

THis Writ, except the Title of it, is like that of *Ed. 2d.* yet I have thought fit to enter it for ſome reaſons particularly.

1ſt. For the Eminent nature of the Titles which this Cardinal aſcrib'd to himſelf, who had alſo tryed ſeveral experiments to have been made Pope: and probably the Paſſions of *Hen.* 8. and the Cardi-

CHAP. VII.

Cardinals diſappointments therein, might haſten the diſſolution of the Abbots, and other proceedings in order to the leſſening the Popes intereſt here; and this refuſal of the Cardinal, may juſtly give an occaſion to ſay that the *Engliſh* have always had hard meaſure in their Attempts therein; for though the Conclave have admitted above 50. *Engliſh* men to be Cardinals, yet (it ſeems) their Policy hath been not to admit of any *Engliſh* man to be Pope (except one in our *Henry* 2. time) called *Nicolas Brakeſpear*, who being Pope, Intituled himſelf *Adrian* the *4th.*) ſo that from *Higynus*'s time there hath been but one *Engliſh* man made Pope (unleſs *Johannes natione Anglicus*, *officio Papa*, *Sexu Fœmina quæ ſedet in Papatu An.* 20. *Menſ.* 6. who in Engliſh we call Pope *Joane*) be allow'd for one of the 246. Popes to this time, yet the Pope hath exerciſed the higheſt Juriſdiction here that *England* could afford, which is a very Partial and unequal way of dealing. *Guſſarus.*

2. The 2*d.* reaſon of Entring this Writ, is to ſhew that the Archbiſhop of *York*, was herein the Exemplar to the Archbiſhop of *Canterbury*, of which there is no Precedent before; for the three Cardinals which were Archbiſhops, *viz.* in the time of King *John*, *Edward* the 3*d*, and

and *Hen.* the *6th.* were all three Archbishops of *Canterbury*, ſo as this precedency muſt be attributed to the Cardinals Dignity above all Archbiſhops, and not to any irregularity in placing the Exemplar. And here it may be obſerved, that as the Title of Archbiſhop did long ſince leap over the Title of Biſhop, and the Titles of Patriarch and Pope, over Archbiſhops, afterwards, *viz. Anno Chriſti* 1099. when the Title of Cardinal firſt began (by Pope *Paſcal* the *2d.* his inſtitution) the Title being rais'd by him, of certain Parochial Prieſts in *Rome* (of whom he had more confidence) did in effect leap over all the Four other Degrees, and by it had the ſole power of Electing Popes, being under their management; ſo as the Pope hath only the Title left, and the 70 Cardinals the power of Electing him, in which they are unwilling to admit of any *Engliſh* man, although if they did, he would be ſo overballanc'd, that there were no great hazard of his Election. In the mean time, the Conclave is ſo kind to its own Intereſt, as to appoint one of thoſe Cardinals to be Protector of *England*, he being at this day Stiled, *Eminentiſſimus Dominus Franciſcus Cardinalis Barbarinus Angliæ Protector.*

3. It may be obſerved that amongſt many other Titles he Intitled himſelf *Presbytery,*

byter, to gratifie all interests.

4. Though *H.* 8. might intitle himself *Fidei Defensor* 8 years before this Writ, yet this is the first Writ on Record wherein this Title is given; and this also is the last Writ, that I find was sent to any Cardinal to sit in Parliament; for though Cardinal *Pool* was Cardinal, and Archbishop of *Canterbury* in Queen *Mary's* time; yet he had no Writ, either as Cardinal, or Archbishop, or both; but the Exemplar was in that Parliament, to the Bishop of *Winchester*, and no Writs to the Bishops of *Canterbury*, *York*, *London*, or *Durham*.

5. When this Writ was made, he was Lord Chancellor, yet it is not inserted in the Writ, possibly because Sir *Thomas More* was in Prospect to be Lord Chancellor, and was actually so before the Parliament met. And now having shewn the first Writ among the *Pawns*, I shall proceed to the Writs in the subsequent *Pawns*, and then shew the alteration of them.

The second *Pawn* or bundle of Writs extant in the Pettibag is of the 31 of *Hen.* 8*th*. wherein the first Writ is to *Thomas* Archbishop of *Canterbury*; and this Writ also agrees with the former (except in the Titles) and with all the Writs to Archbishops, from *Edward* the 2*ds*. time to this, as they are in the Clause Rolls.

The

The third *Pawn*, or Record of Writs in the Pettibag, is of the 36 of *Hen.* 8*th.* which is the remarkable Writ, becauſe it differs from all the former Writs ſince *Ed.* 2*ds.* time, both in the Titles and the Præmonition; for in this Writ he is intituled King of *Ireland*, and Supream Head; but before this, only Lord of *Ireland.* Now as to the Title of King of *Ireland*, *Hen.* the 2*d.* did give the ſame to his Son King *John*, but the Pope would not let him enjoy it; nor did any of his Succeſſors aſſume it, till *Hen.* the 8*th.* reſolved to reaſſume it in defiance of the Pope, and writ himſelf King of *Ireland*, inſtead of Lord of *Ireland*; becauſe, as I ſaid in the former Section, he would not place the Title of *Defender*, before *Ireland*, as the Pope had directed him in his Bull; or it may be in reſpect the Pope pretended a Title under King *John* to *Ireland*; and as for the other Title of *Supream Head*, though it was given him by the Parliament 12 years before, yet I find it not in any Parliament Writ till this year of the 36. *H.* 8. So that the Preamble, or Titular part of the Writ is thus, *Henricus Dei gratiâ Angliæ Franciæ & Hiberniæ Rex, fidei Defenſor, & Eccleſiæ Anglicanæ & Hiberniæ Supremum Caput.* Then for the Premonition, whereas the words *Priorem*

CHAP. VII.

CHAP. VII. *Capellanum* or *Capitulum* were plac'd next unto *Præmonentes*; in this Writ the words were *Præmonentes Decanum & Capitulum*, becauſe Abbies and Priories were newly diſſolv'd, and Deanaries Conſtituted and ſo the Writs thus alter'd have continued till this Writ for the year 1661. But before I ſet down the Writ for 1661, I muſt a little repeat ſome ſhort progreſſes and methods uſhering in that Writ, for though the Biſhops were in the year 1641. by an Act of King *Charles* the Firſt, with the Conſent of the Lords Temporal, and Commons, diſabled from Exerciſing any Temporal Juriſdiction or Authority; and thereupon, ſoon after put out of the Lords Houſe (as I have ſhewn) yet there was no occaſion of new Writs to them till the year 1661. and then there could be no new Writs made for their Reſtauration, till they were reſtor'd by the ſame power of King, Lords Temporal, and Commons, by repealing that Act; in order to which the remnant of the Parliament of 1640 (which ſtill continued in ſeveral ſhapes) was by the Kings Conſent diſſolv'd, his Majeſty appointing another to begin in *April* 1660. So the 29*th*. of *May* 1660. he came ſucceſsfully from beyond Seas to confirm it, and this Parliament laſted till *December* following, in which time, as Preparatories

tories to the Bishops Introduction, provisions were made for restoring Ministers who had been outed of their Livings, and also Commissioners were appointed (who did sit accordingly) to compose the differences which might arise between the Purchasers of the Bishops Lands and the Bishop, wherein they us'd so great Lenity, that the Bishops did come into their Temporalities; (with some satisfaction to both Interests) (after they had been injoyed by the Purchasers near Twenty Years) and in the same Month his Majesty did also set out a Declaration before mention'd, concerning Ecclesiastical Affairs; and after these Preparatories, that Parliament consisting of the King, Lords Temporal, and Commons, being also Dissolv'd, as I said, in *Decemb.* His Majesty was pleas'd in *February* following, to Summon another Parliament of the Lords Temporal, and Commons, to begin the Eighth of *May* 1661. before which time, his Coronation was Solemniz'd, *viz.* the Twenty third of *April* 1661. yet before the Ceremony was perform'd, he thought himself oblig'd to take Care for the Bishops, (for many Ceremonies essential to his Coronation were to be perform'd by them) and thereupon

CHAP. VII. upon at a full Council in *Whitehall*, the Tenth of *April*, this Order was made:

ORdered by his Majeſty, That the Lord Chancellor do forthwith give directions to the Clerk of the Crown, to draw up Writs of Summons to paſs his Majeſties Great Seal, directed to the moſt Reverend Father in God, William *Lord Archbiſhop of* Canterbury, *and* Accepted *Lord Biſhop of* York, *for Convocation of the Lords, Biſhops. Deans, Archdeacons, and the Clergy of their reſpective Provinces in uſual Form.*

Accordingly, the Parliament met the ſaid Eighth of *May* 1661. and did ſit till the Thirtieth of *July*, where amongſt other Acts, one did paſs for Repealing the Act of Aboliſhing Biſhops, and Reſtoring them to their Eſtates, Dignities, and Places; and ſo the Parliament Adjourned to the Twentieth of *November* following; after which Adjournment, upon the Twenty ninth of *Auguſt* following, the Writs which were ordered the Tenth of *April* aforeſaid, did paſs under the Great Seal, and were diſtributed, ſo as the Twentieth of *November* 1661. they did take their places in the Houſe of Lords, and have continued

tinued ſo to do during this Parliament; and notwithſtanding this long deprivation, (wherein the King himſelf, the Temporal Lords, and the chief of the Commons were Sharers) they may be ſaid to be in the Houſe of Lords upon an Intereſt of Right, though the Intereſt of Form in their Introduction was wanting, that Act of Abolition being partly Authentick, and partly not, (for Acts of Parliament are good *Abſente Clero*, though not *Excluſo Clero*,) and ſo next I ſhall ſhew the Exemplar Writ, as it is entered in the Crown Office, (for it was too late to enter it amongſt the *Depoſits* or *Pawns* in the Pettibag.)

SECT. XX.

The Form of the Writ to the Archbiſhop of Canterbury *the* 29th. *of* Aug. 1661.

REx Reverendiſſimo in Chriſto Patri prædilecto & fideli Conciliario noſtro Gulielmo eadem gratia Archiepiſcopo Cantuarienſi totius Angliæ Primat' & Metropolitano Salutem. Quia de Adviſamento & Aſſenſu Concilii noſtri pro quibuſdam arduis & urgentibus negotiis nos Statum & defenſionem Regni noſtri Angliæ & Eccleſiæ Anglicanæ concernen' quoddam Parliamentum noſtrum apud Civitatem noſtram Weſtm'

CHAP. VII. Weſtm' octavo die Maii præterito teneri ordinavimus & ibidem nobiſcum cum cæteris Prælat' Magnatibus & proceribus dicti Regni noſtri Colloquium habere & tractare Vobis in fide & dilectione quibus nobis tenemini rogando Mandamus quod conſideratis dictorum negotiorum arduitate & periculis imminentibus Ceſſante excuſatione quacunq' dictis die & loco perſonalit' interſitis nobiſcum ac cum PrælatisMagnatibus & Proceribus prædictis ſuper dictis negotiis tractatur' veſtrumque Concilium impenſur' & hoc ſicut nos & honorem noſtrum ac Salvationem & defenſionem Regni & Eccleſiæ prædict' Expeditionemque dictorum negotiorum diligetis nullatenus omittatis Præmontes Decanum & Capitulum Eccleſiæ veſtræ Cantuariæ ac Archidiaconos totumq; Clerum veſtræ Dioceſis quod idem Decan' & Archidiaconi in propriis perſonis ſuis ac dictum Capitulum per unum idemq' Clerum per duos procuratores idoneos plenam & ſufficientem poteſtatem ab ipſis Capitulis & Clero diviſim habentes prædictis die & loco perſonaliter interfuerint ad conſentiendum hiis quæ tunc ibidem de Communi Concilio dicti Regni noſtri divina favente Clementia contigerint ordinari Teſte meipſo apud Weſtm' viceſimo nono Auguſti Anno Regni noſtri 13. Annoque Dom. 1661.

SECT.

CHAP. VII.

SECT. XXI.

Conſimilia Brevia dirigenda.

TO the Archbiſhop of *York*; *Reverendiſſimo* Accepted *Archiepiſcopo Eborum Angliæ Primati*, (leaving out *Totius* before *Angliæ*) as in the former.

To each of the other Biſhops *Reverendo*, &c. as they are entred in the Memorials of the Chancery Crown Office in this following order.

Reverendo	Epiſcopo		
Gilberto	Londini		All theſe Writs dated 29. *Aug.* 1661. except the laſt.
Johanni	Dunelmenſis	Vulgo Durham	
Briano	Winceſtriæ		
Gulielmo	Bathon & Wells		
Roberto	Oxoniæ		
Gulielmo	Bangor		
Johanni	Ruffenſis	Rocheſter	
Mattheo	Elienſis		
Henrico	Ciceſtriæ	Chicheſter	
Humphrido	Sarum	Salisbury	
Georgio	Worceſtriæ		
Roberto	Lincolniæ		
Georgio	St. Aſaph		
Gulielmo	St. Davids	Minuenſis	
Benjamino	Burgi Petri	Peterborough	
Hugoni	Llandaff		
Richardo	Carlioniæ	Carlile	
Briano	Ceſtriæ		
Johanni	Exoniæ	Exeter	
Gilberto	Briſtoll		
Edwardo	Norwici		
Gulielmo	Gloceſtriæ		
Nicolao	Herefordiæ		

Johanni Epiſcopo Lichfeildiæ & Coventriæ Jan. 30. 1662.

CHAP. VII. There is alſo the Biſhop of *Man Iſland*, but in reſpect he hath no Writ to ſit in the Lords Houſe, I have not entered him.

Note, That except the two Archbiſhops and the Biſhops of *London*, *Durham*, and *Winchester*, whoſe Precedencies are ſetled by the Act of 33. *H.* 8. all the other Biſhops are entred into the *Pawns* according to the dates of their Conſecrations.

SECT. XXII.

Obſervations on the Writ.

UPon comparing the Writ of *Edw.* the Second, with the middle Writ of 21*th.* of *Hen.* the Eighth, and the Writ of the 13. *Car. Secundi*, theſe follow- Particulars may be obſerv'd.

Firſt, The Titles of ſeveral Kings in their Writs, as well to the Lords Temporal as Spiritual, have varied according to the Succeſſive Kings Increaſe or Decreaſe of their Dominions, but more remarkably in *Hen.* the Eighths time, relating to the Clergy (as I have ſhewn.)

Secondly, All Writs concerning Biſhops, from *Edward* the Seconds time and before, to the 13. of *Car. Secundi* incluſive, were directed to the Archbiſhop of *Canterbury*, as the Exemplar Writ, in in respect of his Dignity, except where any Cardinal was a Bishop of *England*, or the Popes Vicar-General, or that the See of *Canterbury* was void, or that a Bishop was Chancellor; and then the Exemplar Writ was directed to that Bishop, and to neither of the Archbishops; or if both Archbishopricks were void, then to the Bishop of *London*. CHAP VII.

Thirdly, The Exemplar and Consimilar Writs to Bishops, have been generally plac't in the Clause-Rolls, and in all the *Pawns* extant before any Degrees, except Princes of the Blood, though their places in the Lords House are otherwise.

Fourthly, Sometimes the Writ to the Archbishop was without any Epethit to his Christian name; but the Epithet of the most constant Application was *Venerabili Archiepiscopo*, and the like to Bishops; but in *Hen.* the Eighths time it was alter'd, *Reverendissimo* to Archbishops, and *Reverendo* to Bishops.

Fifthly, Also an other Title is usually in the Bishops Writs; as in the Writs to the Lords Temporal, *viz. Prædilecto & fideli Conciliario*, which is not in the ancient Writ; but of late it is entred as an addition to such as are of the Kings Privy Council, whereof the Bishop of *Canterbury* is for the most part one.

CHAP. VII.

Sixthly, In the 36. of *Henry* the Eighth, the Writ is, *Primati & Metropolitano*, which latter word was not extant till that Writ.

Seventhly, In the latter Writs, the words *de adviſamento & aſſenſu Concilii noſtri*, are entred, which are not in the old Writs, and ſome other words which are in the Dukes Writ, and not in the old Writs, as may be obſerved in the Figures which I have placed in that Writ.

Eighthly, And in the *Mandamus*, inſtead of *Firmiter injungentes* to the Temporal Lords, the Writs to the Biſhops are *Rogando Mandamus*; and inſtead of *Fide & ligeantia* to the Temporal Lords, it is, *In fide & dilectione* to the Lords Spiritual; ſo that to the word *Præmonentes*, the Writs both to the Lords Spiritual and Temporal do agree, as well in the Originals, as Alterations, except in thoſe particulars before nam'd.

Ninthly, From the word *Præmonentes* in the Writ, there is a greater Latitude of power granted to the Lords Spiritual, than to the Lords Temporal; for the Lords Temporal are not impowred by their Writs to Summon the Laity, (who ſit in the Houſe of Commons as Repreſentatives of the Commonalty) but the Lords Spiri-

tual

tual are impowred by their Writs, to Summon Deacons, Archdeans, and Proctors to attend the Parliament, (as Representatives of the Clergy) who being met at places appointed, (distinct from the House of Lords, or House of Commons) those places where they meet, have the Titles of Convocations; the Bishops making the upper Convocation, the Representatives of the Clergy, the lower; Suting to those two of the Laity; one called sometimes, the House of Lords or Peers, or upper House, the other sometimes the House of Commons, or lower House.

The General Writs for this Parliament were dated (as I have shewn) the 18*th.* of *Febr.* 1661. to meet the 8*th.* of *May* 1661. but the Writs to the Bishops were not dated, till the 29. of *August* following; yet by these Writs, they are appointed to meet (*die & loco*) at the day and place, *viz.* on the Eighth of *May*, and at *Westminster*, as in the General Writs; so as the latter Writs seem to command an Impossibility; but this is to be understood in a Parliament-sence, *viz.* That the first day of the Meeting of a Parliament, continues to the end of a Session, or Prorogation, and is accounted but as one day, for an Adjournment is but

CHAP. VII. but the continuance of that day; and a passing of Acts upon an Adjournment (as in this case) was not a determining the Session, because they were passed by way of Proviso, That it should not thereby discontinue the Parliament; so that the Bishops being admitted before any Session of determining the Parliament, or before any Prorogation of it; it is to be esteem'd in a Parliament-sence, (as I said) as one day. And so it is in Law; where a Sum is due the Eighth of *May*, payable at *Westminster*, and not paid till the 29. of *August*, and then paid in *London*, and then accepted by the Creditor; it doth bar all breaches or punctilios in Law or Equity, between the Creditor and Debtor.

Besides, If a Parliament continues some Months without Adjournments or Prorogations, in which time many Members of both Houses Dye, so as there is a necessity to send out Writs for a Supply of Members; if the Writs should not issue in a certain Form, with respect to a certain day, though past, it would produce many inconveniencies, attending the Discretion or Indiscretion of Clerks who are to form such Writs; and therefore all Writs though after Prorogations, though many years subsequent, have still reference to the first day of the Parliament, as will be further shewn;

ſhewn; for it hath been the Wiſdom of Parliaments to admit of no variation in that point. CHAP. VII.

Next, As to the place of Meeting; the Biſhops are Summon'd to meet *Cum Prælatis Magnatibus & proceribus*, at *Weſtminſter*, which the Biſhops do as to their Co-Intereſt in the Houſe of Lords; but in relation to the inferior Clergy, the Biſhops do meet at *Weſtminſter*, and ſometimes Adjourn to ſuch places out of *Weſtminſter*, as the Archbiſhop or his Vicar appoints; which before the Fire in 1666. was at the *Convocation-Houſe* on the South-ſide of *St. Pauls* Church in *London*, but ſince, in *Weſtminſter-Abby*. The Biſhops in all this Parliament ſit in *Henry* the Sevenths Chappel, (as the upper Convocation) the Deans, &c. in St. *Benedicts* Chappel, on the North-ſide of the *Abby*; (as the lower Convocation) ſo as they have diſtinct Houſes or Places from the Houſe of Lords, and Houſe of Commons, as alſo diſtinct days of meeting; but always after the Parliament firſt meets; and ſo of ſitting ſome days after any Adjournment, or Prorogation, or Diſſolution, which is appointed beyond the Lords or Commons, as will be ſhewn in the Chapter of Convocations.

11. Con-

CHAP. VII.

11. Concerning the alteration of *Priorem* into *Decanum*, I have given an account.

12. Inſtead of *favente deo* the later Writs ſay, *favente divina clementia.*

13. In the old Writs the year of Chriſt is not added, for it was more than 300 years after Chriſt, before the Computation was us'd; but in the later Writs it is not omitted.

14. Till about the year 855. there was not above 16 Biſhopricks, and then they increas'd to 19 and 21, and in *Hen.* 8. time to 26, and ſo they have continued ever ſince; but in all times there have been ſeveral Tranſplacings, and Tranſmutations; ſo as the names of the Biſhopricks of *Dorcheſter*, *Dunwich*, *Hagleſted*, *Sydnaceſter*, and *Leiceſter*, *Landasfirm*, *Selſy*, *Sherborn*, *Cheſter* in *Durham*, *Crediton*, and St. *Petrocks*, 10 in all, are utterly loſt and drown'd in the now remaining 26 Biſhopricks.

15. The Biſhops being men well Educated, in all Sciences Divine and humane, were ſtil imployed by our Succeſſive Kings, as well in matters Temporal, as Spiritual; for I find that of 153 Chancellors, and Keepers of the Great-Seal (from *William* the Conquerours time) there have been 62 Archbiſhops, and Biſhops employ'd in theſe Offices; and from the firſt Inſtitution of Treaſu-

Treasurer (in *William* the 2*d's*. time to Ed. the 4*ths*. time) there have been 42. Archbishops and Bishops, Treasurers, but from *Ed.* the 4*th's*. to this time, no Bishop hath been Treasurer, except *William* Archbishop of *Canterbury*, in *Charles* the 1*sts*. time, then Bishop of *London*; they have been also Chief Justices, &c. But for other Offices, in respect I find them not mention'd in any of their Writs of Summons to Parliaments, as additional Titles: I shall not make any further inquiries; but indeed anciently most of the Judicial Offices in the Kingdom or State, were under the Care, and Management of the Clergy; and therefore the Chancellor, Treasurer, Privy-Seal, &c. were called *Clerici*, or Clerks, as a distinction from the Laity. And being men generally of the greatest Knowledge and Learning, were thereupon chosen into Offices of the highest nature.

16. That though (for many Ages before the end of *Hen.* the 8*th's*. Reign) the Bishops were then of the *Roman* Religion, yet whenever they had the least encouragement from the present Kings of *England* (and sometimes without it) they still oppos'd the Superintendency, and Supremacy both of the Church and Court of *Rome* (as to the Dominions of the respective

CHAP. VII. ſpective Kings of *England*) proteſting that the ſame was a deſtruction of the Realm, and Crown of *England*, which hath always (ſaid they) been Free, and hath no earthly Sovereignty, but onely God in all Regalities, as may be ſeen in the Parliament Rolls of *Rich.* 2*d*, *Hen.* the 6*th.* and in other Kings Reigns, and ſince *Hen.* the 8*th.* the Biſhops and Clergy under them, have been almoſt the only Bulwark againſt the Storms, and Incroachments of *Rome* upon us.

17. It appears by a long concatenation of Records that they have had theſe various Titles of Honour, *viz.* in the Latin Records *Archiepiſcopi*, & *Epiſcopi*, *Prælati*, *Pares*, and in ſuch Records as are writ in *French* or *Engliſh*, *Archeveſq*; & *Eveſq*; Archbiſhops, Biſhops, Prelates, Peers, Grantz, Grandees, or Great ones, in diſtinction of the Leſſer Peers, or Houſe of Commons (of which I ſhall ſpeak more) alſo *Seigniors* ſingly, and *Signiors du Parlement*, alſo Lords, and Lords Spiritual, and Barons claiming onely a Vital Feudal, Tenurial, and not Nobilitated Peerage, in diſtinction of the Lords Temporal, whoſe Peerage is Perſonal, Hereditary, and Nobilitated.

18. Though they abſent themſelves from the Houſe of Lords upon Tryals of blood,

blood, yet it was, and is ſtill in obedience to the morality of the Canon-Laws; for though thoſe Canon-Laws were practiſed in times of *Popery*, yet the reaſonableneſs, and conſcientiouſneſs of that Law ſtill continues; and now we are free from the bondage of *Popery*, the *Proteſtant* Biſhops ſtill think themſelves obliged to it, as the *Papal* Biſhops were before, like the *4th.* Commandment, which ſtill morally obligeth Us, as formerly it did the *Jews*; yet where they do abſent themſelves in Caſes of blood, it is done by leaving Proxy, or proteſtation of their Right of Sitting, &c.

19. And laſtly it may be very well obſerved, though their influence and Intereſt (upon a Spiritual, and Temporal account) is ſpread over this whole Kingdom, their Revenues great; and thereby their Tenants, Officiates, and Dependents very numerous; yet I do not find in Hiſtories, that the Biſhops of *England* did ever raiſe an Army, to juſtifie their intereſt againſt any of our Kings, or againſt the other two Eſtates, of Lords Temporal, or Commons, by Sword, or Force; but ſtill ſupported it by their Pen, or Prayers.

20. Thus I have given an account of the Managers of Religion in this Iſland; and

CHAP. VII.

and of the Writs, whereby they were Summon'd to Parliaments; and of other great employments wherein they have been intruſted, of a mixt nature, part Civil, and part Eccleſiaſtick; and both tending to Religious Duties. I ſhould now proceed to the Writs which concern Abbots and Priors, which till the 36. *Hen.* 8. were ever entred next the Biſhops in the Clauſe-Rolls, and *Pawns*; but there having been no Writs directed to them ſince the ſaid 36. of *H.* the 8*th.* (except two in Queen *Mary's* time; one to the Abbot of *Weſtminſter*, the other to the Prior of St. *John's* of *Jeruſalem*) I ſhall follow the Method of the *Pawns*, ſince the ſaid 36*th.* year, referring the Diſcourſe of them to the Chapter of Diſſolutions; and here proceed to the third Exemplar Writ, *viz.* to the Lord Chancellor, being the firſt Officer of State, and Principal Aſſiſtant, and now annext to a Barony, and after to his Title of Earl, as will be ſhewn.

CHAP. VIII.

The Third Exemplar of the Lord Chancellor, *or* Lord Keeper.

AMongſt the *Romans* this great Officer was called *Actuarius*, *Scriba*, *Notarius*, *Principis præſentis Vicarius*, & *Cancellarius*; and ſo it came into *France*, and amongſt the *Saxons* it had the name of *Referendarius*; but in *England* we do not find this Title of Chancellor, till the firſt of King *John An.* 1199 (though *Lambert*, and others derive it from *Edward* the *Confeſſors* time. This Officer continued in ſo high an eſteem, that in the 5*th.* of *Richard* the 2*d.* The Commons in Parliament in their Exhibits to the King, deſired that the moſt wiſe and able man in the Realm might be choſen Chancellor, which made *Budæus* (one of *Hen.* the 8*ths.* Orators) to give this Deſcription, *Hunc* (ſaith he) *rerum omnium cognitione, omni Doctrinarum virtutumq; genere inſtructiſſimum & ornatiſſimum, ingenioq; ad omnia verſatili, omnia in numerato habere oportere fatendum eſt.*

This Diſcription is alſo to be applyed to the Keeper of the Great Seal, which in-

CHAP. VIII. vention of a publick Seal, as it was more ancient with the *Romans*, ſo it ſeems to be very ancient with us in *England*, (that Office being Conſtituted by *William* the Conquerer in the Year 1067.) and for the honour of both, (as it is ſhewn in this Section) *Geffrey* a Natural Son to *Hen.* the Second was Chancellor, and the Queen to *Henry* the Third was Keeper of the Seal.

2. Theſe two Offices were ſometimes kept diſtinct, and ſometimes united in one Perſon, till the Fifth of *Queen Eliz.* and then it was Enacted, That both thoſe Offices ſhould be accounted but as one and the ſame, and that hereafter both ſhould not be uſed at one time by diſtinct Perſons.

3. Whilſt they were diſtinct, they had two Seals; the Chancellors was of Gold, and the Keepers of Silver; the Court eſteemed *Officina Regis*, and the Seal, *Clavis Regni*; but whenever they were either united, or diſtinctly executed, ſtill this high Office was managed by Archbiſhops or Biſhops, or by the moſt eminent Laicks for Learning, Integrity, and Abilities, as may be ſeen by comparing the Hiſtory of them with their Catalogues.

4. To manifeſt their Eminency, it is evident from the Rolls, that in the opening

of

of all Parliaments, the Lord Chancellor or Lord Keeper, did constantly, by the Command of the King, shew them the reasons of Summoning them, (unless in a Vacancy, or on a special account of Absence, and then it was performed by one of the Chief Justices.

5. But to pass these, (being more fully shewn in my Annotations) I do not find in any of the Clause-Rolls, or in the *Pettibag-Pawns*, that a Chancellor or Keeper had any distinct Writs of Summons to a Parliament, till the 28. of *Eliz.* (when Sir *Tho. Bromley* Knt. being the Queens Sollicitor, was made Lord Chancellor, and Summoned by a distinct Writ, in the same Form as is hereafter set down, which very Form hath continued ever since. And in the 35. of *Eliz.* Sir *John Puckering* being but Serjeant at Law, was made *Custos Sigilli*, and had a particular Writ of Summons to that Parliament; and in the 39. of *Eliz.* Sir *Tho. Egerton* Knt. being then Master of the Rolls, was made *Custos Sigilli*, and had this assisting Writ of Summons for that Parliament; and the like in the 43. of her Reign; and so in the 21. of King *James*; and in the First of *Caroli Primi*, particular assisting Writs were sent to the Bishop of *Lincoln*, in these words: *Reverendo in Christo Patri*

CHAP. VIII. *prædilecto & fideli Conſiliario noſtro Joanni Epiſcopo Lincolniæ magni ſigilli Angliæ Cuſtodi*: So as he had this Writ as an aſſiſting Writ, and another Writ *virtute Baroniæ*.

6. It may here be obſerved, that this was the only Biſhop that was either Keeper or Chancellor, from the Firſt of *Eliz.* to this time; whereas before Queen *Eliz.* for the moſt part Biſhops or Eccleſiaſticks did execute thoſe Offices; but whenever it was conferred upon the Laicks, choice was made out of the moſt eminent Families; as in the 26. of *Hen.* the Second, (as I ſaid) *Geffrey*, Natural Son to *Henry* the Second, was made Chancellor; and in the 15*th.* of King *John*, *Ralph de Nevile* was made Keeper of the Great Seal; and in 22. of *Henry* the Third, *Geffrey* a Templer, and *John de Lexington*, were made Keepers of the Great Seal; and in the 37. of his Reign, his Queen, upon the Kings going into *Gaſcoine*, (which is remarkable, as I ſaid) had the Cuſtody of the Great Seal; and in the 45. of that King, *Walter de Merton* was made Chancellor; and in the 49. of that King, *Thomas de Cantilupe* was made Chancellor; and in the 53. *Richard de Middleton* made *Cuſtos Sigilli*; and in the 56. *John de Kirkley*, and *Peter de Winton*, made Keepers of

of the Seal; and in the 2. of *Edward* the Third, *Henry de Bughersh* made Chancellor. In the 14. of *Edw.* the Third, *John de St. Paul* made Keeper of the Seal; in the same year, Sir *Robert Burgtheire* Knt. made Chancellor and Keeper of the Seals; and the like in the 15*th.* to *Robert Parning*, and in the 17*th.* to *Robert de Sadington*, and in the 19*th.* to *John de Offord*, and in the 20. to *John de Thoresby*. In the Records of the same year, it is said that Sir *Lionel* Duke of *Clarence*, the Kings Son, (then Lord Keeper of *England*) gave Command by Proclamation, That no Arms should be worn sitting that Parliament; (whose name is omitted in the Catalogue of the Lord Keepers, by Mr. *Selden* in his Discourse of the Office of Chancellor and Keeper) and in the 45. to Sir *Robert Thorpe*, and in the 46. to *John Knivet*; and in the 2. of *Rich.* the Second, to Sir *Le Scroop*; and in the 6. of *Rich.* 2. to Sir *Michael de la Pool*; and in the 11. of *Hen.* 4. to Sir *Thomas Beaufort*; and in the 32. *H.* 6. *Richard* Earl of *Salisbury* was made Chancellor singly; and in the 21. of *Hen.* the Eighth, Sir *Thomas Moor* Knt. made Chancellor and Keeper; and in the 24. of *Hen.* the Eighth, *Thomas Audley* made Chancellor and Keeper; and in the 36. *Hen.* 8. *Thomas* Lord *Wriothesly*

CHAP. VIII.

 made Chancellor and Keeper; and in the First of *Edw.* the Sixth, Sir *William Pawlet* Knt. Lord *St. John* of *Basing*, made Keeper; and in the ſame year, Sir *Richard Rich* made Chancellor; and in the Firſt of *Eliz.* Sir *Nicholas Bacon* Keeper; and the 21. *Thomas Bromley* Chancellor, who continued ſo to the 28. of her Reign, and was the firſt that I find, (as is before mentioned) that had a particular Writ of Aſſiſtance; and though in the Fourteenth of King *James*, Sir *Francis Bacon* was Keeper, (in the Eighteenth of *Jac. Henry Viſcount Mandevile*, Lord Preſident of the Council, and *Lodowick* Duke of *Richmond*, *William* Earl of *Pembroke*, Sir *Julius Cæſar*, had jointly the Cuſtody of the Great Seal; and in the firſt *Car.* 1. Sir *Thomas Coventry*; and in the 16. *Car.* 1. Sir *Edw. Littleton*; and 21. *Car.* 1. Sir *Rich. Lane*, were Keepers of the Great Seal) yet we find no particular Writs in the Pettibag directed to any, but ſuch as I have before mentioned, and to theſe which follow, *viz.* in 15. *Car.* 1. Sir *John Finch* Knt. Chief Juſtice of the *Common-Pleas* was made *Cuſtos Sigilli*, and had a particular Writ of Summons to attend that Parliament.

7. As to this Writ of 13. *Car.* 2. of which I am to treat, it is to be obſerved that the

the Warrant (before mentioned) sent to Sir *Edward Hyde* Knt. and Chancellor, to impower him to send out Writs, was directed in these words, *To our Right Trusty and Well-beloved Counsellor, Sir* Edward Hyde *Knt. Chancellor of* England; but in his *Latine* Writ of Assistance, the words are, *Prædilecto & perquam fideli Consiliario suo Edwardo Domino Hyde Cancellario suo Angliæ*: leaving out *Militi* or *Equiti aurato*, and putting in *Domino*; and the reason of this variation (as I conceive) was, That the Warrant was agreed on by the King and Council before the Third of *November*, at which time he was Baron of *Hindon*; and therefore in the Warrant he is named only Sir *Edward Hyde* Knt. but in the Writ, *Domino Hyde*, which is the Adjunct Title of a Baron, as he then was; and I find before the Parliament met, he was created Viscount *Cornbury* and Earl of *Clarendon*, and thereupon had another Writ in relation to those Dignities, which was entered in the *Pawn*, and the entry dated the 12*th*. of *April* before the Parliament met, and in the latter Writ he had also his additional Titles; so that I observe, that if the Chancellor or Keeper be above the Degree of a Baron, he hath his Writ according to his Degree, and therein only

CHAP. VIII.

intimating his Chancellorſhip or Keeper-ſhip, (as is before ſhewn in the 36. of *Hen.* the Eighth. 1 *Mariæ*, &c. But if he be not a Baron, then he hath this Aſſiſting Writ, *Quatenus* Chancellor or Keeper, as may be ſeen in the former Precedents, from the 28. of *Eliz.* to this Writ of 13. *Car.* 2. If he be a Baron, as I ſaid, he hath or may require a Baronial Writ beſides this Aſſiſting Writ; The form of his Aſſiſting Exemplar Writ is as follows: the other will be ſeen among the Barons.

S e c t. VIII.

The Form of the Aſſiſting Writ to the Lord Chancellor *or* Lord Keeper.

C*Arolus Secundus* Dei Gratia Angliæ Scotiæ Franciæ & Hiberniæ Rex fidei defenſor, &c. Prædilecto & perquam fideli Conciliario ſuo Edwardo Domino Hide Cancellario ſuo Angliæ ſalutem Quia de adviſamento & Aſſenſu Concilii noſtri pro quibuſdam arduis & urgentibus negotiis nos ſtatum & defenſionem regni noſtri Angliæ & Eccleſiæ Anglicanæ concernentibus quoddam Parliamentum noſtrum apud Civitatem noſtram Weſtmonaſterium octavo die Maii proximè futuro teneri ordinavimus & ibidem

ibidem voibſcum ac cum Magnatibus & Proceribus dicti Regni noſtri Colloquium habere & tractatum. *Vobis Mandamus* firmitur injungend' quod omnibus aliis prætermiſſis prædictis die & loco perſonaliter interſitis nobiſcum ac cum cæteris de Concilio noſtro ſuper dictis negotiis tractatur' veſtrumque Conſilium impenſur' & hoc nullatenus omittatis Teſte apud Weſtmonaſterium decimo octavo die Februarii Anno Regni ſuo decimo tertio.

Grimſton.

SECT. IX.

Obſervations on this Writ.

FIrſt I ſhall ſhew how it differs from the Writs to the Nobles; Secondly, How it differs from the Writs to the other Aſſiſtants. Firſt, It differs from the Writs to Dukes, Marqueſſes, Earls, Viſcounts, in theſe particulars.

Firſt, To Dukes and Marqueſſes, the Writ is directed *Præchariſſimo Conſanguineo*, to Earls and Viſcounts, *Chariſſimo Conſanguineo*, to Barons, *Prædilecto & fideli*; and to Aſſiſtants only *dilecto & fideli*, but this Writ is directed as to a Baron, *viz. Predilecto & perquam fideli*, yet the body of the Writ differs from the Barons; the

CHAP. VIII. the word *perquam* is added to *fideli*, being in no other former Writs, but is a proper word to expreſs our *Engliſh Right Truſty*; and here it may not be improperly hinted, that in *Engliſh* Superſcriptions, *Right Truſty* is placed before *Well-beloved*, but in *Latine Well-beloved*, (or *Prædilecto*) is before *Right Truſty*, or *Perquam Fideli*.

Secondly, The words *Sub fide & ligeantia*, are in the Lords Writs next to *Vobis Mandamus*, but in all the Aſſiſting Writs, thoſe words are omitted; probably becauſe in former times, the Aſſiſtants had not Tenures, but only knowledge of the Laws which occaſioned them to be ſent for by Writ *Pro Concilio*.

Thirdly, The words (*Conſideratis dictorum negotiorum arduitate & periculis imminentibus ceſſante excuſatione quacunque*) in the Lords Writs) are left out in the Aſſiſtants Writs, and inſtead thereof, (*omnibus aliis prætermiſſis*) are inſerted. In the Mandatory part of the Writ, the words in the Writ are (*ac cum cæteris de Concilio noſtro*) inſtead of (*ac cum Magnatibus prædictis*) which is the chief diſtinction between the Peers and the Aſſiſtants.

Fourthly, In this part alſo of the Writ, the Words are only in ſhort, *& hoc nullatenus*

tenus omittatis, but in the Lords Writs, (*& hoc ſicut nos & honorem noſtrum ac Salvationem regni & Eccleſiæ prædictæ expeditionemque dictorum negotiorum diligitis*) their Lordſhips being more eminently concerned in the Kingdoms Intereſts.

Fifthly, In all the *Pawns* extant, and in moſt of the Clauſe-Rolls, (after the Exemplar Writ of every Degree or Quality is named,) theſe words are added, *Conſimilia dirigenda*; but there is no Conſimilar directed to this Writ, and although the Maſter of the Rolls is an Officer very little differing in many things from the Office of the Chancellor or Keeper, yet his Writ is made a Conſimilar to the chief Juſtice of the Kings Bench his Writ, and not to the Lord Chancellor; the Lord Chancellor ſtanding Exemplar without any Conſimilar, (and there are but Two of the ſame nature in all the *Pawns*, from the 36. of *Hen.* the Eighth to this time, *viz.* That to *Cheſter* and to *Lancaſhire*, as will be ſhewn in their order) the true reaſons thereof are (as I conceive;)

1*ſt*. That this Officer is of ſo tranſcendent a nature, that a Conſimilar thereunto were improper, becauſe the Original Warrant for iſſuing out Writs (as is before recited) is made from the King only to the Lord Chancellor or Lord Keeper, and the

CHAP. VIII. the like Warrant not to any others of the Aſſiſting Degrees.

2dly. His Lordſhip uſually, and in moſt Caſes, is neceſſarily the chief Miniſter of of State.

3dly. He is the Supream Aſſiſtant of all the Aſſiſtants in the Houſe of Lords; for he is not only Lord Chancellor and Aſſiſtant, but of late years conſtantly Speaker of that Houſe.

4thly. His Grandeur is ſuch that he hath four places in the Lords Houſe, one behind the King of *Scots-Chair*, the other next to the Dukes of the *Blood*, the third on the firſt *Woolſack*, *4thly*. at the Table (as will be ſhewn) whereas each of the other Aſſiſtants have but one ſingle place, different from thoſe provided for the fixt Nobility (as will be ſhewn in the Local part.)

6. I cannot conclude this Chapter better, than from Sir *John Davy* (an Eminent Lawyer, in his Epiſtle to his *Excellent Reports*) who Deſcribes a Chancellor in theſe words, Saith he, *Is he not* ad Latus Principis, *to attend him?* Auricularius Principis, *to adviſe him? Doth not the King make him the Conduit of his Wiſdom, when he uſeth his Voice, and Tongue to declare his Royal pleaſure? Doth he not make him the* Organ *of his goodneſs, when he truſteth him*

him with his Mercy, and Conscience in sweetning the bitter waters of summum jus, *and in mitigating the rigour of Law to his people? Doth he not represent* Reverentiam Principis *in the Power and Authority of his Office? In a word, if the greatest honours do belong to the greatest vertues (for what is honour but a reflection and reward of vertues) How vertuous a person must he be, with what Gifts and Graces, with what Abilities, with what Ornaments, both of Art and Nature must he be indowed and furnisht?* viz. *with all Learning, Law, Policy, Morality, and especially Eloquence to impart and Communicate all the rest: he must withall have a long, and universal experience in all the Affairs of the Commonwealth; he must be acceptable and absolute in all points of Gravity, Constancy, Wisdom, Temperance, Courage, Justice, Piety, Integrity, and all other vertues fit for Magistracy and Government; yet so as the same be seasoned with Affability, Gentleness, Humanity, Courtesie, without descending or diminishing himself, but still retaining his Dignity, State, and Honour. Briefly, he must be a person of such vertue and worthiness (that not only his Writ may be exemplar to other Assistants) but his Life, and Conversation a Mirrour, and Example to all Magistrates.*

He

CHAP. VIII. 7. He performs all matters which appertains to a Speaker of that Houſe, whereby he may be ſaid to be the Eye, Ear and Tongue of that great Aſſembly.

8. He is the Inlarger, Explainer, Interpreter, or Pronouncer of the Kings Commands or Pleaſure; and that which is further obſervable, of 72. Officers under his Juriſdiction, more than 44. of them are imployed in Parliament concerns; either upon its Summoning, or during its Sitting; (as will be ſhewn in my Annotations) And as his Warrant is the ſecond Warrant that gives life to a Parliament, and vivacity to its continuance by Seſſions and Receſſes; ſo he gives the ſecond *Fiat* to its Diſſolution: he hath alſo an appartment near the Lords Houſe (as will be ſhewn) for himſelf to retire to, and for his Serjeant at Arms and others of his Attendants.

Thus having conſidered the Lord Biſhops and Lord Chancellors Writs, I muſt obſerve how exquiſitely and harmoniouſly theſe two Degrees are interpos'd; (both in their ſitting in the Lords Houſe, and in the method of their Writs in *Pawns*, and in the *Act of Precedency*) being placed in all of them between the firſt and ſecond Rank of the Lords Temporal: (as it were) to ſhew that the Lords Temporal are always to embrace and maintain Religion and

and Equity, as the two chief Supporters of a Parliament. CHAP. IX.

I have ſpoken of the firſt Supporters to Religion and Equity, *viz.* Princes of the Bloud: and now I ſhall ſpeak of the other Supporters, (*viz.* the Nobles not of the Bloud, diſtinctly five Titles, *viz.* Dukes, Marqueſſes, Earls, Viſcounts, and Barons) but more eſpecially of their Writs which Summon them to ſit in Parliament, which will guide me into ſeveral obſervations.

CHAP. IX.

Of the Fourth Exemplar Writ to the Nobles not of the Bloud-Royal; To the Lord-Treaſurer, *&c.*

IN the Eighth Chapter I ſhewed the Exemplar Writs to Princes, Dukes, and Earls of the Bloud-Royal; I am now according to the method of this *Pawn*, to ſhew the Exemplar Writs to Dukes, Marqueſſes, Earls, and Barons not of the Bloud. I ſhall begin with that in *Anno* 1661. being agreeable to that Exemplar (before recited) to the Dukes of the Bloud, from the word (*Salutem*) to the end of the Writ; but the Preambles to that word do afford variety almoſt in all

Writs,

CHAP. IX. Writs, and therefore before I make the Obſervation upon it, I ſhall give a view of the Writ at large (being only abbreviated in the *Pawn.*)

CArolus Secundus Dei Gratia Angliæ Scotiæ Franciæ & Hiberniæ Rex fidei defenſor, *&c.* Præchariſſimo Conſanguineo ſuo Thomæ Comiti Southampton Theſaurario Angliæ Salutem Quia de Adviſamento & aſſenſu Concilii noſtri pro quibuſdam arduis & urgentibus negotiis nos ſtatum & defenſionem regni noſtri Angliæ & Eccleſiæ Anglicanæ concernen' Quoddam Parliamentum noſtrum apud Civitatem noſtram Weſtm' 8. die Maii prox futur' teneri ordinavimus ac ibidem vobiſcum ac cum Magnatibus & Proceribus dicti Regni noſtri, Colloquium habere & tractatum, vobis ſub fide & ligeantia quibus nobis tenemini firmiter injungendo mandamus Quod conſideratis dictorum negotiorum arduitate & periculis imminentibus ceſſante excuſatione quacunque dictis die & loco perſonaliter interſitis nobiſcum ac cum Magnatibus & Proceribus præ dictis ſupra dictis negotiis tractatur' veſtrumque Concilium impenſur' Et hoc ſicut Nos & honorem noſtrum ac Salvationem & defenſionem Regni & Eccleſiæ prædictæ expeditionem; dictorum

negotiorum

negotiorum diligitis nullatenus omittatis. CHAP Teste Rege apud Westm' 18. die Febr. IX. Anno Regni nostri 13.

SECT. II.

Observations.

1. ALl Parliamentary Exemplar Writs of this nature which are extant from the 15. of *Edward* the Second, to the 21. of *Henry* the Eighth, if they were not directed to some one of the Heirs of the Crown, or to Princes, Dukes, or Earls of the Bloud, were still directed to an Earl not of the Bloud, (except Three to Three Dukes in *Henry* the Sixths, and *Edward* the Fourths time) it being evident from what hath been said, That Earls, called in *Latin Comites*, was a more ancient Title in this Kingdom, than Dukes; (*Richard* the Eldest Son to *Edw.* the Third, being the first that was so created) but Earls long before; and though *Edward* the Third did create many Dukes more than his Son, which were of the Bloud; yet still to keep the old Title of Earl, and in veneration thereof, (as may be supposed) he in the Fourty Seventh of his Reign did think fit, (as the King usually appoints the Sword to such a Person as he

CHAP. IX. directs to carry it before him) to grant the Exemplar Writ to an Earl not of the Bloud, for the Parliament to be holden that year, and ſo did his Succeſſor, as may be ſeen in this following Table, *viz.*

47. *Edw.* 3. *Richardo Comiti Arundel*, who ſat one Parliament.

18. *Rich.* 2. *Henrico Comiti Darby*, who ſat one Parliament.

3. *Hen.* 5. *Radulpho Nevile Comiti Weſtmerland*, and the like Writ in the ſame year, ſo he ſat two Prrliaments.

7. *Hen.* 5. *Henrico Percey*, *Comiti Northumbr.* and the like in the ſame year, and in the Eighth and Ninth of this King, and Twelfth of *Hen.* 6. ſo he ſat five Parliaments; (note that the Chriſtian names and Sirnames of *Nevile* and *Percey* are in this Writ, which is not uſual to Earls, only the Chriſtian names.

The three Exemplars to Dukes not of the Bloud are in time ſubſequent to Earls; for the firſt Exemplar to a Duke was not till,

28 *H.* 6. *Gulielmo Duci Suffolciæ*, who ſat one Parliament.

38 *H.* 6. *Henrico Duci Oxoniæ*, who ſat one Parliament.

1 *Edw.* 4. The third *Johanni Norfolciæ*, and the like in the ſame year, ſo he ſat two Parliaments. And

And then after these Three Dukes, again to an Earl, *viz.*

CHAP IX.

3 *Edw.* 4. *Richardo Comiti Warwick*, who sat one Parliament; so from the 47. of *Edw.* 3. to *Rich.* the 3. there was Eight not of the Bloud, *viz.* Five Earls and Three Dukes, who had Exemplars.

From *Richard* the Third to the 21. of *Hen.* 8. there is (as I have shewn) a want of Records in the *Tower*; so as the first Exemplar that appears to us in the Pettibag, of such as had Exemplar Writs being not of the Bloud, do begin at the 36. of *H.* 8. *viz.*

36 *Hen.* 8. *Thomæ Wriothsley Militi Domino Wriothsley Cancellario*, he sat one Parliament, and was the year before made Baron of *Titchfield*, and in the first of *Edw.* 6. Earl of *Southampton*.

1 *Edw.* 6. *Gulielmo Pawlet Militi Domino Senescallo magni hospitii nostri ac Præsidenti Concilii nec non Custodi magni Sigilli*: He was then Lord *St. John* of *Bazing*, and afterwards created Marquess of *Wincester*.

6 *Edw.* 6. *Gulielmo Marchioni Winchester*, *Thesaurario Angliæ*, (*Thomas Goodrick* Bishop of *Ely* being Chancellor, and had his distinct Writ) this Marquess had his several Writs, *viz.* in the 6 of *Edw.* 6. and 7 of *Edw.* 6. and 1 *Mariæ*, and 1 *M.* 1. and 2 *Phil.* and *M.* and 2 and 3 *P.* and *M.* and 4 and 5 *P.* and *M.* (in which time the Bi-

CHAP. IX. ſhops of *Ely*, *Wincheſter*, and Archbiſhop of *York* were Lord Chancellors and had diſtinct Writs, it being not proper for them, being Lords Spiritual, to be Exemplars to the Lords Temporal;) beſides he was Exemplar in the 28. 30. 35. 39. and 43. of *Eliz.* and *Primo Jacobi*, (in which time Sir *Thomas Bromley*, and Sir *Chriſtopher Hatton* were Lord Chancellors, and Sir *John Puckering*, and Sir *Thomas Egerton* Lord Keepers, and each of them had diſtinct Writs) ſo as it is remarkable, that this *William* Lord *Pawlet* Marqueſs of *Wincheſter* was Exemplar in all the Parliament *Pawns* which are extant in the Pettibag, from the firſt of *Edw.* the Sixth, to the firſt of King *James* incluſive, which is 55. years, and was in that time Lord Treaſurer 22. years, which was longer than any of his Predeceſſors continued in that Office, except *Cicil*, who continued 27. years.)

1 *Car.* 1. *Georgio Duci Buckingham*, for one Parliament, (Sir *Thomas Coventry* being then Lord Keeper, and had a diſtinct Writ, and Sir *Richard Weſton* Treaſurer, who was then in *Scotland*.)

15 *Car.* 1. *Johanni Marchioni Wincheſter*, for one Parliament (Sir *John Finch* being then Lord Keeper of the Great Seal, and had a diſtinct Writ) alſo *Will.* Biſhop of *London* was Lord Treaſurer, and had his Writ.

13 *Car.*

13 *Car.* 2. *Thomæ Comiti Southampton*, CHAP. IX.
for this Parliament, (Sir *Edward Hyde* being then Lord Chancellor, and had his distinct Writ) this Earl was Grandchild to that *Wriothesly* mentioned in the 36. of *Hen.* 8. and died without Issue *Anno.*166---

So from the 36. of *H.* 8. to this Parliament of the 13. of *Car.* 2. there were three Exemplars, to Three Barons, (Two of them being Chancellors, and one Lord Keeper) and to Two Marquesses, to one Duke, and to one Earl; (and all these not of the Blood) Now as to the three Barons having Exemplars, (which Degree had not any before the 36. *H.* 8.) it may be presumed that the Exemplars were given them in relation to their Offices, as Lord Chancellor, or Lord Keeper, or President of the Kings Council.

And as to the two Marquesses having Exemplars, (who had not any till the 6. of *Edw.* 6.) one was as he was Treasurer, and the other in the 15. of *Car.* 1. only as Marquess, because there was no Duke Summon'd to that Parliament; (and Sir *John Finch* was then Lord Keeper, and *William* Bishop of *London* Lord Treasurer, and both had distinct Writs;) so there was none of the three great Officers of State remaining to be Exemplars, except *Henry* Earl of *Manchester*, then Lord Privy-Seal,

CHAP. IX. who according to the fore-mentioned *Act of Precedency* is placed in the Lords Houſe before all Dukes, Marqueſſes, *&c.* (not of the Blood) but I ſuppoſe, becauſe there was no Preſident wherein the Lord Privy-Seal had been Exemplar ſince its firſt Inſtitution in the 11. of *Hen.* 4. and being not called Lord Privy-Seal, nor that place in the Lords Houſe allotted to him, till the 31. *H.* 8. poſſibly for thoſe reaſons it was not given to the Lord Privy-Seal, but to the Marqueſs ſingly, or elſe it was an omiſſion in not minding the *Act of Precedency.*

Theſe latter Writs from the 36. of *Hen.* 8. did ſeem to break the method of the former; for before that *Pawn* of that year, no Dukes or Marqueſſes were made Conſimilars, where an Earl was made Exemplar; but in the Exemplar of the 36. *H.* 8. *Wriotheſly* Earl of *Southampton* was made Exemplar, and the Duke of *Norfolk* then Lord Treaſurer of *England*, (and *Charles* Duke of *Suffolk* the Great Maſter of the Kings Houſhold, and Preſident of the Council, were (beſides the Marqueſs of *Dorcheſter*, and Thirteen Earls, and Twenty eight Barons) made his Conſimilars, ſo as the precedency of his Exemplarity muſt be aſcribed to his Chancellorſhip, which according to the *Act of Precedency* was

was to be before all Dukes, &c. (not of the Blood;) and upon the same reason, Pawlet Lord *St. John* in the first *Edw.* 6. being then Lord Keeper, had the Exemplar Writ, and the Duke of *Somerset* (though the Kings Uncle) Governor of the Kings Person, and Protector of *England*, (as also the Marquess of *Dorchester*, and Marquess of *Northampton*, and Thirteen Earls and Thirty Barons) were his Consimilars, which is the only President (which I know of) where the Lord Chancellor or Lord Keeper had the Exemplar to a Duke of the Bloud; and upon the like reason, as (I conceive) in the 6 of *Ed.* the 6. *William* Marquess of *Winchester*, being Lord Treasurer, (the next in Precedency to the Lord Chancellor, by the Act of 31. *H.* 8.) had the Exemplar to two Dukes, one Marquess, Fourteen Earls, One Viscount, and Thirty one Barons, all which were his Consimilars: and it is probable the reason why this Exemplar was given to the Treasurer and not to the Chancellor, was, because *Thomas Goodrick* Bishop of *Ely* was then Lord Chancellor; and so it was not proper for that Bishop to be Exemplar, for the reasons before alledged.

Now in the first *Car. primi*, *Thomas Coventry* being Lord Keeper, and having a distinct Writ, the Duke of *Buckingham*

CHAP. IX. had the Exemplar, who had one Marqueſs, Thirty ſeven Earls, Eleven Viſcounts, and Fourty ſeven Barons to his Conſimilars.

Alſo in the 15. *Car.* 1. *John* Marqueſs of *Winchester* (Son to the former Marqueſs of *Winchester*) was made Exemplar, (Sir *John Finch* being Lord Keeper, who had a diſtinct Writ, (and *William* Biſhop of *London* being in *Scotland*) but he had no Duke or other Marqueſs, but Fifty eight Earls, Five Viſcounts, and Forty four Barons his Conſimilars, and ſo reduced the proper Conſimilars to its former method.

But the 14. *Car.* 2. *Thomas Wriotheſly* Earl of *Southampton* Lord Treaſurer (Grand-child to the former Earl of *Southampton*) altered it again: (there being now alſo a diſtinct Writ to Sir *Edward Hyde* Lord Chancellor) for this Earl had three Dukes, (one being General) Four Marqueſſes, Fifty five Earls, Eight Viſcounts, and Sixty eight Barons his Conſimilars; (I conceive as Lord Treaſurer) for according to ancient Practice, (as I have ſhewn) an Earl had not any Dukes entred as his Conſimilars.

The number of all the Exemplar Writs extant, from the 15. of *Edw.* the 2*d.* in *An.* 1322. to the 13. of *Car.* 2*di.* *An.* 1661. are but Twenty, and but Fourteen Kings from whom they were granted; The num-

number of the Parliaments in which the Nobles did Sit, to whom ſuch Exemplars were iſſued, were 107. and theſe 107. Parliaments were in the ſpace of 341. Years. CHAP. IX.

As concerning the years when theſe Exemplars were firſt iſſued to the reſpective degrees of Nobles before mentioned, they are in this order of time.

15 *Edw.* 2. This firſt Exemplar Writ, as I have ſhewn, was [illegible] was of the Bloud, *viz* [illegible] of *Cheſter*, Eldeſt Son [illegible] ter King *Edw.* the 3*d.* for there [illegible] no Duke in *England.*

3 *Edw.* 3. The firſt Exemplar Writ to a Prince of the Bloud, was to the ſame Earl being then made Prince of *Wales.*

37 *Edw.* 3. The firſt Exemplar Writ to a Duke of the Blood was not till this year, though the firſt Duke in *England* (diſtinct from that of Earl, (as Mr. *Selden* ſaith) was the Eleventh of *Edw.* 3*d.* and then *Edward* the Kings Eldeſt Son was in Parliament created Duke of *Cornwall*; (yet *Speed* in his Chronicle of *Edw.* 3*d.* makes this Creation in the 3*d* of *Edw.* 3*d.* when (ſaith he) he was created Prince of *Wales*, Duke of *Aquitain* and *Cornwall*, which agrees with the Records of the *Tower*, and therefore I conceive there is ſome miſtake in Mr. *Selden*) but however the miſtake be,

CHAP. IX. be, the firſt Exemplar Writ to a Duke was not till this year; for though *Edward* Prince of *Wales* was Duke in the Third or Eleventh year of his Father, and *Thomas* Earl of *Norfolk* ſoon after was created Duke of *Norfolk*, and *Henry* Earl of *Lancaſter* ſoon after created Duke of *Lancaſter*, yet they had not any Exemplar Writs as Dukes, but before as Earls; ſo as *John* Duke of *Lancaſter* in this Parliament of the 37. *Edw.* the 3*d.* was the firſt Duke which had an Exemplar Writ.

47 *Edw.* 3: As I have ſhewn the firſt Exemplar to an Earl of the Bloud, ſo this ſhews the firſt Exemplar to an Earl not of the Bloud, which was this year to *Richard* Earl of *Arundel*; for though there were many Earls before not of the Bloud, yet they had only Conſimilar Writs, but no Exemplars extant to any of them till this Year.

28 *H.* 6. And though there were many Dukes not of the Blood ſince the firſt Creation of that Title, yet the firſt Duke not of the Blood who was thought fit to be an Exemplar, was not till this Parliament, and the Predeceſſor of this Duke was an Earl in *Edw.* 3*ds.* time, and even this Duke was Earl in the time of his Predeceſſors, before any Duke was created.

6 *Edw.* 6. Though the firſt Marqueſs (created

(created in *England*) was in the *9th.* of *Rich.* 2*d.* yet none were thought fit to be Exemplars, till this 6. of *Edw.* the 6*th.* that *William* Marquess of *Winchester* was made the first Exemplar in Parliament of that Dignity, but his Exemplar had the additional Title of Lord Treasurer, who is the second Officer of State. CHAP. IX.

36 *H.* 8. Although a Baron is a more ancient Title with us in *England*, than any of the other Degrees of the Nobles, yet we find no Record now extant, wherein a Baron, singly as Baron, had the Exemplar Writ; for (as I said) *Thomas Wriothesly* Baron of *Tichfield* being Chancellor, *William Pawlet* Baron of *Bazing* being Lord Keeper, were Exemplars in those Parliaments, and had Consimilars appointed them; but *Edward Hyde* Baron of *Hindon* having a distinct Assisting Writ, had no Consimilar allotted him, either in respect of his Barony or Assistancy.

Thus we find that Earls, Dukes, Marquesses and Barons have been Exemplars, but we do not find any Viscounts to be so in any Parliament since the creation of that Dignity, which was (as I said) in *Hen.* 6*ths.* time to *John de Beaumont.*

And the reason is, because the word *Vicecomes* doth imply a Consimilar to *Comes*, so it were improper for *Comites* to be Consimilars to a *Vicecomiti.* Con-

CHAP. IX. Concerning the additionals of the Titles to thoſe Nobles mentioned in their Exemplars, it may be obſerved, That in all thoſe Writs to *Hen.* the 8*ths.* time, the words *Conſanguineo Chariſſimo Prædilecto Dilecto & Fideli*, were not ſo poſitively fixt to the ſeveral Degrees in their Writs, but ſince that time they have paſt in a more conſtant method, *viz.* to Dukes and Marqueſſes, *Præchariſſimo Conſanguineo*; to Earls and Viſcounts, *Chariſſimo Conſanguineo*; to Barons, *Prædilecto & Fideli*; and to the Lord Chancellor as chief Aſſiſtant, *Prædilecto & perquam Fideli*; but to all the other Aſſiſtants, of which I ſhall ſpeak more, only *Dilecto & Fideli.*

SECT. III.

Obſervations on the Conſimilars to the former Exemplars.

WHen Princes of the Blood were made Exemplars, there was ever ſome Prince of the Blood in the Conſimilars, and then followed in the ſame Regiſter in every Clauſe-Roll or *Pawn*, the other Dukes, Marqueſſes, Earls, Viſcounts and Barons, without interpoſition of the Lords Spiritual and Eccleſiaſtical, to the Princes of the Blood, and the Temporal Lords

Lords not of the Bloud; so it continued in that method till the 21. of King *James*, but then the Exemplar (being to the Prince of *Wales*, and no Consimilar to him, there follows the Exemplar and Consimilars to the Lords Spiritual, (of which I have spoken) and after them follows the particular Writ to *John* Bishop of *Lincoln*, as Lord Keeper, and after that, the Exemplar to *Lodowick* Duke of *Richmond*, who had one Duke, one Marquess, Thirty eight Earls, nine Viscounts, and Fourty seven Chevaliers his Consimilars, and ever since the 21. *Jac.* there hath been an interposition either of the Lords Spiritual or Lord Chancellor between the Dukes of the Blood and the Nobles that were not of the Blood; and so in the 13 *Car.* 2. though the Bishops were deprived from that Roll, (as I have shewn) yet the Lord Chancellors Writ did interpose; and it may further be observed, That when Princes or Dukes of the Blood, or not of the Blood, were Exemplars, other Dukes, Marquesses, Earls, Viscounts and Barons were Consimilars; but when Earls were Exemplars, there were no other Consimilars admitted of Degrees above them, but still under them, *viz.* of Earls, Viscounts and Barons; and yet when the three Dukes beforementioned were made Exemplars, 'tis true the

CHAP. IX. the Duke of *Suffolk* and *Oxford* had Dukes to their Consimilars, as formerly; (being *pari gradu*) but the Duke of *Norfolk* had no Duke to his Consimilar, for he had only four Earls, one Viscount, and Thirty one Barons, of which there is no other precedent that I can find.

2. As to the different Titles of these six Degrees, *viz.* Princes of the Blood, Dukes, Marquesses, Earls, Viscounts and Barons, of whom I have spoke more in the Fifth Chapter; it is fit to be hinted here, that Prince in *English*, and *Principi* in the *Latin* Writ, Duke and *Duci*, Marquess and *Marchioni*, Viscount and *Vicecomiti*, have little difference in their Orthography; but *Comiti* in all their *Latin* Writs, and Earl (which is their general appellation in *English*) have very great difference; concerning which and the other Degrees I have writ more at large before, and in my Annotations, to which I refer the Reader; and so Baron and *Baro* have but little variation, yet this may be observed here of this Title *Baro*, that in all the Consimilar Writs in Clause Rolls or *Pawns* wherein those of that Degree are enumerated from the 15*th.* of *Edw.* 2*d.* to the 13. of *Car.* 2. neither the Titles or words *Baro*, nor of *Banerettus* are mentioned in the Writs; but either the Articles *De* or *Le*

Le or *La*, or the words *Dominus*, *Miles*, *Equies Auratus*, or *Chevalier* are added to the Barons name, *viz. Hugo de Spencer*, *Johanni de Bello Campo*, *Johanni de St. John de Bazing*, *Roberto de Monte albo*, *Johanni de Sancto amando*, *Willielmo de la Souch de mortuo mare*, *Nicolao de Cantilupo le Quint*, *Johanni de Insula de rubro monte*, *Nicolao de Sancto Mauro*, *Michaeli de la Pool*, (who was then Banneret) *Admirallo Maris*, *Johanni de Moubray Mariscallo*.

CHAP. IX.

Petro de malo lacu le Quint, *Hugo de le Spencer*, *Willielmo la Zouch de mortuo mare*, *Johanni le Strange*, *Johanni le Shelton*, and many more, and some only in their Christian names and Sirnames, *viz. Richardo Gray*, *Richardo Talbot*, *Gulielmo Aincourt*, *Richardo Percey*, *Johanni Fitzwater*, *Radulpho Dacres*, yet these were all Barons or Bannerets, though the Title of *Baroni* was not in their respective Writs.

3. Thus they continued without any other adjuncts to their names (than what I have mentioned) till the first of *Richard* the Second, and then *Willielmo de Morley*, *Willielmo de Alborough*, *Hugo de Dacres* were writ *Chevaliers*; (amongst 48. others that were Intituled as before) After, in the 7th. of *Rich.* the 2d. *William Botereaux* was brought in, and with the other Three written *Chevaliers*; and in the second Parliament

CHAP. IX. liament of that year, that Title of *Chevalier* increas'd to three more, *viz. Johanni Falſly*, *Henry le Scroop*, and *Thomæ Camois Chevaliers*; ſo there were then ſeven *Chevaliers* in all, the reſt of the Barons being then Fourty five, were Intituled as before, and ſo they continued, not exceeding nine *Chevaliers*, till the third of *H.* 6. and for that Parliament there were but twenty Barons Summoned, whereof eleven were Stil'd *Chevaliers*; and in the fourth of his Reign, all the Barons but two were Stil'd *Chevaliers*; and in the ſixth year, all the Barons were Stil'd *Chevaliers*; and ſo to the Twenty third, wherein all the Barons were written *Chevaliers* except *Thomas de Scales Miles*, (who was then Lord *Scalds*) and *Dominus de Molins*, ſo here came in *Dominus* for a Baron; and in the Twenty fifth, there were Twenty ſix *Chevaliers*, whereof two Stil'd *Milites*, and three *Domini*; in the Twenty ſeventh *Henry Percey* is Writ *Militi & Domino*, and ſome others, which ſhews that the words *Militi*, *Domino*, and *Chevalier*, having Writs to Sit in the Lords Houſe, had one Denotation of a Baron; and in the third of *Edw.* 4. almoſt all the Barons are written *Domini* and *Chevaliers* jointly, yet in the end of theſe Conſimilars, it is writ in the Record, *Milites omnes*, except

Audley

Audley and *Clinton*, and so in the 3*d.* of *Ed.* 4. all are *Chevaliers*, but in the Post-script is, *Equites aurati omnes præter Dominum Scales*, by which must be understood, that all the rest which were Summoned to those Parliaments, and their names not entred in those Rolls, were *Milites* or *Equites Aurati*: Except *Audley*, *Clinton*, and *Scales*, which latter in the Record of the 23*d.* of *Hen.* 6. before mentioned, is written *Miles*, which shews there was a distinction then between *Miles* and *Eques Auratus* (as may be seen in Mr. *Seldens* Titles of Honour) and so in the 7*th.* and 12. 22. and 23*d.* of *Ed.* 4. all *Chevaliers*, but two *Milites*, which do argue some distinction, though all intended to signifie a *Baron*.

Then passing over other Records to the 21. of *Hen.* 8. all the Barons are stil'd *Chevaliers*; but in the 36. *Hen.* 8. the words *Domini*, and *Chevaliers* are mixt, and so they continued to the 28. of *Eliz.* and then all the Barons are writ *Chevaliers*, and so have continued to this time singly, with that Title of *Chevaliers* in all their Writs, without adding *Dominus miles*, or *Eques Auratus*.

Though the Title of *Baro* for *Baron* is not us'd in these Parliament Writs, no more is *Bannerettus* or *Banneret*; yet it is

CHAP. IX. as evident, that as *Dominus* does signifie a *Baron*, so the word *Miles* and *Chevalier* did signifie a *Knight Banneret*, and so I presume it was originally intended. For by comparing the Writ in the 8*th*. of *Rich*. 2*d*. to *William Botereaux*, with the Writ to him in the 15*th*. of *Rich*. 2*d*. where in one he is called *Chevalier*, in the other *Miles*; it may be presumed that the Titles are one and the same, the words *Chevalier* and *Miles* being so interchangeably used, and sometimes joyntly, yet either being applicable to Denote a *Baron* or *Banneret*.

8. This Identity of *Chevalier* and *Banneret*, may be evident from the Writ to the Sheriff of *Surry* (hereafter transcribed) Cited by the Learned Mr. *Selden*, where *Thomas Camois* (beforementioned) sometimes Stil'd *Chevalier*, sometimes *Miles* (for brevity omitting *Bannerettus* (being then Lord *Camois* or *Baron*) and being chosen Knight of the Shire for that County to serve in Parliament in the 8*th*. of *Rich*. 2. the Sheriff was commanded by this Writ, to make an Election of another Knight for that County, because his place was in the *Lords-House* as a *Banneret*; which Writ he sets down in these following words.

The

The Writ to the Sheriff of Surry 8. Rich. *the* 2d. *concerning* Thomas Camois *Banneret, his being Elected Knight of the Shire.*

REx Vic' Surr' Salutem Quia ut accepimus tu Thomam Camois *Chevalier* qui *Bannerettus* est sicut quam plures Antecessorum suorum extiterint ad essendum unum militem venientium ad proximum Parliamentum nostrum pro Comunitate Comitatus predicti de assensu ejusdem Comitatus. Elegisti Nos advertentes quod hujusmodi Banneretti ante hæc tempora in militis Comitatus ratione alicujus Parliamenti eligi minime consueverunt ipsum de Officio Militis ad dictum Parliamentum pro Communitate Comitatus predicti ventur' Exonerari volumus Et Ideo tibi precipimus quod quendam alium militem idoneum & discretum gladio cinctum loco ipsius Thomæ eligi & eum ad diem & Locum Parliamenti predicti venire facias cum plena & sufficien' potestate ad consentiend' hijs quæ in Parliamento predicto fient juxta tenorem primi Brevis nostri tibi pro electione hujusmodi milit' directi & nomen ejus nobis scire facias. Teste Rege apud Westm' octavo die Octobris septimo Regis. 8. *R*. 2.

R 2 *Accord-*

CHAP. IX.

Accordingly the Parliament did sit the 3d. *of* March, *and* Thomas Camois *in the Lords House: but that which Mr.* Selden *observes in this Writ is, that this is not to be understood of any other* Banneret *than a Parliament* Baron, *or a* Banneret *of that time. The expressing of* hujusmodi Bannoretti *shews, that it is not meant of all* Bannerets, *but such only as have the Title, either by inheritance, or in such a kind, that an inheritance might be of it, which is apparent also by the precedent words in the Writ;* Bannerettus est sicut quam plures Antecessorum suorum extiterint, *for it was never conceived, that the Title of* Banneret *as it denotes a* Knight-Banneret *was ever hereditary.*

However, another Knight for *Surry* was Chosen; and this *Thomas Camois* being Lord *Thomas Camois*, did sit that Parliament in the Lords House, as his Ancestors had done; for I find, that in the 15*th.* of *Ed.* 2*d*, and 4*th.* of *Ed.* 3*d. Radulphus Camois* was Summon'd by Writs, and did sit in those two Parliaments; but I find none in 54 years after, *viz.* till the 7*th.* of *Rich.* 2*d.* and then that name continued in 37 successive Parliaments, *viz.* to the 8*th.* of *Hen.* 6. as may be seen in the Records. I shall make no further use of this Writ here, than that

that of the words, *Thomas Camois Chevalier qui est Bannerettus*, doe make it clear, that *Banneret* was denoted by the word *Chevalier*, and that that word *Chevalier* amongst the Lords did shew the difference between *Banneret* and an Ancient or Hereditary *Baron*. Now in respect it is evident that the Title of *Banneret* was first brought into use for some meritorious action, in bearing, preserving, or retaking the Kings *Banner* in time of War; whereupon he received the honour of Knight *Banneret*, and thereupon as an additional honour was also thought worthy to sit amongst the hereditary *Barons*; and in respect many Martial exploits were about that time done in *France* (the word *Chevalier* being borrowed from the *French Tongue*) came into so great repute, that such as did merit it, did justly Challenge it, and those of less merit did Covet it, and by meer interest and favour obtain'd it, and so by degrees (as I have formerly shewn) the word *Chevalier* upon the account of merit or favour, did swallow up the other Titles; and in process of time, and favour of Kings, it grew to be fixt and hereditary, which was intended at first but Titulary and Temporary, which hath been the fate of most of our Titles of Honour.

CHAP. IX.

Chap. X. Thus having diſpatcht the *Brevia Clauſa*, or Cloſe Writs of Summons, to the Lords Spiritual and Temporal before the Parliament is ſitting (for theſe are different from the Writs which are ſent out whilſt a Parliament is ſitting, as will be ſhewn.) I ſhall proceed to the *Brevia aperta* or open Writs, commonly called Patents, by which (ſuch as are Created) are inabled to ſit there; yet even thoſe Lords, which by their Creations are ſo priviledg'd, have alſo Cloſe Writs of Summons ſent them *pro forma*, leſt they ſhould fail of their duties for want of intimation, and the Writ is and hath been anciently Cloſ'd, leaſt (as I conceive) the Writ ſhould contain ſuch private matter, or cauſes of Summons as are not fit to be known by the conveyor of them to their Lordſhips.

Chap. X.

Of Patents of Creation Impowring the Lords Patentees to ſit in Parliament.

Sect. 1. HAving ſhewn the Form of the Cloſe Writs of Summons, for ſuch as are to ſit in the Lords Houſe, either *Ratione ſanguinis regalis*, or *Ratione tenuræ*, or *Ratione Nobilitatis & Honoris*, I am now to to ſhew how ſome of theſe ſit there *Ratione Creationis* (not Excluſive of the others) viz. by vertue of their Open Writs, or Patents of Creation; for though Cloſe Writs of Summoning to a Parliament were thought ſufficient to Nobilitate the perſons and their Heirs, who had the benefit of them; yet ſince Tenures and Preſcriptions, and Writs only, were not found ſo ſafe and convenient, the way of Creation by Patent hath much increaſed. CHAP. X.

2. Theſe Lords Patentees having Writs of Summons, as Memoirs of their Duty to the publick, their Patents do not only intile them to ſit in Parliament, but direct them where they ſhall ſit, which their Writs of Summons do not expreſs; for the Writs do only appoint a place, and time where and when to meet, but not their diſtinct places where to ſit, both in reſpect to their own, and to the other degrees of Nobility.

3. Theſe are called Patents of Creation, ſignifying ſomething which was not before; now it is evident by what I have ſhewn, that there were perſons called *Dukes*, *Marqueſſes*, *Earls*, *Viſcounts*, and *Barons*, both in Foreign parts, and in this Kingdom, long before thoſe Degrees were Erected by Patent; but till then (as Mr. *Selden* ſaith) they were to be eſteemed

CHAP. X. rather Official than Nobilitated Dignities, and therefore it muſt be underſtood that the Form of making them *Earls*, *Dukes*, *&c.* by theſe Letters Patents, were not in uſe here in *England*, till *Dukes*, *Marqueſſes*, *Earls*, *&c.* did accept of this inſtrument or Form; and thereupon call'd *Dukes*, *Earls*, *&c.* by Creation.

4. I find theſe Patents to be of three ſorts. Firſt, of Titles Confirm'd (*viz.* ſuch as were before their Patents) Secondly, of Titles Reviv'd (*viz.* which were before, but were extinct for want of Iſſue, or Eſcheated to the Crown for Treaſon, *&c.* (which often happened in the Barons-wars, and at other times) Thirdly, Titles Created or given where none was before. As to the firſt, *viz.* of ſuch Titles as were before their Patents of Creation, it appears that *Awbry de Vere* (as Mr. *Cambden* ſaith) had the choice of four Earldoms, *viz.* *Dorſet*, *Wilts*, *Berks*, and *Oxfordſhire*, of which four Shires (there having been Official Earls both in the *Saxons*, and afterwards in the *Normans* time) he choſe *Oxfordſhire*, which being granted to him by *Henry* the 1*ſt.* it was confirm'd to him by Patent of Creation by *Hen.* the 2*d.* according to this following Patent.

The

The Patent to Awbry de Vere, *Confirming him Earl of* Oxford.

HEnricus Secundus Rex Angliæ & Dux Normaniæ & Aquitaniæ & Comes Andigaviæ Archiepiscopis Episcopis Abbatibus Comitibus Baronibus Justiciarijs Vicecomitibus Ministris & omnibus Fidelibus suis totius Angliæ Franciæ & Angliæ Salutem. Sciatis me dedisse & concessisse Comiti Comitatus Oxenford-scire ut sit inde Comes quare volo & Firmiter præcipio quop ipse & hæredes sui habeant inde Comitatum suum ita libere & quiete & honorifice sicut aliquis Comitum Angliæ liberius & quietius & honorificentius habet Test. Attested by the Chancellor, three Earls, and ten others of Quality. 5. *H.* 2.

Mr. *Selden* observes, that this Patent was rather a Confirmation than a Creation; and further saith, that in a *Chancery-stile*, a Creation and Confirmation signifie the same; however though the words in the Patent are not *Confirmasse*, but only *Dedisse*, and *Concessisse*, yet I conceive it plainly appears to be a Confirmation from the words in the Patent, *viz. habeant inde Comitatum suum*, which implies that that County *Selden* 1. *H. p.* 539.

CHAP. X. County was his before this Confirmatory Creation.

The second sort of Creation Patents, are the reviving of a Title which had been before, but lay Dorment as in this following Patent, of Creating *Edward* call'd *Edward* the Black-Prince, Son to *Edward* the *3d.* to be Duke of *Cornwal*, there being Official Dukes of *Cornwal* before.

The Preamble to the Creation of Edward, *Son to* Edward *the* 3d. *Duke of* Cornwal.

Sect. 6. 11. *Ed.* 3. EDwardus Dei gratia, *&c.* inter cætera Regni insignia illud arbitramur fore potissimum ut ipsum ordinum dignitatum & Officiorum distributione, congrue vallatum sanis fulciatur consilijs & robustorum potentijs teneatur, plurimis itaq; gradibus hæreditarijs in regno nostro cum per descensum hæredetatum secundum legem regni ejusdem ad cohæredes & participes tunc deficiente exitu, & alijs eventibus varijs ad manus regias devolutis passum est a diu in nominibus honoribus & graduum dignitate defectum multiplicem dictum regnum Nos igitur ea per quæ regnum nostrum decorari idemq; regnum ac Sancta ejusdem Ecclesiæ aliæ etiam terræ nostro subjectæ Dominio contra hostium & adversa-

versariorum conatus securius & decentius CHAP. X.
defensari paxq; nostra inter nostros ubiq; subditos conservari illæsa poterint meditatione solicita intuentes ac loca ejusdem Regni insignia pristinis insigniri honoribus. Cupientes nostræ considerationes intuitus ad personam Dilecti & Fidelis nostri Edwardi Comitis Cestriæ filij nostri primogeniti intimius convertentes volentesq; personam ejusdem honorare eidem filio nostro nomen & honorem Ducis Cornubiæ de Communi assensu & Consilio Prælatorum Comitum Baronum & aliorum de Consilio nostro in presenti Parliamento nostro apud Westmonasterium die Lunæ proxime post festum Sancti Matthæi Apostoli proxime preterit' convocato existentium dedimus ipsumq; in Ducem Cornubiæ prefecimus & Gladio cinximus sicut decet &c. Dedimus itaq; &c. Castra &c. juxta generis sui nobilitatem valeat contenere & onera in hac parte incumbentia facilius supportare, *viz.* ut faciat Vicecomites predicti Comitatus.

7. It is affirm'd by our History, that there were Dukes of *Cornwal* (as I have shewn in the *Brittish* times) but afterwards intituled Earls, but both the Titles of Dukes, and Earls of that County being long extinct, *William* the 1*st*. rais'd it to an Earl-

CHAP. X. Earldom, and after *Edward* the 3*d.* Erected it to a Dukedom, and thereupon had a preamble, and this was done alſo by aſſent and conſent of the Prelates, Earls, Barons, and others of his Council (which I preſume doth include the Commons). but it may be obſerved, that here was no other Inveſtiture mention'd than *Gladio cinximus*, which is the ſame Ceremony of a Knight Batchelor; but many great Royalties and priviledges were herein granted, as may be ſeen in the Patent at large.

That to the Earl of *Oxford* needed no preamble, or Conſent of the Earls and Commons, or mention of the Form of Inveſtitures, or of particulars of Lands and Caſtles granted, being only a Confirmation of that honour which he injoyed; but it was convenient, that this to the Duke of *Cornwal* ſhould have a preamble, in reſpect the Title had lain dead for a long time in the Crown, as may be Collected from the words, *ad manus Regias devolutis.*

The like Patent of Reviver, was of the Barony of *Abergaveny* by *Richard* the 2*d.* to *John de Beauchamp* ſecond Son to the Earl of *Warwick*, from whom by Marriage of the Daughter and Heir, it came into the Family of the *Nevils*, where it yet continues; but this was a Barony long before,

before, for in the time of King *William* the 2*d.* call'd *Rufus*, *Hamelius de Balon* was Baron of *Abergaveny*, and from him it descended to *Brian de Insula*, then to the *Bruce's*, *Cante Lupes*, and *Hastings*, in which last name it continued many descents, till *John Hastings* then Earl of *Pembroke*, and Baron of *Abergaveny* died without Issue; and then as I said, *Richard* the 2*d.* Conferr'd it *John Beauchamp* according to this following Patent. CHAP. X.

6. *Richardus Secundus*, &c. *Sciatis quod pro bonis & gratuitis servitijs quæ Dilectus & Fidelis Miles noster Johannes de Beauchamp de Holt Senescallus Hospitij nostri nobis impendit ac loco per ipsum tempore creationis nostræ huc usq; impenso & quem pro Nobis tenere poterit infuturum in nostris Consiliis & Parliamentis nec non pro nobili & Fideli genere unde descendit ac pro suis magnificis sensu & Circumspectione ipsum Johannem in unum Parium ac Baronum Regni Angliæ nostri præfecimus volentes quod idem Johannes & hæredes masculi de corpore suo Exeuntes statum Baronis obtineant ac Domini de Beauchamp & Barones de Kiderminster nuncupentur in cujus rei*, &c. *Teste*, &c. 11. R. 2.

10. Thus having given instances of Confirming,

CHAP. X. firming, and Reviving of Titles by Patents of Creation, I shall speak of the third sort of Creating, or Erecting of new Titles by Patent of Creation also.

The third sort of Creation Patents, is more properly call'd a Creation than the other; and for this, I instance the Patent to the Prince of *Wales*. 11. *Ed*. the *3d*. for though *Wales* had been an ancient Principality in it self, and their Natives were Princes thereof; and this being the first time that that Title was transferr'd to an *English* man, and a Patent granted by an *English* King which had never been done before; it might properly be call'd a Creation, the Preamble of the Patent is Transcrib'd *Verbatim*; but the *Habendum* (being very long) I have only given a short abstract of it.

The Preamble to the Creation of Edward *Prince of* Wales.

Sect. 11. 17. *Ed.* 3. REx &c. Archiepiscopis &c. salutem de serenitate regalis praeeminentiæ velut ex Sole radii sic inferiores prodeunt principatus ut regiæ claritatis integritas de Luce Lucem proferens Ex Lucis distributione minoratæ Lucis non sentiat detrimenta Immo tanto magis Regale Sceptrum extollitur & Solium Regium sublimatur

quanto

quanto tribunali suo plures subsunt Proceres eminentiæ clarioris Hæc autem consideratio condigna Nos qui nominis & honoris Edwardi ducis Cornubiæ & Comitis Cestriæ primogeniti nostri charissimi incrementum appetimus (in quo potius Nos ipsos conspicimus honorari & domum nostram Regiam & subditum nobis populum nostrum speramus per Dei gratiam sumpta de gloriosis suis auspiciis conjectura honorifice roborari) allicit & inducit ut ipsum qui reputatione juris censetur eadem persona nobiscum digno proveniamus honore & fæcunda gratia persequamur de Consilio itaq; & Consensu Prælatorum Comitum Baronum & Communitatum Regni nostri Angliæ in Generali Parliamento nostro apud Westmonasterium die Lunæ in Quindena Pasche proxime præterita Convocato ipsum Edwardum Principem Walliæ fecimus & creavimus & dictum principatum sibi dedimus & concessimus & per Chartam nostram confirmavimus ac ipsum de dicto principatu ut ibidem præficiendo præsideat & præsidendo dictas partes derigat & defendat per fertum in Capite & annulum in digito aureum ac virgam argenteam investivimus juxta morem, habend' & tenend' de nobis sibi & hæredibus suis Regibus Angliæ in perpetuum cum omnibus Dominijs & terris

CHAP. X.

CHAP. X. ris noſtris Northwalliæ Weſtwalliæ & Southwalliæ, &c.

The like was in *Richard* the 2*ds.* time, when the Earldom or County of *Lancaſhire* was Erected into a Dutchy Palatine, which was not ſo before, the Preamble of which Patent, I ſhall here inſert; aſwell to ſhew the Latin Style of the Age, as for other reaſons, which I ſhall hereafter have occaſion to mention.

The Patent of Creation to John *Duke of* Lancaſter. *Anno* 1389.

Sect. 12. 13. *R.* 2. INter Glorioſæ Reipublicæ curas & ſollicitudines varias. Regiis humeris incumbentes firmat potiſſime Regale ſolium effluens á juſtitia condigna premiatio merritorum ibinamque continue virtus creſcit & colitur ubi a debito ſibi præmio non fruſtratur. Cum igitur honor ſit virtutis præmium conſtat quod virtuoſis & ſtrenuis ex Regali juſtitia debentur faſces honorum & præmia dignitatum quæ utiq; ſi dignis conferantur non debent ſimpliciter æſtimari donum ſeu exhibitio favorum, ſed potius debita compenſatio meritorum Quid enim in retroactis ſæculis & felicium Principum temporibus Rempublicam amplius provexiſſe comperimusquam quod

quod pie regnantes virtuosos & strenuos sub se habebant oneris ijs injuncti participes, quos postmodum juxta Exigentiam meritorum honore & distributionibus dignitatum successive fecerunt ex debito Regalis Justitiæ gloriosos. Quia quod soli non poterant, provida virtuosorum hujusmodi provisione supplebant. CHAP. X.

Hijs igitur considerationibus inducti ad te præcharissimum patruum nostrum mentis nostræ aciem dirigentes actusq; tuos virtuosos & præclaria merita quibus te virtutum Dominus insignivit in profundæ discussionis liberamine ponderantes, de assensu Prelatorum Ducum Magnatum & aliorum Procerum & Communitatis Regni nostri Angliæ in instanti Parliamento nostro apud Westmonasterium convocato existentium Te predilectissimum patruum nostrum in Ducem Aquitaniæ cum titulo stilo & nomine & honore eidem debitis præfecimus ac inde præsentialiter per appositionem Capæ tuo Capiti ac traditionem virgæ aureæ investimus in præmium eximiæ virtutis tuæ & attinentiæ predictarum toto vitæ tuæ possidendum, &c. Et, &c. Donamus tibi Ducatum, &c. tenendum de nobis ut de Rege Franciæ, &c. ad totum vitæ tuæ.

S Here

CHAP. X. Here was a great Merit expreſs'd, and magnificently rewarded, yet not to his Heirs, but to himſelf only for life, which he took as a ſufficient Recompence for his Services; and this was *Aſſenſu & conſenſu Prælatorum Ducum Magnat'. Et aliorum Procerum & Communitatis Regni noſtri Angliæ.* And I obſerve, That when the Patents were only for Confirmation, the Aſſent and Conſent of the Parliament was not inſerted, but where they were to Revive, or meerly to Create, then the Aſſent and Conſent was expreſs'd.

The like Patent of meer Creation was that of the Ninth of *Richard* the Second, when *Robert de Vere*, then *Earl of Oxford*, was Created *Marqueſs of Dublin*; (which, ſaith Mr. *Selden*, was in him an *Engliſh* Title:) however, it was the firſt that any was Created of that Title here in *England*.

And alſo the like Patent of meer Creation was that of 18 *H.* 6. whereby *John de Beaumount* was created *Viſcount de Beaumount*, the Title of *Viſcount* being before an Official Dignity, but never till this Creation nobilitated. All which may be more fully ſeen in the *Rolls Chappel*, or *Patent Office*.

13. As I have ſhewn three ſorts of Patents of Creation, ſo, for the clearing of ſome

ſome ſubſequent matters, I muſt ſhew, That theſe Patents uſually conſiſted of four parts, (yet ſubject to variations) Firſt, *The King's Stile and Preamble.* Secondly, *Of Inveſtitures.* Thirdly, *Of Places in Parliament.* Fourthly, *Grants of Lands, Annuities,* &c. CHAP. X.

As to the Preambles upon New Creations or Revivals, they were uſually long, expreſſing the Merits of the Perſon, but commonly they were couch'd in few words; and thoſe, *viz.* in generals, *Pro bono & laudabili ſervitio quod dilectus & fidelis noſter* A. B. *nobis nuper impendit*, &c. particularly *Pro rebelles noſtros debellando*, (according to the particular Services) and in others, *Pro gratia noſtra ſpeciali & certa ſcientia & mero motu.*

As for the Second I ſhall have occaſion to ſpeak of them in the Chapter of *Inveſtitures.*

For the Fourth, concerning *Grants, Annuities,* &c. I ſhall have little uſe of them.

But for the Third, concerning *The diſtinct Places of the Degrees of Nobles*, I can find nothing in ancient Patents; but generals, *viz.* That his place ſhould be in *loco quem teneri poterit in futurum in noſtris Conſilijs & Parliamentis*; and ſo they were generally ſet down (except in ſuch as I

 ſhall

CHAP. IX. ſhall mention) till *Edward* the Sixth's time (which was ſoon after that the Act of 31 *H.* 8. concerning *Precedencies* was made) and then the whole frame of the Patents for all the Degrees, from the *Habend'* or *Sciatis*, were ſetled in this following Method, and have ever ſince ſo continued with very little alterations. I begin firſt with *Dukes*.

The Sciatis *to a Duke's Patent of Creation, and his Place in Parliament.*

14. SCiatis pro conſideratione prædicta de ulteriori gratia noſtra ſpeciali ac ex certa ſcientia & mero motu noſtris Præfatum A. in Ducem C. nec non ad ſtatum, gradum, ſtilum, titulum, dignitatem, nomen & honorem Ducis C. ereximus, præfecimus, inſignivimus, conſtituimus & creavimus ipſumq; A. in Ducem C. nec non ad ſtatum, gradum, ſtilum, titulum, dignitatem, nomen & honorem Ducis C. tenore præſentium erigimus præficimus inſignimus conſtituimus & creavimus per præſentes eidemq; A. nomen, ſtilum, titulum, ſtatum, gradum, dignitatem & honorem Ducis C. impoſuimus dedimus & præbuimus ac per præſentes imponumus damus & præbemus ac ipſum A. hujuſmodi nomine ſtilo, titulo, ſtatu, gradu, dignitate & hono-

honore Ducis (per Gladij Cinctùrum, Capæ & Circuli aurei impositionem in Capite & traditionem aureæ virgæ) insignimus investimus & realiter nobilitamus per præsentes. Habend' & tenend' nomen stilum, titulum, statum, gradum, dignitatem & honorem Ducis C. prædict' cum omnibus singulis præeminentijs, honoribus, cæterisq; hujumodi nomini, stilo, titulo, statui, gradui, dignitati & honori Ducis pertinentibus sive spectantibus prefat' A. & heredibus masculis de Corpore suo exeuntibus in perpetuum Volentes & per presentes concedentes pro nobis heredibus & successoribus nostris quod predictus A. & heredes sui Masculi predicti nomen, stilum, titulum, statum, gradum, dignitatem & honorem predict' successive gerant & habeant & eorum quilibet gerat & habeat & per nomen Ducis C. successive vocitenter & nuncupenter & eorum quilibet vocitetur & nuncupetur, & quod idem A. & heredes Masculi sui predicti, successive ut Duces C. teneantur tractentur & reputentur, et eorum quilibet teneatur tractetur et reputetur habeantq; teneant et possideant, *&c.* (*Then as to Parliaments,*) Et quod dictus A. et heredes sui Masculi predicti et eorum quilibet habeat teneat et possideat Sedem locum et vocem in Parliamentis Comitijs et Consilijs nostris heredum

CHAP. X.

B.

CHAP. X. redum et successor' nostror' infra regnum nostrum Angliæ ut Dux C. Nec non dictus A. et heredes sui Masculi predicti gaudeant & utantur et eorum quilibet gaudeat et utatur per nomen Ducis C. omnibus et singulis juribus privilegijs præeminentijs et immunitatibus statui Ducis in omibus rite et de jure pertinentibus quibus Duces hujus Regni Angl' antea hæc tempor' melius, honorificentius et quietius usu sunt et gavisi seu in presenti gaudeant et utuntur.

There is an addition of most of the latter Patents concerning *Annuities* granted, which I shall speak of so soon as I have recited so much as concern the Places appointed to the several Degrees of Nobles to sit in Parliament suitable to what is inserted in the Dukes Patent at the Figure *B*.

Of the Marquess his Place in Parliament by his Patent.

15. After the King's Title and Preamble, in the *Sciatis*, these words are in the Marquess his Patent; *viz. Prefat'* R. *in Marchionem* D. *creavimus*, &c. *per Gladij cincturam & circuli aurei quo Capiti impositionem investivimus*, &c. *Habendum*,

bendum, &c. *honorem Marchionis* D. *&c.* *prefat'* R. *&* *heredibus masculis de corpore suo exeuntibus*, &c. (Then as to Parliaments,) *Et quod dictus* R. *&* *heredes sui masculi predicti & eorum quilibet habeat teneat & possideat sedem locum & vocem in Parliamentis Comitijs & Consilijs nostris heredum & successorum nostrorum infra Regnum nostrum Angliæ, inter Pares Parliament' in gradu celsiori videl't inter Duces & Comites ut Marchio.*

Of the Earls Place in Parliament by his Patent.

16. After the Kings Title and the Preamble in the *Sciatis*, these words are also in the Earls Patents, *viz. Prefat'* N. *in Comitem* A. *&c. creavimus per gladij cincturam & Capæ honoris & Circuli aurei impositionem investimus Habendum*, &c. *honorem Comitis* A. *&c. prefat'* N. *& heredibus masculis de Corpore suo exeuntibus*,&c. (Then as to Parliaments,) *Et quod dictus* N. *& heredes sui Masculi predicti & eorum quilibet habeat teneat & possideat sedem locum & vocem in Parliamentis & Consilijs nostris heredum & successorum nostrorum infra regnum nostrum Angl' inter alios Comites ut Comes* A.

CHAP. X.

Note, It is not here ſaid *inter Marchiones & Vicecomites*, becauſe they were Degrees erected after the Earls.

Of the Viſcounts Place in Parliament by his Patent.

17. After the Kings Title and the Preamble, and the *Sciatis*, theſe words are alſo in the Viſcounts Patents, *viz. Prefat'.* A. *in Vicecomitem* N. *&c. creavimus ac ipſum inſignijs Vicecomitis inveſtimus*, &c. *Habendum*, &c. *honorem Vicecomitis* N. &c. *Et quod idem* A. *& heredes ſui Maſculi gerant titulum Vicecomitis* N. *&c. Et heredes ſui Maſculi predicti.* (Then as to Parliaments,) *Et eorum quilibet habeat teneat & poſſideat ſucceſſive ſedem locum & vocem in Parliamentis & publicis Comitijs* (in the firſt Patent to *Beaumont* it is *Congregationibus noſtris*) *heredum & ſucceſſorum noſtrorum infra Regnum noſtrum Angliæ inter alios Vicecomites & ante omnes Barones ut Vicecomes.*

Of

Of the Barons Place in Parliament by his Patent.

18. AFter the Kings Title and the Preamble in the *Sciatis*, these words are in the Barons Patent, *Prefat'* A. B. *&c. ad honorem Baronis* B. *&c. creavimus ipsumq;* A. B. *Baronem* B. *Creavimus*,&c. (no mention of Investitures) *Habendum*, &c. *honorem* A. B. *heredibus suis Masculis*, &c. *per nomen Baronis* B. *de* C. *& heredes sui Masculi predicti.* (Then as to Parliaments) *Et eorum quilibet habeat teneat & possideat sedem locum & vocem in Parliamentis publicis Comitijs & Concilijs nostris heredum & successorum nostrorum infra Regnum nostrum Angliæ inter alios Barones ut Barones Parliamentorum publicorum Comitiorum & Consiliorum.*

Note, That the word *Chevalier* is in his Writ, but not in his Patent, nor the word *Dominus*, which was us'd in ancient Patents, is alsso disus'd in the latter Patents.

Of

CHAP. X.

Of the Conciseness of ancient Patents.

19. HEre I must observe how wanton the Penmen of these Patents have been in latter days, by multiplying words in them, which former ages thought superfluous, and even the Sages of the Law, who are the most knowing in what is sufficient, have anciently and do still reject them (as may be seen in the Thirteenth Chapter) and yet the Jurisdiction and Priviledges which are granted to those Sages are little inferiour to what is granted in these, whereas those Patents do not contain (besides the names from the *Sciatis* to the *Teste*) above twelve words, and these by the redundancy of Sentences, at least one Thousand two Hundred words.

Of Creation-Money.

20. IN the recital of the *Sciatis* (in *Sect.* 8.) I did omit the extravagant flourishes, which are us'd in many of these Patents about *Creation-Money* and *Annuities* given to the Patentees.

Con-

Concerning an Annuity of twenty Marks *granted in the* Patent of Creation.

21. IMmediately after the words *gaudent* and *utuntur* (in the *Sciatis* at large, a little before mention'd) theſe words follow: *viz.*

Et quoniam aucta ſtatus & dignitatis celſitudine neceſſario creſcunt ſumptus & accedunt onera grandiora: ut predictus A. *& heredes maſculi ſui predicti melius decentius & honorificentius ſtatum honorem & dignitatem predictam Vicecomiti* N. *ac Onera ipſi* A. *& heredibus ſuis maſculis predictis incumbentia manutenere & ſupportare valeat, Ideo de uberiori gratia noſtra dedimus & conceſſimus eidem* A. *& heredibus maſculis de Corpore exeuntibus feodum ſive annualem redditum treſdecim librarum ſex ſolidorum & octo denariorum legalis monet' Angliæ. Habendum & percipiendum annuatim dictum feodum ſive annualem redditum treſdecim librarum ſex ſolidorum & octo denariorum eidem* A. *& heredibus ſuis maſculis de Corpore Exeuntibus de exitibus proſituis, et reventionibus magnæ & parvæ cuſtumæ et ſubſidijs noſtris nobis conceſſis ſive debitis ſeu impoſterum nobis heredibus ſeu ſucceſſoribus noſtris concedendis ſive debendis*

CHAP. X. *bendis provenientibus crescentibus sive emergentibus infra portum Civitatis nostræ Londini per manus Custumariorum sive Collectorum nostrorum heredum et successorum nostrorum custumarumet subsidiorum nostrorum heredum et successorum nostrorum ibidem pro tempore existentium ad festum Pasche et Sancti Michaelis Archangeli per equales portiones volumus*,&c. *absq; fine hanaperio*, &c. *et quod Expressa mentio*, &c. and so concludes, *in cujus*, &c. *Teste*, &c. (too tedious to recite) making above one Hundred words more : and almost the like is to an *Earl* for 20 *l*. *per annum*, so as the Money given will scarce pay for the words written, or but little left to support such a Dignity, unless the meer expression of the uberious munificence of the Donor be sufficient.

Sure it was less chargeable, and as effectual when the words of the whole Patent of Creating the Earl of *Essex*, *tempore H.* 2. and others in other Kings Reigns was only thus : *viz.*

Do & concedo G. *de* M. *pro servitio suo, & heredibus suis post eum hereditabiliter ut sit Comes de Essexia, & habeat tertium denariorum Vicecomitatus de placitis, sicut Comes habere debet in Comitatu suo.* So here was both the Honor, the Service, and the Reward mention'd in less then thirty words.

There

There is nothing alledged for the length of these Patents, but that the latter Ages (as 'tis said) are more cautious than the former, and that *abundans cautela* (say we) *non nocet*, which occasions an abundance of words more than anciently were in use.

As to the smalness of the *Creation-Money*, those who have taken pains in Writing about raising of the price of Money, both *Gold* and *Silver*, since *Edward* the Third's time, tell us, That there are three ways of raising it; First, By *encreasing the Value* of it, that is by giving more parts to it than originally it had, as by ordaining an Angel of *Gold* to be valued at a 11 *s.* which was Coin'd for 10 *s.* or a Shilling, to be valued at 14 *d.* The Second, By *diminishing the Matter*, but leaving the same Name and Value to the Money which it had before, as when Angels or Shillings are Coin'd by the same Name and Value as before, but diminished some Grains in the weight; or if new Names be given to them, and the same Value retain'd, but the weight diminished, for in this case there being really less Gold or Silver in weight in the price than was before, and the value remaining the same, this Silver and Gold which remains hath an high price set upon it. The Third is, When the Value

CHAP. X. lue remaining the ſame, of the Species of Money, and the Weight the ſame, the fineneſs is abated by putting more Allay to it, ſo as really then there is leſs Gold or Silver in fineneſs (for it is ſupply'd by Copper (which is uſually the Allay to either) whereby the Weight is made the ſame as before, but the Fineneſs ſo much leſs. They further tell us, That the Cauſes of theſe Allays, are firſt the Gain which the *States* make by it, the better to ſupply themſelves in their neceſſities for Money; the other Cauſe is an Art which all States do frequently uſe (as it were) to rob one another of their Money, *by vying* one upon another, who ſhall raiſe their Money higheſt; and this occaſions the raiſe and fall of Exchanges of Money among our Merchants, which is a Myſtery worth the knowing, by every one that ſerves in Parliament, thereby to prevent Injuries, and to maintain the Honour and Profit of our Kingdom.

But whatever uncertainties are in the raiſe or fall of Money, this is certain, That 20 *l. per Annum*, in thoſe days, did go as far (if not farther) in managing Mens occaſions (where Money was to be us'd) as 200 *l. per Annum* now; and one great Reaſon was, Becauſe in almoſt all matters of Wars or Peace, the Tenants

were

were obliged by their Tenures, to supply their Lords, especially in Provisions for Hospitality and Labour, without Wages, or very little, so as a little Money was lookt on as a great Reward, as may be seen in the Tenure of the Lord of the Mannor of *Carlton* in *Norfolk*, who is oblig'd every year, with himself and his Servants, to present to the King a certain number of Herrings from the City of *Norwich*, (with which the Town of *Yarmouth* are oblig'd by their Patent to supply that City for that purpose) and after three days stay, upon delivery of the Herrings to the King, the Lord of *Carlton* is to be presented by the Master of the Green-Cloth with a Groat, to buy him a pair of Gloves, as a full Recompence of his Trouble, and this continues to this day.

So as if we look upon the gift of 20 *Mark*, or 20 *l.* according to the present Adequation of Money, to the rates of other things, it may seem a Sum derogatory to the Honour of the King that gives it, as to him that receives it, and therefore it must be considered as the Groat, a Gift of Antiquity, Noble and Liberal in its first Intention; but had the large *Encomium* to it (before recited) been as ancient as the Gift, I should not at this time have taken notice of its exuberancy. However (in pur-

CHAP. X. purſuance of my Deſign) theſe Patents of *Creations* do intitle them where to ſit in the Lords Houſe, &c.

Thus having done with the Patents which concern the Lords Spiritual and Temporal, I intended to have writ ſomething here concerning the Antiquity and preſent Uſe of Seals and Labels to Patents and Writs, and of various Superſcriptions to the Lords and Commons, &c. as alſo of Wax, Parchment, &c. (as neceſſary Utenſils for carrying on the Conſtitution of a Parliament) but I ſhall reſerve the Diſcourſe of them till I have paſt through the Parliament-Writs, as well concerning the Houſe of Lords as Houſe of Commons, and Convocation-Houſes, and ſo now proceed to the General Titles given to the Grandees of the Houſe of Lords, *viz.* *Nobles*, *Lords*, and *Peers*.

CHAP. XI.

Of Nobles, Lords, and Peers.

I Have past through the four first Exemplar Writs in the *Pawn*, concerning the Lords Spiritual and Lords Temporal, and given an account alſo of ſo much of their Patents of Creations as relate to Parliaments. But in reſpect theſe Nobles are ſometimes call'd Lords, and ſometimes Peers, and thereupon the very place where they ſit in their High Judicatory is call'd the *Houſe of Lords* or *Houſe of Peers.* I think fit to hint ſome few Memorials before I proceed to the Fifth Exemplar of *Aſſiſtant Writs.*

1. It is agreed by all Inſpectors of Words, that Lords and Peers are of the ſame ſignification with us, that *Domini* and *Pares* had with the old *Romans*, ſo as we and the *French* are equally beholding to the *Latin* for them: but when the word *Dominus* was chang'd into the word Lord, (having no more affinity of ſound or Orthography than *Comes* and Earl) or when *Pares* into *Proceres* (of a nearer ſound) may be a queſtion, but it may be ſufficiently evident, that the word Lord was the Abbreviation

T of

CHAP. XI. of *Louerd*, which the *Saxons* at their firſt coming, about the year 448. uſed here inſtead of *Dominus*.

2. As for the word *Peer*, we commonly uſe it as ſignifying a Defence, as *Dover*-Peer and *Yarmouth*-Peer, &c. which is from *Petra*, a *Rock*, which the *French* write *Pierre*, and we *Peer*, theſe Artificial Peers being made in imitation of Rocks, to defend the Land againſt Inundations, and it may very aptly allude to the Noble Peers in Parliament, who are the Rocks or Peers of our Safety.

3. To paſs this, it is allow'd, That *Pares* in *Latin*, *Paires* in *French*, and *Peers* in our *Engliſh* Dialect, are all three words of the ſame ſence, ſignifying *Parity* or *Equality*, and as the *French* had it from the *Romans*, by whom they were call'd *Pares Curiæ*, viz. *Qui ab eodem domino feudum retinent*, ſo we had it from the *French*, who in the year 778. when *Charles* the Great (being then King of *France*, and ſoon after Emperour of the *Weſt*) did put all the Government of *France* into the hands of Twelve of the moſt eminent Nobles, who thereupon were call'd by the Title of the *Twelve Peers of France*, being *Pares Gubernatores Franciæ*, or in their Language *Paires d' France*, whereof ſix were Lords Spiritual, *viz.* the Archbiſhop of

of *Reims*, the Biſhops of *Laon* and *Langres*, (who alſo were ſtil'd Dukes) the Biſhops of *Beauvois*, *Chalois* and *Nòyon*, which three latter were alſo ſtil'd *Comtes* or Earls, and ſix were Lords Temporal, *viz.* the Dukes of *Burgundy*, *Normandy*, and *Guienne*, the Earls of *Flanders*, *Champaigne*, and *Tholoſe*; the ſix Eccleſiaſticks do continue to this day, but the Territories of the other ſix being either united to, or alienated from the Crown, do now conſiſt of ſuch Princes of the Blood or Favorits (without limitation by number of ſix) as the King thinks fit; but thoſe who are, do injoy the Privileges of the Original Peers conſtituted by *Charles* the Great. CHAP. XI.

4. From this Conſtitution it is conceived, we in *England*, (upon the *Normans* coming) did make uſe of ſomething of that method, and did then alſo firſt make uſe of the word Peers, although in truth, as I ſaid, both of us had it from the *Romans*; we alſo made uſe of their number Twelve, as may be obſerved in the Eccleſiaſtical Parliamentary Degrees, *viz.* firſt Archbiſhops, ſecondly Biſhops, thirdly Archdeacons, fourthly Deans of Chapters, fifthly Proctors of Chapters, and ſixthly Proctors of the Clergy; and ſix alſo are of the Temporal Degrees, *viz.*

 firſt

CHAP. XI. firſt Princes of the Blood, ſecondly Dukes not of the Blood, thirdly Marqueſſes, fourthly Earls, fifthly Viſcounts, and ſixthly Barons. Theſe being ſo proportion'd into twelve Degrees, but not into twelve Perſons, I ſhall paſs to what others have ſpoken concerning the number of our Peers.

5. In reſpect the Peers of *France* were anciently confin'd to a certain number of ſix and ſix, ſome of our *Engliſh* Writers would alſo confine ours to a certain number, ſome to five and ſome to fifty. But herein we may truſt that learned *Selden*, who ſaith, That *the number of Peers with us, was never confined to any more certainty than the Lords of the Parliament are; for* (ſaith he) *whereas only the number of five Peers are mentioned in ſome Records, that can be no Rule of certainty; becauſe at this day the number Five doth legally expreſs Seven;* (*as it doth in the Parliament Writ to the Warden of the Cingqueports or five Ports; There being in truth* (ſaith he) *Seven of them, and ſo conſequently returned*; whereas there are eight Ports called *Cinqueports*, and ſo returned; (as will be ſhewn in the ſecond Part) but however the miſtake be in that *Grave Author*, yet with ſubmiſſion to his great Learning, I conceive this might have been better reconcil'd:

concil'd: for the old Writers who mention-ed five, might intend the five Degrees of Nobility under the Princes of the Blood, *viz.* Dukes, Marquesses, Earls, Viscounts and Barons, which makes the compleat Temporal Degrees in Parliaments.

CHAP. XI.

And what others write of Fifty, that number without doubt did relate to the number of which those five Degrees did in those days consist; which were now increast to Eighty eight, (as may be seen in this *Pawn*) besides those of the Blood Royal, and the Lords Spiritual, and Assistants, and have varied in number almost in every Kings Reign. But I rather believe, that there was some mistake in making use of this number Five, by applying it *Personally* and not *Virtually*; for anciently, and even to this day, the number five, that is five Lords, do with that number Constitute the House of Lords for the dispatch of lesser Affairs, till a greater number come, fit for greater Affairs; and so the number of fourty Members, whether Knights, Citizens, or Burgesses, or some of either, do Constitute an House of Commons, yet these also do not proceed to weightier matters, till they be supplied with a greater number; so as the number five may be well thought to have its relation to the House of Lords, and the num-

CHAP. ber of fifty to the House of Commons.
XI.

6. But not to insist further about the definite number of Lords or Peers, or about the derivation of the words Lords and Peers; I shall give a touch of the words *Prælati*, *Magnates* and *Proceres* us'd in the *Latin* Writs and Patents; and herein, if we consider the first Institution of this House, it did and still doth consist of Lords Spiritual and Lords Temporal, (diversified into several Degrees) as Archbishops, Dukes, &c. yet the Lords Spiritual were known only by the Title *Archiepiscopi & Episcopi*, *i. e.* Archbishops and Bishops; and the Temporal only by the Titles of *Comites* and *Barones*, *i. e.* Earls and Barons; in general terms the Lords Spiritual were called *Prælati*, *i. e.* Prelates; (in relation to matters which concern the Soul, which hath preference or prelation to that of the Body) and the Lords Temporal were called in general *Magnates & Proceres*, *i. e.* Lords and Peers, (intimating Persons of the greatest Power and Domination) and being the chiefest Peers and Supports (as I said) of the King and Kingdom.

7. But in *Henry* the thirds time, certain Persons called Abbots and Priors, (who were the Fathers, Heads and chief Governers of Monasteries, or of such Houses as were

were possess'd by Monks and Canons living in those Houses, with an intent or pretence of weaning themselves from the World, and disposing their minds to a contemplative life) and these being of a mixt nature, partly Regular and partly Secular, and (in respect of their great access of Territories given by the charity of others to support them) Baronial did step in between the Lords Spiritual and the Lords Temporal, and so were called *Prælati* with the Bishops, and *Magnates & Proceres* with the Lords Temporal. But *Hen.* the Eighth (as I have shewn) did dissolve them, so that the Bishops have now the single Title of *Prælati*; and the Temporal Lords, of *Magnates & Proceres*, for we see in the Summoning of this Parliament, (when Bishops were excluded, the words *Cum Prælatis* was left out, but being restored, then they were equally Summon'd to sit, *inter Prælatos, Magnates & Proceres*, and the preposition *Inter*, is properly inserted; for however their sitting is, yet the Bishops are called over, between Viscounts and Barons.

CHAP. XI.

8. Now as Abbots and Priors were thus interposed in *Henry* the Thirds time; so in the time of *Edw.* the Third (as I have shewn) Dukes began, and as they increased, did step in before Earls and

CHAP. XI. Barons; and in *Rich.* the Seconds time Marqueſſes began, and as they increaſt alſo ſtept in between Dukes and Earls; and in *Hen.* the *6ths.* time Viſcounts began, and as they increaſt did ſtep in between Earls and Barons; ſo as Originally, according to the dates of their Admiſſions, theſe Lords Spiritual and Temporal were all Peers, *i. e. Pares*, *pari gradu*, the Biſhops were *Pares inter ſeipſos pari gradu Epiſcopali*, (the Abbots, &c. in their time, were *Pares inter ſeipſos*, and both of thoſe Degrees were alſo *Pares* upon a Baronial account; (ſo the Dukes and Marqueſſes being Earls or Barons before they were created Dukes or Marqueſſes, in reſpect of their Earldoms or Baronies were Peers to the Earls and Barons; and the Viſcounts alſo, (moſt of them being Barons before they were created Viſcounts) in reſpect of their Baronies were Peers alſo to the Barons; ſo alſo upon a Baronial account they were *Pares pari gradu Baroniali*: Till Patents of Creation did more exactly diſtinguiſh them, without relation to Baronies; ſo as now to ſpeak properly, each Degree are *Pares* or *Prees* to their diſtinct Degrees.

9. I muſt here again make uſe of my former obſervation, *viz.* That in the Writs to Dukes they were Summon'd to be preſent

ſent in Parliament, *Cum Magnatibus & Proceribus*; and ſo are the Marqueſſes, Earls, Viſcounts and Barons, yet the Pattents to the Dukes do place them *inter Proceres & Magnates*, putting *Proceres* or *Peers* before *Magnates* or Lords; and in the Pattents to Marqueſſes, they are placed *inter alios Marchiones*; and the Earls *inter alios Comites*; and the Viſcounts *inter alios Vicecomites*; and the Barons *inter alios Barones*. But none of the Lords Patentees (except the Dukes in relation to their places) do take any notice of the poſition of the words *inter Proceres & Magnates*; for the Earls and Barons Patents have reference only to their own Degrees and not to the three other Degrees; ſo as *Proceres* or Peers is applied only to the Dukes in their Patents of Creation. CHAP. XI.

10. This is all that I can ſatisfie my ſelf in concerning the uſe of the words Lords and Peers, *Prælati*, *Magnates*, & *Proceres*; and that this may be the more ſatisfactory to others, I ſhall recite the words of the learned *Selden*, (in his Titles of Honour) whoſe laſting Credit is beyond exception; (ſaith he,) *Though there be a diſtinction of Degrees in our Nobility, yet in all publick actions they are Peers or Equals*; (*as in the Tryals of Noblemen*, &c. *in which the Spiritual Lords never did*

or

CHAP. XI. *or do concern themselves Personally, because it is against their Canons to act in any matters which relate to Blood*) *yet whatever Acts pass, these words are inserted*, viz. *We the Lords Spiritual and Temporal*, &c. *with the Kings Assent*, &c. *for though the Lords Spiritual consist of Archbishops and Bishops, and the Lords Temporal of Princes of the Blood, Dukes, Marquesses, Earls, Viscounts and Barons, yet they are all included as Peers in the words Lords Spiritual and Temporal*, and so in many cases the word Peers is also generally applied; so that, as the words Lords and Peers have been of latter times intermixedly used, we cannot well make a difference between them otherwise than is before exprest.

11. That the words Lords and Peers have been used promiscuously, in relation to the five Degrees of the Lords Temporal, is evident from the Commissions issued for the Trials of the Earl of *Strafford*, 1640. the Lord *Morley*, *Anno* 1665. the Lord *Cornwallis*, *Anno* 1676. the Earl of *Pembroke*, *Anno* 1678. wherein the words are, *Damus autem Universis & singulis Ducibus, Marchionibus, Comitibus, Vicecomitibus & Baronibus*, &c. (without mentioning *Prælatis*, for reasons before mentioned) and though the Earl of *Strafford* and

and Earl of *Pembroke* were Earls, yet by the Commission they were triable, *per Barones, Vicecomites, Comites Marchiones, & Duces*, and not by Earls only; and so though the Lord *Morley* and Lord *Cornwallis* were only Barons, yet they were triable by Dukes, Marquesses, Earls and Viscounts, and not by Barons only, whereby the word Peers seems to be a word of eminency, giving no real distinction to those five Degrees of Nobility; so as all the Degrees of the Temporal Lords are Peers, and the Peers Lords; to confirm this, I shall cite one passage more from Mr. *Selden*, who saith, *That though we borrowed the word Peers from the twelve Peers in* France, *yet here we apply it to all the Lords in Parliament, and not to any set number of them; because* (saith he) *the number of our Nobles may be more or less, as the King pleaseth*: and as Marquesses and Viscounts were (as I said) interpos'd to Dukes, Earls and Barons, so he may abstract less, or add more, as he thinks most fit, for the support of Nobility, for he is *Dominus Nobilitatis & Honoris*, or the Fountain of Honour; and that this Prerogative may be more fully seen herein, in the 21. of *Jacobi* (it being needless to quote former precedents) five several Writs were issued after the *Pawn* was setled;

CHAP. XI.

CHAP. XI. setled; yet entred in the Margent of the *Pawn* for that year, to five several persons, *viz.* to the Lord *Grandison*, Sir *Robert Chichester*, Sir *John Sucklin*, Knight, Comptroler of the Kings House, to Sir *Thomas Edmunds*, Knight, Treasurer of the Kings Houshold, and to Sir *Richard Weston*, Knight, Chancellor of the Exchequer, to summon and impower them to sit in the Lords House, who otherwise had no right of *Tenure*, *Prescription* or *Creation*. So in the first of *Caroli primi*, six several Writs were issued (and also entred in the Margent of the *Pawn* for that year) *viz.* to *Oliver Lord St. John*, and again to Sir *Thomas Edmunds*, Sir *John Sucklin*, Sir *Richard Weston*, and to Sir *Robert Nanton*, Knight, one of the Kings Privy-Council, and to Sir *Humphry May*, Chancellor of the Dutchy of *Lancaster*; and so in 15 *Car. primi*, two Writs were issued and also entred in the Margent of the *Pawn* for that year, *viz.* to *Charles Viscount Wilmot*, of the Kings Privy-Council, and to *Edward Newburgh*, Knight, then Chancellor of the Dutchy of *Lancaster*, and also of the Kings Privy-Council.

12. To sum up all, I apprehend, That those Lords Spiritual which are summon'd by Writ to sit in Parliament are Vital Peers, and the Lords Temporal so summon'd are

are hereditary Peers, for there are other English Lords, which may be, but are not summon'd, and thereby are no Parliament Peers, yet are Lords, and upon an hereditary account also; for the King (as I said) can summon or not summon any of them when he thinks fit, unless any Lord claims a right by Patent of Creation, or otherwise, and then upon that right he demands his Writ, and it is seldom denied, if the grounds of their demands be right, if dubious, the Case is debated in the Lords House, as in the Case of the Lord *Abergaveny*, &c. CHAP. XI.

Some are of opinion, That the Lords Temporal are only to be accounted Peers, and not the Lords Spiritual, first, Because they sit there rather by their Writs of Summons than Tenures, as anciently they did; secondly, Their Titles of Lord is but vital at most; thirdly, In case of Treason or Felony committed by a Spiritual Lord or Lord Temporal, the manner of trying them upon Indictment and Judgment upon Conviction are clearly different, as will be shewn in the Chapter of *Trial by Peers*.

13. Notwithstanding these Allegations, it is evident, That the Lords Spiritual are *Pares* or Peers, but *inter seipsos gradu Episcopali & vitali*, but not *Pares* to the Tem-

CHAP. XI. Temporal Lords, who are *Pares gradu hæreditario Nobilitatis & honoris*, either Descendent or Created, so that though all the Lords in the Lords House may be said to be Peers, yet the Lords Temporal being in *gradu celsioris Nobilitatis*, are more properly to be accounted so than any other Degree; in respect that as their Interest is greater than any other Degree, so they cannot be said to be *Pares* to any lesser than themselves, and therefore it may aptly be said, that none but such Dukes, Marquesses, Earls, Viscounts, and Barons as are summon'd by Writ to sit in Parliament, are to be accounted Peers of the Realm, or of Parliament. All other Degrees of Nobility, or Degrees under these five Degrees, are only *Pares sui cujusq; ordinis*, and not *Pares Regni*, and so the House of Commons, in time of Parliament, are *Pares minoris Nobilitatis*, and the Lords of the Lords House, *Pares majoris Nobilitatis*.

The next subject that I am guided to treat of, is concerning Proxees to the Lords Spiritual and Temporal, which may be made either of Lords or Peers, or of neither Lords nor Peers, yet by this Proximation are, *pro hac vice*, nobilitated.

CHAP. XII.

Of Proxees.

I Am now to speak of such as are substituted by the Lords Spiritual or Lords Temporal, to sit in the Lords House, and these are called by the name of *Proxees*.

1. The *Latin* word for *Proxee* is *Procurator*, which is sometimes English'd *Proxee*, and sometimes *Proctor*, according to the Employment of the Person to whom it is apply'd.

Proxee in a Parliamentary sence is constantly apply'd to such a Deputy or Substitute as is chosen by any Lord Spiritual or Lord Temporal (by Licence first had from the King, in case of just occasion alledged for absence) to supply his Deputy in the Lords House, and thereupon his Vote to be as significant to all purposes, as if the absent Lord were present; and therefore the word *Proxee* may well be thought to be only the *Tachygraphy* or short writing of *Proxime*, signifying the next in Judgment, Opinion, Degree, or Quality to the Lord who chooseth him for his *Proxee*.

CHAP. XI. But *Proctor*, which is the moſt literal abbreviation of *Procurator*, hath ſeveral applications, firſt to ſuch as are in ſome ſort a Limb or Branch of Parliaments, *viz.* ſuch as are choſen by the Chapters and Clergy, together with Archdeacons and Deans, to repreſent the whole Clergy, as Knights, Citizens and Burgeſſes do the Laity or whole Commons of *England*; but theſe are more uſually call'd Repreſentatives, the other conſtantly Proctors, both being deputed by diſtinct Degrees to diſtinct Purpoſes, as will be more fully ſhewn.

Secondly, There are alſo Proctors for the two Univerſities of *Cambridge* and *Oxford*.

And Thirdly, Proctors of Eccleſiaſtical Courts, which have no other relation to Parliaments than according as they are concern'd in Elections.

The *Proxees* which are admitted to the Lords Houſe are like thoſe in the old *Roman* Empire, call'd *Procuratores Cæſaris*, (which were the chief of four ſorts of *Procuratores* amongſt them) becauſe that firſt and chief of the four were only imploy'd *ad Res publicas adminiſtrandas*, (the other three for leſſer matters) and ſo the *Proxees* of the Lords Houſe being the chief of all other *Proxees*, are to be eſteemed *Publi-*

carum

carum rerum administratores, as fully as the absent Lords (except in some particulars as to Place, Continuance, *&c.*) CHAP. XII.

2 These Noble *Proxees* are (as I said) lincensed by the King, upon the Petition or Request of some Lord Spiritual or Lord Temporal, and are not usually made of Strangers, (who are not Members of the Lords House) nor of the Assistants of that House.

When the absent Lords occasions of absence have not been just, or his absence inconvenient to the Publick, the King hath often deny'd to License their *Proxees*; but when the Allegations have been just, the *Proxee* hath been sometimes allow'd without the Kings License.

Sometimes it hath been allow'd to the absent Lord, to make a *Proxee* of such a person as is otherwise incapacitated to sit in the Lords House, (for by this he is nobilitated) but there hath been none such allow'd in this Parliament.

3. Generally the absent Lord doth fix upon such a Lord as (I said) doth sit in the Lords House, by his own Right and Writ of Summons, whereby the *Proxee*-sitting Lord hath a double Voice, one for himself, the other for the absent Lord to whom he is *Proxee*.

V 4. These

CHAP. XII. 4. Thefe Noble *Proxees* are made fometimes before the fitting of a Parliament, (after the Writs are iffued) and fometimes in the time of their fitting, and their Deputations both before and after the fitting have feveral Forms, as will be fhewn.

5. In former times the Lords Spiritual had the privilege to make two or three *Proxees*, but fince the diffolution of Abbies, and that Abbots, *&c.* were excluded, no *Proxor*, or abfent Lord, doth make but one *Proxee*.

6. The Licenfes for *Proxees* (as I faid) were granted by the King, upon the abfent Lords Petition; which Petition from *Edward* the Third's time was in this Form:

Sereniffimo Principi Domino Edwardo Dei gratia Regi Angliæ, Franciæ & Hiberniæ Domino, &c. *Quia impedimentis varijs & arduis negotijs*, &c. *fumus multipliciter impediti quo inftante Parliamento veftro apud Weftmonafterium in Quind'*, &c. *proximo futur' perfonaliter effe non valentes.* (And fo others, for other reafons) pray that he may be allow'd his *Proxee*; whereupon Licenfe was granted, as may be feen in ancient Journals, but more lately in Queen *Elizabeth*'s time, thus:

Right-

Right-trusty and well-beloved, We greet you well. Whereas we are inform'd, That by reason of Sickness you are not able to make repair hither to this our Parliament, to be holden at Westminster, *We have thought good, by these our Letters, to dispense with you for your absence, and to License you to remain still at home for this time, so nevertheless that you send up your* Proxee, *of such Personage as may be for you in your Name, to give his Voice and Assent, or Denial, to such Matters as shall be concluded on in our said Parliament. And this our Letter shall be your Warrant.*

Given under our Signet at our Palace at Westminster, *the* 20th *of* November, *in the Eighth Year of Our Reign.*

8. These Licenses are usually entred in the Signet or Privy-Seal-Offices, (and pass no further) but are certified to the Lords when sitting.

9. This regular Method of Licenses continued till about the end of Queen *Elizabeth*'s Reign, but by the kindness (or connivance of her Successors to the Nobles) there hath been of late no more Ceremony us'd than a Verbal Motion to the King; and some Nobles by that Indulgence have constituted *Proxees* without application

CHAP. XII. to the King, only adding in their Deputations to their *Proxees* (viz. *per Licentiam Domini Noſtri Regis*) conceiving that the very mentioning of the Kings Licenſe was a ſufficient acknowledgment of his Prerogative herein; however theſe following *Proxee-Deputations*, or derivative Writs (which I cite as Precedents) were regularly obtain'd.

The Form of a Proxee-Licenſe *from one Lord Temporal to another before the ſitting of a Parliament.*

10. OMnibus Chriſti Fidelibus ad quos hoc præſens ſcriptum pervenerit, Rupertus Palatinus Rheni, Dux Bavariæ & Cumbriæ, Comes Holdernes in regno Angliæ ſalutem Noveritis me præfatum principem (per Licentiam Sereniſſimi Domini noſtri Regis) a ſuo Parliamento tenendo & inchoando apud Weſtmonaſterium in dicto regno Octavo die Menſis Maij proximo futuro ſufficienter excuſatum abeſſe; Nominare ordinare & conſtituere dilectum mihi in Chriſto prænobilem & honoratiſſimum virum Jacobum Ducem, Marchionem & Comitem Ormondiæ, Comitem Oſoriæ, Carrickiæ & Breconiæ Dominum Thurles Baronem, meum

meum verum certum & indubitatum Factorem, Attornatum & Procuratorem, eidemq; Procuratori meo dare & concedere plenam Authoritatem & Potestatem pro me & nomine meo, & de super quibuscunq; causis exponendis seu declarandis tractandis, tractatibusq; hujusmodi mihi factis seu faciendis, Concilium nomine meo impendendum. Statutisq; etiam & ordinationibus quæ ex maturo & deliberato Judicio Dominorum in eodem Parliamento Congregatorum, inactitari seu ordinari contigerint nomine meo consentiendum, eisdemq; (si opus fuerit) subscribendum, Cæteraq; omnia & singula quæ in præmissis necessaria fuerint, aut quomodolibet requisita facienda & exercenda, in tam amplo modo & forma prout ego ipse facere possem, aut deberem si præsens personaliter interessem, ratum & gratum habens & habiturus totum & quicquid dictus Procurator meus statuerit & fecerit, in præmissis. In cujus rei testimonium præsentibus subscripsi, Sigillumq; meum apposui datum apud Westmonasterium decimo sexto die Aprilis Anno Regni dicti Domini nostri Caroli Secundi Dei gratia Angliæ, Scotiæ, Franciæ & Hiberniæ Regis fidei defensoris, &c. decimo tertio Annoq; salutis nostræ 1661.

CHAP. XII. 11. This was ſubſcribed (*Rupert*) and ſealed with his Seal at large upon an annext *Label.*

12. All *Proxee-Writs* of this nature are given into the Clerks of the Parliament before the *Proxees* are admitted, and their Licenſes either produced to the Lords (if written) or affirm'd by ſome other Lords that the Kings conſent was thereto.

13. This was the only derivative *Proxee-Writ* which was made by a Lord Temporal of this Parliament, 1661. before the Seſſions, and though the Foreign Titles of the *Proxor* and of his *Proxee* are mention'd in the Writ *Honoris Gratia*, yet it operates nothing in this Caſe; for as the *Proxor* could not make a *Proxee* without the Kings Licenſe, written or verbal, ſo he could not be a *Proxee* by virtue of his Foreign Titles, but only by their *Engliſh* or *Welſh* Titles, *viz.* as Duke of *Cumberland* he was *Proxor*, not as Palatine of the *Rhine*, or Duke of *Bavaria*, and the Earl of *Brecknock* was his *Proxee*, as Earl of *Brecknock*, not as Duke of *Ormond.*

14. Had there been more of theſe Derivatives before the Seſſions, they muſt have been in the ſame words, differing only in the Titles of the *Proxor* and *Proxee*; and thoſe that were made the Parliament ſitting,

ſitting, *viz.* the 10th of *May*, the Earl of *Holland* (before any Prorogation) made the Earl of *Suffolk* his *Proxee*, and are alſo in the ſame words with the other Form, *mutato nomine*, and by changing the future to the preſent, *viz. Tenendo & Inchoando*, to *tento & inchoato*, but after a Prorogation the words are as in the next Writ (at *inde prorogato*, &c.) And theſe two Derivatives are ſufficient to ſhew the difference between Writs made before the Parliament, or before any Prorogation, and the Writs made after a Prorogation. CHAP. XII.

15. The recital of Prorogation or Prorogations are not only ſo in Derivatives, but in all original Writs which are iſſu'd after a Prorogation, by reaſon of the death of any Lord, to ſummon another.

I have entred this Writ to the Archbiſhop here, though I ſhall ſpeak more of it when I come to treat of Writs made in time of Parliament, becauſe it contains many Clauſes different from the Derivatives to the Lords Temporal, eſpecially in the laſt Paragraph more obſervable.

CHAP. XII.

The Form of the Archbiſhop of Canterbury's *derivative* Proxee-Writ *to the Biſhop of* London *after a Prorogation.*

16. OMnibus in Chriſto Fidelibus ad quos hoc præſens Scriptum pervenerit Gulielmus providentia divina Cantuarienſis Archiepiſcopus totius Angliæ Primas & Metropolitanus Salutem in Domino ſempiternam, Cum Sereniſſimus Dominus noſter Rex, quibuſdam de cauſis ſublimitati ſuæ intimatis licentiam a præſenti hoc ſuo Parliamento tento & inchoato apud Weſtmonaſterium octavo die Maij Anno regni ſui decimo tertio & continuato ad decimum nonum diem Maij Anno decimo quarto dicti Domini Regis & inde prorogato ad decimum octavum diem Februarij proxime inde ſequentem nobis abſentandi ex ſuo ſpeciali gratia & favore nuper conceſſerit dummodo fidelem aliquem Procuratorem, vice locoq; meis ponerem ordinarem & conſtituerem, Noveritis Igitur me præfatum Archiepiſcopum dilectum mihi in Chriſto Reverendum in Chriſto Patrem Gilbertum eadem divina providentia Dominum London Epiſcopum meum verum certum & indubitatum Factorem, Actorem, Procuratorem, Attornatum, nego-

negotiorumq; nostrorum Gestorum & Nuntium specialem, nominare ordinare facere & constituere per p'sentes, dando & concedendo eidem Procuratori meo plenam authoritatem & potestatem de & super quibuscunq; causis & negotijs statum & utilitatem dicti Domini nostri Regis Reipublicæ incolumitatem & Ecclesiæ Anglicanæ quietem concernentibus, quæ in præfato Parliamento qualibet ejusdem sessione per dicti domini Regis statum agitari contigerint tractandi, tractibusq; hujusmodi mihi factis seu faciendis concilium & auxilium nomine meo imponendis etiam & ordinationibus quæ Communi statu prædicta ordinatione ibidem fieri & ordinari contigerint nomine meo consentiendi, & ijsdem si opus fuerit subscribendi vel dissentiendi, Cæteraq; omnia & singula quæ in præmissis aut in aliquo præmissorum necessaria fuerint seu quomodolibet requisita faciendi expediendi & exercendi in tam amplis modo & forma prout ego ipse facere possem & deberem si præsens personaliter interessem, Promittoq; me ratum gratum & firmum perpetuo habiturum totum & quicquid dictus meus Procurator statuerit aut fecerit in præmissis, & sub Hypotheca & obligatione omnium & singulorum bonorum meorum in ea parte cautionem expono per presentes, In cujus rei Testimonium

CHAP. XII. nium manum & ſigillum meum Appoſui. Dat apud Lambeth' viceſimo primo Novembris Anno regni dicti Domini noſtri Caroli Secundi Dei gratia Angliæ, Scotiæ, Franciæ & Hiberniæ Regis fidei defenſoris, *&c.* Annoq; Dom. 1662.

17. All derivative *Proxee-Writs* made either from a Lord Spiritual or Temporal, to any of their own Degrees, or of other Degrees, do not continue longer than one Seſſion, without a new Derivative Licenſe, or Proxee-Inſtrument.

18. As to the places of the *Proxees* in the Lords Houſe, they are not mention'd in the Act of Precedency, ſo I ſhall conclude with Mr. *Elſing*, That ſurely they did not ſit in the Lords Seat whoſe *Proxee* he was, yet in all Councils and Dyets beyond the Seas he does.

19. Though they are Nobilitated by ſitting as *Proxees*, yet they are not to be accounted Peers, unleſs they were Peers before they were *Proxees*.

Thus having ſaid as much as I think fit of Writs to the Lords Spiritual and Temporal, both Original and Derivative, I am come to the Fifth Exemplar, concerning the Aſſiſtants to thoſe Lords, Peers, and Proxees.

CHAP. XIII.

Of the Assistants to the House of Peers, comprized in the Fifth Exemplar *of the* Pawn.

1. HAving done with all the Degrees which are mention'd in the Act of Precedencies, and given an account by four *Exemplars* of the Writs to the Princes of the Blood, of the Writs to the Archbishops and Bishops, of the Writ to the Lord Chancellor, of the Writs to the Hereditary Nobles of Parliament, (*viz. Dukes, Marquesses, Earls, Viscounts*, and *Barons*) as they are mention'd in the *Pawn*, and also given an Abstract of such Patents of Creation as Intitle some of them to be the more capable of Summons, as also of Peers and their Proxies, I come now to the Degrees which are not mention'd in the Act of Precedency, but are compriz'd under the fifth *Exemplar-Writ*, recited in the foremention'd *Pawn*, *viz.* to the Lord Chief Justice of *England*, and of the *Consimilars* to his Writ; and these are different from all the former (except the Lord Chancellors, of which I have spoken) because these do not sit in the Lords House by vertue of any Tenure or Patent of Crea-

CHAP. XIII. Creation, or according to the Act of Precedency, but only by Writs, as Aſſiſtants, (for none do ſit there without Original Writs, except Proxies, and Maſters of Chancery, &c.) as will be ſhewn. But before I treat of them diſtinctly, I ſhall ſet down ſome Obſervations on their Profeſſions.

1. Theſe Aſſiſtants do all profeſs the Study and Knowledge of Laws, and therefore have their Places allotted in the very heart of the Lords Houſe, that they may with the more eaſe give their Advice to that Noble Body, in all Matters which concern either the Theory or Practice of what is juſt or fit to be done.

2. Now there are certain Faculties and Vertues ſpringing from the Profeſſion of theſe Aſſiſtants (*viz. Jus*, or Right; *Juſtitia*, or Juſtice; *Judicium*, or Judgment; *Ratio*, or Reaſon; *Prudentia*, or Prudence; *Æquitas*, or Equity; *Diſcretio*, or Diſcretion; *Sapientia*, or Wiſdom; and *Scientia Legum*, or Knowledge of the Laws:) to whith (it is preſum'd) they have attain'd, and are thereby made fit for Aſſiſtants; yet that theſe Vertues may be the more diſtinctly diſcern'd, I ſhall take the freedom to explain them.

Jus, (the *Latin* for Right) is the foundation on which *Juſtitia*, or Juſtice, is built.

Juſtitia

Justitia is *status*, or *statio Juris*, *quia Jus stat vel exercetur per Justitiam.* So that *Jus* is the principal, *Justitia* the Efflux of it. CHAP. XIII.

Judicium, or Judgment, is the fix'd resolution, determination, or sentence of what is true, or false, good, or evil, just, or unjust.

Reason is a Ray of Divine Light, which guides a man to judge what is Just or Justice.

Prudence is in the nature of Providence, (from *Providere*) to foresee the conveniencies or inconveniencies of so doing or not doing right to one man, that it may do good to one, and not hurt another.

Discretion is also to discern the nature or difference of things represented, and to manage them to their right end, and by this

Equity is usher'd in, which is a conscientious care that all things may be equally and proportionably done towards those who exspect Justice, when the matter concerns distinct persons, or interests, and then

Sapientia or Wisdom advanceth it self, and includes the *Scientia Legum*, or Knowledge of the Laws, and that imploys all the Faculties of the Soul, and hath a particular

CHAP. XIII. ticular Intellect and Inſpiration to ſee, improve and manage all things to a juſt and right end, and teacheth the Profeſſors to inſtruct others in the principal Rules of perfect Converſation with each other, *viz Honeſte vivere, neminem lædere, & ſuum cuiq; tribuere*, which is to live ſoberly, and temperately, to offend no man wilfully, and to give tribute to whom tribute belongs, and to every man what is their right to enjoy, or in our power to perform.

All theſe do conſtitute a wiſe man, and the Profeſſors of Laws have more opportunities to demonſtrate them to others, and by theſe Vertues they become Accompliſh'd Aſſiſtants to a Parliament both in Divine and Human Matters.

3. But the Imbecility of our Human Nature is ſuch, that no man is ſo univerſally knowing in all things, as to give a true Judgment of all particulars, without a light or information from others, whereby to judge of what is juſt, right, or fit to be done; eſpecially in the contentions ariſing from the Mechanick Arts, or Trades, and ſome other Sciences, which are a ſignificant part of the Fabrick of any Kingdom, or State; for ſuppoſing two Artificers, profeſſing different Arts, are both imployed to the perfecting of ſome Publick Work, wherein their

their joint Skills are necessarily required, in which they are at variance upon some mystical parts in their Trades, and without determination of their differences and concerns, neither of them can proceed in the joynt Design; and thereupon they refer themselves to one of the Professors of the Law, to settle the matter between them.

But it is vulgarly thought beneath one of these eminent Professors to dive into Mechanick Trades or lesser Sciences; yet both of these Artists informing him of the true state of the mysteries of their respective Trades, the Judge from thence makes a rational determination of what is fit to be done, as well for the support of their Trades, as for the common good to others, by preventing fallacies, or circumventions, or the like contests; and this he gains from the impartments and arguments of these Artists, and so weighing their alternate allegations in one balance, and the common good in another, he makes so peculiar a determination and Sentence, as to convince both parties, and this from the ground of their different Arts and Impartments.

Now the Judge or Justice, even by these dayly accidents, and references, doth dayly gain Knowledge, and by justly managing

CHAP. XIII. naging this Knowledge grows to be generally eſteem'd a *wiſe Man*, not only from theſe lower particulars upon which the Opinion of the Vulgar is founded but from his inſight and tranſacting in matters of a more tranſcendent nature, which dayly alſo come before him (either of Publick or Private Concerns.)

But in all Tranſactions in this World there is a Right and a Wrong, which latter is term'd Unjuſt, and ſometimes it may be poſitively judg'd to be ſo; yet it may ſo happen that *ſummum jus* may do injury, whereupon there is a neceſſity of interpoſing Equity, leſt the Wrong by Cuſtom ſhould prove an eſteem'd Right, or that Right by neceſſary fix'd Rules, (which may be ſafe at one time and not at another) or an unlimited uſe or power, ſhould ſlide into Wrong; ſo as the due and critical time of applying this Equity to *ſummum jus* (which is gain'd by reading Law and Precedents) doth ſtill improve and exalt the Character of a *wiſe Man*.

4. But becauſe moſt men are either negligently or wilfully ignorant in the way of attaining theſe excellent Vertues, the wiſdom of all Governours hath (by the help of theſe learned Profeſſors) eſtabliſh'd certain Rules to direct men (which the *Latin* call *Regulæ*, from *Regere*) intima-

ting

ting the care of Governours in Exhibiting such Rules for the good of those who are under Tuition, but generally such Rules are called Laws (which the *Latins* term *Leges*, from *Legere*, to Read) so as every man, who is not careless of his own Felicity or Justice towards others, may thereby be instructed to what he ought to perform. CHAP. XIII.

5. In ancient times when People were not dispers'd into various Regions, nor into great Societies of Towns, Cities and Kingdoms, but consisted of some few Families, or Villages, it was no hard matter to transmit those Rules or Laws to one another, by singing them in Meeter, or some other ways of Tradition; but when those lesser Societies grew into the greater forms of Government, their Legislators invented a more certain way or art of communicating their just Rules or Laws, by legible Characters, Words, and Sentences, either Writ or Printed, (containing those Rules) which (as I said) were originally, only certain tunable unwritten Instructions; and after, when mens dispositions grew more and more deprav'd, there was something of Coertion added to those Laws, which Coertions (or inflicting of Penalties for disobedience to those Laws) increas'd with the increase of un-

CHAP. XIII. conformable tempers: and herein there is nothing so great an argument of a wise and good disposition, as when he makes it his study to satisfie himself (and thereby able to inform others) in the knowledge of such Laws or Rules as may make our Lives in this World happy and conscientious, which can no ways be obtain'd, but by knowing and obeying good Laws.

6. For these are they (as the learned Sir *John Davies* says) to which all Kingdoms and Common-wealths are indebted for all their temporal blessings of Peace, Plenty, Civility, and all moral parts of honesty. By these (saith he) we injoy our Relations, Lands, Goods, good Names, or what ever is sweet or dear unto us, for *quid sunt Regna nisi magna latrocinia sine Justitia & Legibus*; the Land would be full of Thieves, the Sea of Pyrats, the Commons would rise up against the Nobility, the Nobility against the Crown; without these there would be nothing certain, no Contracts, no Commerce, no Conversation, but Confusion, and even Dissolution of Human Society: for good Laws are Comforts to the Griev'd, Counsel to the Perplex'd, Reliefs to the Circumvented, Preventions of Ruin to the Improvident, Preservations to the Innocent, Supports to the Impotent; they Relieve the Oppress'd,

Oppress'd, protect the Orphan, Widow, and Strangers, they are *Oculi Cæcis*, & *Pedes Claudis*; (Cures for lame and blind) To sum up all, they are the Secular Arms to defend both the Church, True Religion, and the Common-Weal of the Kingdom or State.

CHAP. XIII.

7. For these reasons, the Successive Kings of this Island have constantly (as rewards) set such a mark upon those who are Professors of the Laws, and whose study and experience in Laws have attain'd to so great a sagacity, (as to know how to apply them to the publick good) that the chief of them is made Lord Chancellor, or Lord Keeper of the Great Seal of *England*; (of whom I have spoken, who for the most part hath been a Professor of Divinity, Law, or Equity) the next (of whom I am now to treat) is made Chief Justice of *England*; his very Title *Justice* rendring him in one sence even Superior to the Law it self; (for the Law it self is but *Lex tacens*, but he that distributes that Law, is *Lex loquens*.

8. This Title of *Justice* (given also to every one of the twelve Judges or chief Dispensers of Laws) is so ancient, that in former times they were call'd *Justitiæ*, (as containing that vertue not only in the singular, but in the plural number) and

CHAP. XIII. afterwards they were call'd *Justitiarii Angliæ*, and *Justitiarii*, (without addition of *Angliæ*) and after *Justitiarii Regis*, which last Title was to the four Justices of the *Kings Bench*; the chief of which four was anciently called *Summus*, and at this day *Capitalis Justitiarius Angliæ*; (which generally we term in *English*, the Lord Chief Justice of *England*) there was also anciently another sort of *Justitiarii ad placita*, (applyed only to the four Justices of the *Common Pleas*, (the chief of which was, and is to this day also called *Capitalis Justitiarius*, (omitting *Angliæ*) and which we in *English* term, the Lord Chief Justice of the *Common Pleas*.

And to ease the People from going for Justice to them, these Justices did go to the People, to distribute Justice.

These Motions in process of time were call'd their Circuits, because they did in a manner go round the Kingdom; and for these Motions they were called *Justitiarii Itinerantes*, & *Justitiarii ad Assisas, Juratas* & *Certificationes*. There were also anciently another sort of *Justitiarii*, (which it may be for distinction sake were called *Barones Scaccarii*) consisting also of four; and this Title is applied only to the Exchequer, where their Justice was to be shewn

ſhewn in the management of the Revenue of the Crown; and theſe four alſo were and are conſtantly mixt with the other Eight, in their *Itinerancìis* : in all making Twelve. CHAP. XIII.

9. And for further Honor to theſe Eminent Profeſſors, as well out of Parliament as in Parliament, they have peculiar Courts, (as *Regalias* allotted to them) wherein they have daily opportunities to manifeſt their Wiſdom.

Theſe Profeſſors I divide into three Orbs, and their Courts accordingly, *viz.* to the Lord Chancellor or Lord Keeper, the Court of *Chancery*; to the Lord Chief Juſtice of *England*, the Court call'd the *Kings Bench*; to the Maſter of the Rolls (or Keeper of the moſt eminent Office of Records) the *Rolls Chappel*; (in the nature of a Court) to the other Lord Chief Juſtice, the Court of *Common Pleas*; to the Lord Chief Baron, the Court of *Exchequer*; and theſe are the five Courts or *Regalias* belonging to five of the firſt Orb of that Profeſſion; yet not excluding the other Nine: ſo as,

The ſecond Orb conſiſts of Nine more, *viz.* three Juſtices of the *Kings Bench*, three of the *Common Pleas*, and three other Barons of the *Exchequer*; and theſe have gradual intereſts in thoſe three Courts, (as will

CHAP. XIII. be shewn) and with the other five do make fourteen, of the first and second Orb; and as a further addition of Honor, twelve of these fourteen (in their Circuits twice every year) have Courts also provided for them, almost in every County of *England* (as will be shewn.)

The third Orb of the Professors of Law, are not usually above six in number; (yet sometimes more, sometimes fewer (as will be shewn) I mean of such only as have Summons to sit in Parliament,) and these have Courts also allotted for them, *viz.* the Kings Serjeants at Law, the Kings Attorney General, the Kings Sollicitor General, have the Inns of Courts, (though common also to under Graduates and Students) and the two principal Secretaries of State have the Kings Court or Palace for their *Regalias*; so as the before mentioned five of the first Orb, and nine of the second Orb, and six of the third Orb, (these three Orbs being the most eminent of that Profession) have not only the Jurisdiction and an Interest in the said Courts, but as an higher mark of Honour and Esteem, though they were no Lords, or Barons of the Realm, yet they were and are usually Summon'd by Writs to the High Court of Parliament, when ever it Assembled, and there they are

are also dignifi'd with peculiar Places appointed for them, and many Priviledges: of which, with their Number, and the Causes of Variation of that Number, I shall give an Account in the ensuing Sections.

10. These (as I said) are imploy'd in the Lords House to be Assistants with their sage advices, who are perfect knowers both of general and particular Laws, *viz.* in the Laws of God and Nature, the Civil Laws, (practised in most parts of *Europe*) the Ecclesiastick Laws of other Nations, but more particularly of our own, of our Common Statute, Municipal, and Customary, (and By-Laws, which are *alteræ Leges*) and many others of other Titles, which we derive and still retain from the old *Roman* Empire, *Saxons*, &c. And thus fraught with knowledge of Laws, they bring them for the most part into the Hive, or compass of our Common and Statute Law, and their universal knowledge makes them esteem'd Learned, their Learning indues them with Wisdom, their Wisdom enables them to be Justices or Judges out of Parliament, and in Parliament to be Assistants there, for the better carrying on of Publick Actions and Consultations; so as the present Laws may be preserved, or such new ones made

CHAP. XIII. as their Wisdoms shall think fit to advise; there being sometimes as much necessity of making new, or correcting, altering, explaining, or inlarging the old, as in possitively preserving them; for when a Buttress hath sustain'd an House many years, and is it self decayed by time, it is to the safety of the House, to have another Supporter in its room; for *tempora mutant mores*, and *mores* may justly *mutare leges*, (considered according to the diversity of circumstances) and herein consists the great Master-piece of advice, by turning a *nolumus mutare*, into a rational *volumus*.

11. Having now given a short discourse of Law, and the Professors of it in general, occasioning just grounds for their Assistance, I shall proceed to the particular Titles of the chiefest Professors of it, and according to my first propos'd Method, go on with the fifth *Exemplar*, mention'd in the aforesaid Parliament *Pawn*, *viz.* to the Lord chief Justice of *England*.

The Form of the Fifth *Exemplar-Writ* to the Lord chief Justice of *England*.

CArolus *Secundus Dei gratia Angl' Scot' Franc' & Hibern' Rex fidei defensor'*, &c. *Dilecto & fideli suo Roberto Foster Militi Capitali Justiciario nostro ad placita coram nobis tenend' assign' salutem. Quia de advisamento & assensu Consilij nostri pro quibusdam arduis & urgentibus negotijs nos, statum, & defensionem Regni nostri Angliæ & Ecclesiæ Anglicanæ concernen' quoddam Parliamentum nostrum apud Civitatem nostram Westm' octavo die Maij prox' futur' teneri ordinavimus, & ibidem vobiscum & cum magnatibus & proceribus dicti Regni nostri Colloquium habere & tractatum, vobis mandamus firmiter injungend', quod omnibus alijs pretermissis predictis die, & loco personaliter intersitis nobiscum, ac cum cæteris de Concilio nostro super dictis negotijs tractatur', vestrum Consilium impensur'. Et hoc nullatenus omittatis Teste me ipso apud Westm' decimo octavo die Februarij Anno regni nostri tertiodecimo.*

The next words in the foremention'd *Pawn* are *Consimilia Brevia diriguntur personis subscriptis.*

But

CHAP. XIII. But before I speak of those *Consimilars*, I shall add some few Observations on this *Exemplar*.

Observations on the Exemplar *and it's* Consimilars.

I Did think to have made distinct Observations on this and the following *Consimilars*, but finding how curiously they, in their Jurisdictions, Power, Authorities, and Operations are intermix'd, separated, and yet united, I shall speak of them as they spring up from my Recollections, on which others may graft more, as best suiting to theirs.

1. Neither this chief Assistant, nor any of the following Assistants (which are call'd *Consimilars* in the *Pawns*) are mention'd in the Kings Warrant to the Lord Chancellor for summoning a Parliament, otherwise than in these words:

Wherefore We Will and Command you forthwith, upon receipt hereof, and by warrant of the same, to cause such and so many Writs to be made and seal'd under our great Seal, for the accomplishment of the same, as in like cases hath been us'd and accustom'd, as may be seen in the first Chapter.

And

And thereupon the Lord Chancellor (according to the ancient Custom, and such Precedents as I have and shall set down) sends his Warrant to the Clerks of the Pettibag (*in hæc verba*) as in the first Chapter. CHAP. XIII.

You are hereby required forthwith to prepare for the great Seal of England *the several Writs of Summons for the Lords Spiritual and Temporal, as also for the Judges and others, to appear at the Parliament to be holden,* &c. *in such method and form, and directed to such persons as are and have been usual in such cases,* &c.

Now that the Lord Chief Justice (and the *Consimilars*, of which I am to speak) have been anciently and usually summon'd, I have and shall shew in their following order.

2. In the Act of Precedency there is no mention made of the Places of these Assistants, but there having never been any dispute among themselves of their Places or Precedencies (for they are perfect in their own Regularities and Seniorities, &c.) it had been but expense of time and Paper to insert them, and therefore according to the constant order by which they have sat anciently in the Lords House

I

CHAP. XIII. I shall treat distinctly of them, so soon as I have ruin through some few mix'd Observations.

3. This great Minister of Justice was anciently made by Letters Patents, with the Clause of *Quam diu nobis placuerit*, and so it continued till about the end of *Henry* the Third, and then, and ever since, he hath not been constituted by Commission or Patent, (as all the other Judges are) but by Writ only, in this form.

Rex, &c. R. F. *Militi salutem Sciatis quod constituimus vos Justitiarium nostrum Capitalem ad placita coram nobis tenend' durante bene placito*, &c. *Teste*, &c. And this Writ makes him capable of his Parliament-Writ before recited.

4. The Lord Chancellor or Lord Keeper of the Great Seal (as I said) is admitted Chancellor or Keeper by delivery only of the Great Seal to him, and taking his Oath, without Patent or Writ; but this Lord Chief Justice is admitted to his Office by Writ only, and all the other Assistants (of whom I shall speak) do injoy their Offices in their respective Courts by Patent only, and all of them *durante bene placito* (except the Master of the *Rolls*, whose Patent is *durante vitâ*) as will be shewn.

5. But

5. But neither the delivery of the Great Seal to the Lord Chancellor, or Lord Keeper, nor the aforeſaid Official Writ to the Lord Chief Juſtice of the *Kings Bench*, nor the reſpective Patents by which the other Juſtices enjoy their reſpective Offices, do intitle them to ſit in the Lords Houſe, without ſuch an eſpecial Parliament Writ of Aſſiſtance, as is ſhewn in the Exemplar before recited, (to which all the other Aſſiſting Writs have a Conſimilitude.) CHAP. XIII.

5. This Parliament, or Aſſiſting Exemplar Writ to the Lord Chief Juſtice of the *Kings Bench*, and all the Conſimilars to it (*mutato nomine & titulo Officii*) agrees in all parts with the Writ to the Lord Chancellor, (as I have before ſhewn) except the alteration of the words, *Prædilecto & perquam Fideli*, into *Dilecto & Fideli*, which are in this and in all the Writs to the following Aſſiſtants.

6. The differences between this Writ and that to the Hereditary Lords in Parliament, are partly ſhewn in the Obſervations on the Lord Chancellors Writ, the reſt will be ſhewn.

7. This Parliament writ differs but in few words from the form of the writ iſſued in the 15*th.* of *Edw.* 2*d.* (from whence I take my riſe (nor from the

Succeſſive

CHAP. XIII. Successive Writs to this time) which for the satisfaction of others, (whereby they may see that no new form is obtruded on them) I have set here down *Verbatim.*

Rex Dilecto & Fideli suo Willielmo de Bereford salutem Quia super diversis & arduis negotiis nos & statum Regni nostri specialiter tangentibus in instante Parliamento nostro die Dominicâ prox' futur' ante Festum sancti Laurencii prox' futur' fecimus summoneri, vobiscum & cum cæteris de Concilio nostro colloquium habere volumus, & tractatum, vobis mandamus firmiter injungentes quod omnibus aliis pretermissis dictis die & loco personaliter intersitis nobiscum, & cum ceteris de Consilio nostro super premissis tractatur' vestrumque Consilium impensuri Et hoc nullatenus omittat' Teste, &c.

In this Writ the words after *Regni nostri*, (viz. & *Ecclesiæ Anglicanæ* are omitted;) for the Church in those days was almost wholly manag'd by Ecclesiastick Persons, who were Conversant in the Civil, and Canon Laws, &c. but in the 26*th.* of *Henry* the Eighth, when the power of the Pope was here abridg'd, those words, & *Ecclesiæ Anglicanæ* were entred and continued to this day.

Also

Also after the word *Vobiscum* these words, *ac cum Prælatis Magnatibus & Proceribus* are omitted; but (as near as I can collect) some of the most eminent of the Professors of the Law, (as the Lord Chief Justice, and Lord Chief Baron, *&c.*) were sometimes Summon'd by Peeral Writs, that is by such Writs that were sent to the Nobles, and then the words *ac cum Prælatis*, &c. (as in *Richard* the Seconds time to *Jo. Cavendish Capital' Justic'*; and in *Henry* the Fifths time, to *William Hanckford* and many more) were inserted; but when ever they were Summon'd meerly as Assistants, the words *cum Prælatis*, &c. were left out, and so have been ever since *Edward* the Fourths time.

8. This Parliament Writ is directed, *Capitali Justitiario nostro ad placita*, &c. and so is his Writ by which he enjoys that great Office, yet his common and general appelation is, *Capitali Justitiario Angliæ*, which we call Lord Chief Justice of *England*, and sometimes, Lord Chief Justice of the *Kings Bench*, and by some one of those Titles; he is called so in several Acts of Parliament, and ancient Records; (as I have hinted) and though the word Lord be added to his appellation, both in his Assistancies and Office, (and so to some

other

CHAP. XIII. other of the Aſſiſtants) yet neither he nor they are to be counted Lords of Parliament; for his Writ by which he enjoys his Office (which is the Inducement to his Aſſiſting Writ) is but *durante Placito*, (*& honore Officii*) and his Aſſiſtance being but *durante Parliamento*, neither of them can fix the Title further than the continuance of his Office or Aſſiſtance.

And here it may be obſerved, that the word *Vos* (a word of great eminency, always ſignifying a plural, though ſometimes apply'd to a ſingle Perſon) is us'd in this Official Writ (before mentioned) to the this Lord Chief Juſtice, but is not in his Parliament Writ, nor in any of the Patents or Parliament-Writs to the other Juſtices, of whom I ſhall ſpeak in order.

9. The antiquity of this great Miniſter of Juſtice, and his Court, is doubtleſs more ancient (under various Titles) than from *Hen.* the Thirds time; (from whence we vulgarly compute it,) for the Civilians do acknowledge that, *Juſtitiarii ſunt umbræ quædam illorum qui olim* νομοφύλακες *apud Græcos dicebantur, deſignati ad Cuſtodiam Juris & æquitatis.* However, Sir *Edward Coke* to prove its antiquity, tells us of an Epitaph in *Ramſy* Abby, ingraven on Stone in theſe words, *Alvinus incliti*

Regis

Regis Edgari Cognatus, totius Angliæ Aldermannus, (saith, that by *Aldermannus* is meant, *Capitalis Justitiarius Angliæ*, and consequently his Assistance in all Councils before the name of Parliament, (and since that name) hath always been esteem'd necessary, and (as he saith) all these Courts of *Justice* are so ancient, that they seem to have their Originals from Custom, rather than by Commission.

10. His Jurisdiction is so great, as well out of Parliament as in Parliament, that often times the Lords do wave their own Power and Priviledges of using their own Officers, and do direct the Chief Justice to send out his single Warrant to Seize on Persons in case of Treason, or Suspicion of it, or for other high Crimes or Misdemeanors; and the *House of Commons* have likewise sent to him to come to their *House* upon the like occasions, as happened when by their directions his Lordship sent out Warrants to Seize the five Lords, of whom I shall speak in the Chapter of Tryals.

11. Other uses are also made of him, and some other of the Assistants in Parliament; for when the *Lords* have any matter of importance to impart to the *House of Commons*, then the Lord Chief Justice with the other Chief Justice, or Lord Chief

 Baron,

CHAP. XIII. Baron, or some other of the Judges (but always one of them, and no more) is joyn'd with him in delivering the same; but in matters of less importance, two Masters of Chancery are imployed (as will be shewn.)

12. When any Writs of Error, or Writs of *Habeas Corpus*, or Tryals of Peers, or when any Pleas of the Crown, or other cases Criminal, Civil, and sometimes Ecclesiastick, or indeed any matters of Law are to be heard and determin'd in Parliament; as also in the penning of new, and altering, explaining or repealing of former Statutes, their assistances are required, and more especially the Chief Justice.

13. The number of Assistants Summon'd by Writ to appear in Parliament, (*Cum cæteris de Consilio*) from the time of *Henry* the Third, to the 21. of *Henry* the Eighth, consisted of an uncertain number, sometimes above fourty, sometimes under; but from the 21 of *Henry* the Eighth, (from which time the extant *Pawns* do give an exact account of them) they never exceeded 27. and sometimes were not above 13. or 14. But in all Parliaments since *Edw.* the Firsts time, some of them were Summon'd, and very likely before; For Mr. *Prin*, (though in his Breviary of Parliament Writs, *pag.* 36. he tells

tells us of Twenty four Parliaments, (from the 49. of *Hen.* the Third, to the 49. of *Edw.* the Third) and many more which he saith he omits; of which Parliaments, he saith, there is no mention of Writs of Summons to any of the Kings Council, Justices, Officers, or others in the Rolls of these Parliaments; yet he kindly ascribes it to the negligence or slothfulness of Clerks, in omitting the entries of their Writs. This he saith, but he had done much better for his own justification and others satisfaction, (being intrusted by his Majesty with the Records of the *Tower*) if those Records which he cites, (both in his *Breviary*, and many others mention'd by him in Sir *Robert Cottons Abridgment*) now wanting, might have been restored by him to their ancient Repositories there. CHAP. XIII.

14. As to the Lord Chief Justice, and the Assistants Places in the *Lords House*, none of them, as I have said, have their Places there by the Act of Precedency's, but rather by custom and favour; of which I shall speak more, when I come to the actual Sitting of the Parliament, as also of their Priviledges and Employments there.

15. As to the Officers which are under the Lord Chief Justice his Jurisdiction,

 none

CHAP. XIII. none of them are imployed about the Summoning of a Parliament, but many of them are imployed in other matters in time of Parliaments, as in cases of Errors, &c. but more chiefly upon Tryals of Peers, (when only the chief Clerk of the Crown in the *Kings Bench* is the principal Manager of them) as will be shewn.

16. Regularly no Officer or Court, either in Parliament or out of Parliament, have greater Power or Jurisdiction, or more publick affairs to manage; (except the Lord Chancellor in Chancery) and yet in some cases above it: For all appeals from the Chancery and other Courts, are determin'd in this Court, and no appeal from this Court, but to the High Court of Parliament, and all Records which are brought from other Courts into this, are never return'd back into those Courts from whence they were brought, and many others which might be instanc't.

17. To conclude, his Lordship, or the other Lord Chief Justice, or one of them, are constantly appointed to be Speaker of the *House of Lords*, *Pro tempore*, when the Lord Chancellor or Lord Keeper is absent, which is usually done by a particular Writ, which I shall enter amongst emergent Writs, *Chap.* 14.

Thus

Thus having said as much as I think convenient concerning this Exemplar, with some intermixtures of some of the Consimilars, I proceed to give a short touch of each of the Consimilars more distinctly; and first of the Master of the Rolls. CHAP. XIII.

Of the Consimilar Writ to the Master of the Rolls.

1. THE Office of Master of the Rolls is granted by Patent under several Titles, *viz. Clericus parvæ Bugæ & Custos Rotulorum & Magister Domus Conversorum*, and he Sits in the Rolls to hear Causes, *&c.* by vertue of a Commission to that purpose.

2. But his Writ of Summons to a Parliament is directed as in this Pawn, *viz. Harbotello Grimston Baronetto Magistro Rotulorum Cancellariæ suæ*, and then the remaining part of his Consimilar, as also the rest of the following Consimilar Writs, agree in the same words with the Exemplar to the Lord Chief Justice, as in Sect. the Eleventh.

3. This *Magister Rotulorum*, or *Custos Rotulorum*, or *Clericus parvæ bugæ*, is the same which we call in *English* Master of the Rolls, anciently call'd Clerk of the Rolls;

CHAP. XIII. Rolls; but from *Henry* the Sevenths time, when the Clergy did decline in their Temporal Imployments, he was and is still call'd Master of the Rolls.

4. In the absence of the Lord Chancellor or Lord Keeper, he Sits as Judge in the *Chancery*, and therefore by Sir *Edward Coke* is call'd his Assistant, and at other times he Sits as Judge of Causes in the Chappel of that House, which in *Henry* the Thirds time, was imployed as a place of Charity to such *Jews* as should turn to the *Christian Religion*; but those *Jews* being Banish't, *Edward* the Third did dispose of it for the keeping of Records, and joined it to the Office of *Custos Rotulorum*, and of the *Pettibag*, (which Office of *Pettibag* seems to be a lesser Bag or place of Records.)

5. So that he hath three Titles, *viz. Clericus Pettibagæ*, or Clerk of the *Pettibag*; (he being the chief of three Clerks more of that Office) Secondly, *Magister Rotulorum*, or Master of the *Rolls*, (or Clerk or Preserver of such Records as do at any time pass the Great Seal, and are sent to his Custody, either in the Office of the *Rolls*, called the *Rolls Office*, or to the *Pettibag Office*) where his under Clerks do attend on purpose to produce them as occasions require.

Thirdly

Thirdly, His third Title is Master of the *Chancery*, which Title is given to twelve Persons, of which twelve he is te chief. CHAP. XIII.

5. Formerly, and even to this day, the greatest part of these Twelve were Constituted of Doctors of the Civil Law; however Eleven of those are so constantly dispos'd of, as that some of them do Sit in the *Lords House* in time of Parliament, and at other times with the Lord Chancellor in the Court of *Chancery* upon hearing of Cases, others with the Master of the Rolls, when he Sits in the *Chancery*, or at the *Rolls*, where he hath a Jurisdiction to hear or determin Causes, yet appealable to the Lord Chancellor.

5. There are other Masters of *Chancery*, call'd Extraordinary, and six Clerks of eminent Quality, and other Clerks imployed both in the *Chancery* and *Rolls*; but these are not Summon'd to Parliaments; (of whom I shall speak more) but in in those capacities which I have mention'd, the Master of the *Rolls*, as Master of the *Rolls*, or chief Clerk of the *Pettibag*, or both, or chief Master of *Chancery*, or in all three Capacities, he is very Assisting to a Parliament, especially in the business of Summons, &c.

CHAP. XIII. For as I have shewn in *Cap.* 2. whenever the Kings Warrant is sent to the Lord Chancellor to issue out Writs for a Parliament, his Lordship either sends it, or a like Warrant, to the Master of the *Rolls*, who as chief Clerk of the *Pettibag* causeth the other Clerks of the Office to ingross all the Writs, (both for the *House of Lords* and *House of Commons*) so as they may be fit for the Great Seal; and these being thus done, and fairly abstracted and ingross't into a Roll, (which is call'd the Parliament *Pawn*, and lies there as a Memorial and Record of what they have done, and as a President for the future) all the particular Writs mention'd or intimated in that *Pawn* (being fitted) are carried to the Lord Chancellor; and being in his presence Seal'd, they are immediately delivered to Messengers belonging to the Chancellor, who do take care to dispose some to the Persons to be Summon'd for the *Lords House*, and others to the respective Sheriffs of all Counties, and Comitated Cities, for Elections of such as are to sit in the *House of Commons*, and so the Master of the *Rolls* and the Clerks of the *Pettibag* having done all their parts, and the Messengers and Sheriffs theirs, the same Writs which concern the *Lords House* are or ought to be return'd to the Clerk

Clerk of the *Lords House* at the first Sit- ting, and the Writs for Elections are to be return'd by the respective Sheriffs to the Clerk of the *Chancery Crown Office*, and not to the *Pettibag*, (as hath and will be shewn) for they come no more there till some time after Dissolution of a Parliament; and then for ease of that Office, and more safely preserving them, they are order'd to be carried to the Rolls, and from thence to the *Tower*, all which will be more fully shewn; which method I often repeat in this Treatise, because I find it so much neglected.

CHAP. XIII.

As to the Imployment of the other Eleven Masters of the *Chancery* in time of Parliament, I shall shew it in a distinct Chapter.

This Master of the *Rolls* doubtless hath been anciently Summon'd to Sit in the *Lords House*; yet I find no Writs issued to him till the 36*th*. of *Henry* the Eighth, and then as Master of the *Rolls*, not as chief Master of *Chancery*; and after that he was Summon'd to all Parliaments except the 39*th*. of *Eliz*. and first of King *James*; and in this very Parliament a Writ was prepared for him, but being Elected a Member of the *House of Commons*, his attendance was not requir'd in the *House of Lords*, for what reason I know not; but

but he hath his place whenever he Sits there, next to the Lord Chief Justice of *England*, upon the second Woolsack, as will be shewn in the Chapter of Places.

The Consimilar Writ to the Chief Justice of the Common-Pleas.

THE Patent which invests this Chief Justice to his Imployment in this Office, is *in hæc verba.*——— *Carolus*, &c. *Omnibus ad quos Patentes Litteræ nostræ pervenerint salutem Sciatis quod Constituimus dilectum & fidelem Orlandum Bridgman Militem Capital' Justitiarium nostrum de Banco suo, Duran' bene placito Teste*, &c.

Observations.

HIS Writ of Summons to Sit in Parliament, is also *Capitali Justitiario nostro de Banco*, (*mutato nomine*, in all other words agreeing with the Exemplar) and here it may be again observed, to prevent vulgar misunderstandings, That the Lord Chief Justice of *England* is Chief Justice of the *Kings Bench* or upper *Bench*; and this is Chief Justice of the *Common Bench*;

Bench; and sometimes one is call'd Chief Justice of the *Pleas of the Crown*, as in the *Latin* words, *De placitis Coronæ*, and this Chief Justice of the *Common-Pleas*, or *Communia Placita*, yet in the *Latin* Writ it is *de Banco*; so as both Courts are call'd Bancks or Benches, and both call'd also Courts of Pleas, in respect of Pleas or Pleadings; one properly concerns the King in matters Criminal; the other concerns the Pleas or Pleadings of the Commonalty or Common People among themselves in matters Civil, and one also is call'd the Upper Bench, the other the Common Bench, and therefore (what ever the Patent or Writs are, yet for an easier distinction) I here intitle one, the Chief Justice of the *Kings Bench*, the other Chief Justice of the *Common-Pleas*. CHAP. XIII.

2. As for the names *Bench* or *Banc*, *Pleas* or *Placita*, I refer them to my *Annotations*.

3. The Chief Justice hath three more Justices to assist him in this Court.

4. That which makes the eminency of this Court is, That only the learned Serjeants of the *Coife* (of whom I shall speak in order, being the next Degree to Judges) do Plead in this Court, (yet not prohibited from Pleading in all other Courts) but all other Graduans of Law have

CHAP. XIII. have the liberty to Plead in all other Courts, but not in this.

5. The Pleas of this Court cannot be so well ascertain'd, as that of the *Kings Bench*, because the Pleas held by Common Persons, or between Subject and Subject, are devided into as many Branches as Actions, and the Actions into as many Causes as there are variety of Contests in the Kingdom; yet all these Actions, Causes and Contests, are included under three notions, Real, Personal, and Mixt, which are here tried as they happen according to the strict Rules of Law. As for Personal and Mixt Actions they are tried in other Courts, but Real Actions are only Pleadable here, nor are any Fines of Concord (which is observable) levied in any Court but this, so that (as Sir *Edward Coke* saith) the Motto of this Court may be, *Hæc est finalis Concordia.*

6. Upon these and other considerations, the necessity of requiring Assistances from the Justices of this Court may appear: For as the Justices of the *Kings Bench* may acquaint the Lords with what concerns the King; so the Justices of the *Common Pleas* may most properly acquaint them with what concerns the People, whereby Laws for either may be corrected, repeal'd, or made *de novo*, as shall be thought most expedient.

The

7. The Justices of this Court are not concern'd in the managing of any Summons to a Parliament, as the Lord Chancellor and Master of the *Rolls* are. CHAP. XIII.

Of the Consimilar Writ to the Chief Baron of the Exchequer.

THE Title of this is different from the two Chief Justices, for his Pattent is thus.

Carolus, &c. *Omnibus ad quos Patentes Litteræ nostræ pervenerint Sciatis quod constituimus Matthæum Hale Militem Capitalem Baronem Scaccarij nostri duran' bene placito Teste*, &c. (*Scaccarius* being that which we call *Exchequer*.)

But his Writ of Summons to a Parliament is (with this addition, *Dilecto & Fideli Matthæo Hale*, (then as in the Exemplar Writ omitting *Durante bene placito*) and so in all the Assisting Writs, because the continuance of a Parliament (as I said) is but *Durante Placito Regis*, therefore needless to insert it.

Obser-

CHAP. XIII.

Observations.

THIS Chief Baron hath four more Barons to assist him in his proper Court of the *Exchequer*, whereof the puisne, or youngest made Baron of the four, is not an *Itinerant Justice*, nor accounted in the number of the Twelve Judges.

2. These Barons are not such as are before mention'd of the next Degree to Viscounts in the *Lords House*, nor such as are meerly Barons by Courtesy, or Barons of Court Barons, or Barons of the *Cinqueports*, (of whom I shall speak more, when I treat of them in the *House of Commons*) but are great Officers of Justice; and so his Writ calls him *Baro Scaccarij*, or Baron of an Officiate Place; but the Writ to the noble Baron before mention'd, is to an Hereditary Place, *viz. John Nevil, Baro de Abergaveny*, and so to others of that Degree.

3. Some think they were call'd Barons, because the Court of *Exchequer* was anciently manag'd by noble Barons; but as *Okham* saith, that these Barons were to be *Majores & Discretiores*, &c. being either cull'd out of the Clergy or Laity, or the Kings Court; and for many ages, the chief

chief of these five Barons was call'd as now, (both in his Patent and Writ) *Capitalis Baro*, and generally is Intitled the Lord Chief Baron: the other four Barons do assist him in all matters between the King and his Subjects, in cases properly appertaining to Assize, Exchequer, or the Kings Revenue. CHAP. XIII.

4. He is the chief Judge of that Court in matters of Law, as also of Informations of any abuses therein, and of Pleas upon them, and solely gives order for Judgment, (wherein the Lord Treasurer thinks not fit to concern himself.)

5. He alone without other Barons in Term time, Sits in Afternoons at *Guildhall*, upon *Nisi prius*, (upon cases which arise in *London*, and cannot be dispatch't in the Mornings) he takes Recognizances of Debt, Appearances, and Observances of Orders, he takes the Presentations of all Offices unto himself, and causeth an Oath to be given to the Lord Mayor of *London*. He takes Audits, Accounts, &c. in his absence, and sometimes to ease him, the second and third Baron hath the like power, and the fourth takes the Oath of Sheriffs; and as I said, the three first of the five have constantly their Writs of Summons to a Parliament, yet the fifth is also of good use in that Office, but hath

CHAP. XIII. hath no Writ of Summons as the other.

6. That which is most observable of this Court is, that all Cases of great difficulty in the *Kings Bench* or *Common-Pleas*, are still Adjourn'd to the *Exchequer Chamber*, and there with the Barons Debated, Argued, and Resolved by all the Twelve Judges, (whereof the four first Barons make four of the Twelve.)

7. This Court consists of two parts, the upper *Exchequer* and the lower; the upper is that wherein these Barons do execute their Justice: but herein the Lord Treasurer, as Supervisor, may Sit as oft as he pleaseth, however once in every Term he seldom fails to Sit, and hear Matters; but the lower *Exchequer* is chiefly under the care of the Lord Treasurer, (the Offices of upper and lower being distinct) yet both of them (considered jointly under the Title of the *Exchequer*) do include eight Courts or Offices, *viz.* A *Court of Pleas*; (in some manner like the *Kings Bench* and *Common-Pleas*) Secondly, The *Court of Accounts*; Thirdly, The *Court of Receipts*; Fourthly, The *Court of the Exchequer Chamber*; (being for the Assembly of all the Judges of *England* (as I said) for Matters in Law for special Verdict; Fifthly, The *Court of Exchequer Chamber*, for Errors in the Court

Court of *Exchequer*; Sixthly, The *Court* CHAP. XIII.
of Exchequer Chamber, for Errors in the Court of *Kings Bench*; Seventhly, The *Court of Equity*, in the *Exchequer Chamber*; Eighthly, That which was, but is not now call'd a Court, yet is an Office much of the ſame nature, (and of as great concern as ſome of the other) Intituled the *Remembrancers Office of the firſt Fruits and Tenths*, who takes all Compoſitions, and makes out all proceſs for ſuch as do not pay the ſame; ſo that the buſineſs of this Court and incluſive Courts and Offices doth imploy above 200. Officers and Clerks.

8. From which may be computed what variety of buſineſs this Court doth afford to a Parliament, though not in the troubles of Summoning it, yet by bringing in and iſſuing out of Money, (which are the Nerves of a Kingdom, and Arteries of a Parliament) ſo as the Progreſſes of this (and the incluſive Courts) do occaſion more Debates in Parliament, than what ever do ariſe from the *Chancery*, *Rolls*, *Kings Bench*, or *Common-Pleas*.

Having done with the firſt Orb or Rank of Degrees of ſuch Profeſſors of the Law as are Summond to Parliaments, conſiſting of five, *viz.* Lord Chancellor, Lord Chief Juſtice of the *Kings Bench*, Maſter

CHAP. XIII. of the *Rolls*, Lord Chief Justice of the *Common Pleas*, and Lord Chief Baron; I shall proceed to the second Orb or Rank of Degrees usually Summon'd; and these are three Justices of the *Kings Bench*, three Justices of the *Common Pleas*, and three Barons of the *Exchequer*, whose Writs are also Consimilary to that of the Lord Chief Justice of the *Kings Bench*.

The Consimilar Writ to the three Justices of the Kings Bench.

EACH of these Justices have their distinct Patents in these words.

1. *Carolus*, &c. *Omnibus*, &c. *Sciatis quod constituimus*, &c. *Tho. Mallet Militem unum Justitiariorum suorum ad placita coram*, &c. *Teste*, &c.

2. His Parliament Writ hath also the same words in the Dative Case, *Uni Justitiariorum suorum*.

3. *Tho. Twisden Miles*, had his Patent and Parliament Writ in the same words, *Unum & Uni*.

4. *Wodham Windham*, had also his Pattent and Writ in the same words, *Unum & Uni*.

Of

CHAP. XIII.

Of the Consimilar Writs to the three Justices of the Common Pleas.

1. ROB. *Hide Mil.* had his Patent of Constituting him, *Unum Justiciarium suorum*, and his Parliament Writ, *Uni Justitiariorum.*

2. *Tho. Tyrrill Mil.* had the like Patent of Constituting him, *Unum*, and his Parliament Writ, *Uni.*

3. *Samuel Brown Mil.* had the like Patent of Constituting him, *Unum*, and his Parliament Writ, *Uni.*

Of the Consimilar Writs to the three Barons of the Exchequer.

1. EDward *Atkins Mil.* had his Patent of Constituting him, *Unum Baronum de Scaccario*, and in his Parliament Writ, *Uni Baronum de Scaccario.*

2. *Christopher Turner Mil.* had the like Patent of Constituting him, *Unum*, and his Parliament Writ, *Uni.*

3. This place was vacant, so but eight of the nine Judges were Summon'd to this Parliament at the time of Summoning.

CHAP. XIII.

Obſervations.

1. ALL their Patents and Writs (except the mutation of their Names and Titles) are *verbatim* the ſame, eſpecially in the words, *Unum & Uni*, *viz.* one of the Juſtices, ſignifying that they were all ſo equally preſum'd to be juſt, that they are rendered to us rather by an Unity than a Priority, *viz.* by one and one, and not by *1ſt. 2d. 3d.* and *4th.* yet in the *30th.* and *39th.* of *Eliz.* and 1. *Jacob.* I find the word alter, next to *Capitalis*, *& Unus*, in the *Kings Bench* and *Common Pleas* only, but in the *Exchequer*, in the 43. *Eliz.* next *Capitalis Baro*, is *Secundus & tertius Baro.*

2. Of theſe fourteen which are of the firſt and ſecond Rank of the Profeſſors of the Law, two of them are properly Judges of matters of Equity, *viz.* the Lord Chancellor, and Maſter of the *Rolls*, the other Twelve are call'd the Twelve Judges of the Common-Law; the two Judges of Equity have been conſtantly Summon'd to Parliaments; (except as I have ſhewn) but as to the Twelve, ſometimes all, and ſometimes but ſome of them are Summon'd, according to the Kings Pleaſure, or the vacancy of their

Places

Places, or imployed in their *Itinerances*. I need not begin higher than *Henry* the 8. and then there were nine Summon'd, and the 30*th*. of *Henry* the Eighth, twelve; the 36*th*. of *Henry* the Eighth, but six; the first of *Edward* 6*th*. nine; the 6*th*. of *Edward* the Sixth, nine; the 7*th*. of *Edw*. 6*th*. but seven; the first of *Mary*, but eight; the first of *Mary*, but five; the first and second of *Phil*. and *Mary*, but 6. the second and third of *Phil*. and *Mary*, 8. the 4*th*. and 5*th*. of *Phil*. and *Mary*, but eight; the 28*th*. of *Eliz*. eleven; the 30*th*. *Eliz*. eleven; the 35*th*. *Eliz*. twelve; the 39. *Eliz*. eleven; the 43. *Eliz*. ten; the first of *James*, the full number of 12. (but in respect of the changing of them before the Parliament sate, there were two Writs made for the several Judges before the Parliament sate;) the 21. *Jac*. eleven; the first *Car. primi*, twelve; the 15*th*. *Caroli primi*, eleven; and the 13*th*. *Caroli Secundi*, also eleven; as I said, accounting the two Chief Justices and chief Barons in all these years.

3. In all these Writs, I do not so much trust to the several *Pawns*, as to the Writs themselves, where I doubt of any mistakes in the Clerks.

CHAP. XIII. 4. To conclude this Section; as in all the Judicial and Equitable Courts, (before mention'd) there are diftinct Jurifdictions and methods of managing the concerns of their refpective Courts; fo in many things, there are alfo excellent intermixtures and concurring Authorities of their Courts and Powers, whereby they make up the Harmony of Juftice, (as in cafes of Confult in the *Chequer Chamber*, Writs of Error, and other matters which I have hinted) and whoever will take a full furvey, not only of their Jurifdictions, but of the number of their Clerks, Attorneys, or other Officers of various Appellations, belonging to their refpective Courts; may think that they are fo many Principalities within our Kingdom, and thereby fee how neceffary it is for thefe Affiftants (who have fo great influence over the whole Kingdom) to be Summon'd to this *Supream Judicatory*, to Advife either the Corroborating the old Laws, or altering them, or making new, where there is juft occafion (as I have fhewn) of Reviving, Correcting, or inlarging them, according to the fluctuations of Affairs, which not only happens in this Kingdom, but in all other Kingdoms and States, fo as Laws are ftill fuited to the tempers and difpofitions of thofe who are to be govern'd; for

Tempora

Tempora mutantur, & nos mutamur in illis, there being a secret confederacy between time and human affairs, which can scarce be discovered; the time was, is, and to come, being so nice, that the future reverts into a Præ-existence, that to an existence, and so into a circular perpetuity of notional gradations. CHAP. XIII.

And thus having, as briefly as I could, dispatch't the first and second Orb of Professors of Law; I proceed to the third, which consists of the Kings Serjeants at Law, the Kings Attorney General, his Solicitor General, and his Secretaries.

Of the Consimilar Writs to the Kings Serjeants, &c.

I Am now to treat of the third Orb or Degrees of the Professors of the Law, *viz.* the Kings Serjeants at Law, the Kings Attorney General, the Kings Solicitor General, and the Kings Secretaries, (and some others of the Kings Council upon emergent occasions.)

These Serjeants at Law in the *Latin* appelation are call'd, *Servientes ad Legem,* for Serjeant and Servant are the same,

CHAP. XIII. only differing by a vulgar Pronunciation, or the Idiom of our Language, which often renders an A. for an E; for properly Servant ought to be writ Servient, from *Servio* to Serve, or from *Servare* to Keep, ſo as they may be ſaid to be as well Keepers of the Laws, as Servients to the Law.

As theſe are *Servientes ad Legem*, ſo there are another ſort, (of which I ſhall ſpeak) who are Attendants in the *Lords Houſe*, call'd *Servientes ad Arma*, but *Cedant Arma togæ*; therefore I proceed to Serjeants at Law.

The Gradations to this Title are thus attain'd, *viz.* After the young Students of the Law have continued Seven Years in the Inns of Courts, and have done their Moots, or *Motus ad Literarum*, and other exerciſes, they are called or admitted to plead at the Bar of any Court, (except the *Common-Pleas*) and are thereupon called Barreſters, and thereby alſo gain the Title of Eſquire. And after that, they are promoted to be Readers of Law in the Inns of *Chancery*, whereof there are eight, *viz. Cliffords*-Inn, *Lions*, *Clements*, *Barnards*, *Staple*, *Furnivals*, *Davis*, and *New-Inn*, which are dependent on the four Inns of Court, *viz.* the *Inner Temple*, *Gray's-Inn*, *Lincolns-Inn*, and the *Middle-Temple*, in ſome one of which they are to be be Benchers and Readers alſo; and thus they are to paſs ſeventeen Years in their Studies, before they can arrive to the dignity of a Serjeant, or *Serviens ad Legem*; but after they have perform'd their Readings, the King taking notice of their Proficiencies, doth by his Writ call a certain number of them to take upon them that Dignity; and the reaſon of making a number of ten or more (at one time) is becauſe the charge to each may be the leſs, becauſe almoſt no Dignity in any Profeſſion (eſpecially of Law) is uſher'd in with greater State, Ceremony, and Charge than this Degree, as may be read in *Fortiſcue de legibus Angliæ*, *Crooks* Reports, &c. The Form of which Writ for Electing of a Serjeant is *in hæc verba*.

Carolus Secundus Dei gratia (as in other Writs) *Fideli noſtro* I. M. *Mil. Salutem, Quia de adviſamento concilij noſtri ordinavimus vos ad ſtatum & gradum Servient' ad Legem immediate poſt receptionem hujus Brevis noſtri Suſcipiend' Vobis Mandamus firmiter injungend' quod vos ad ſtatum & gradum predict in forma predict Suſcipiend' Ordinatis preparatis & hoc ſub pœna mille Librarum nullatenus omittatis, Teſte, &c.*

Barker.

These

CHAP. XIII. These Serjeants at Law are of two sorts, *viz.* Serjeants at Law considered in their General Appellation, and the Kings Serjeants at Law; that is, when the King selects some out of the rest, and appropriates their Service to his occasions; (which he constantly doth at every Call) thereupon they have two Writs, one at the general Call of Serjeants, (which I have shewed) the other as a particular Serjeant (or Servant) to the King, the Form of which Writ also is as follows.

C*Arolus Secundus*, &c. (as in other Writs) *omnibus ad quos*, &c. *Sciatis quod nos de gratia nostra speciali, ex certa scientia & mero motu nostro constituimus dilectum & fidelem nostrum*, J. M. *servientem ad legem, unum Servientem nostrorum ad legem, nec non concessimus eidem*, J. M. *Officium unius Servient' nostror, ad legem habendum occupandum & exercend' dict' officium nec non ad essendum unum' Servient' nostrorum ad legem quamdiu nobis placuerit, capiendum & percipiend anuatim in & pro officio illo exercend' eidem* J. M. *vad' fead' vestur' & regard' dict' officio debito sive pertinend' pro ut aliquis Servient' nostrorum ad legem pro hujusmodi officio exercend' percepit, sive habere, & precipere debeat eo quod expres a mentio non*

non fit, &c. In cujus rei testimonium, &c. Teste, &c. CHAP. XIII.

Per ipsum Regem.

Barker.

And being thus made the Kings Serjeants by a distinct Writ, they are capacitated to have a Writ of Summons to sit in the *Lords House* in Parliament, and though none sit this Parliament, yet Writs were provided for two of them, in this Form following, *viz.*

Carolus, &c. *dilecto & fideli suo* Johanni Glin *Militi* Servienti domino Regi ad legem *Quia*, *&c.* and so *verbatim* according to the Exemplar before recited to the Lord Chief Justice.

The other was *Johanni Maynard militi*, who had the like Writ prepared for him.

Observations.

1. THESE Professors of Law are call'd *Servientes ad Legem* in all Writs, (which are generally Writ in *Latin*) but in *English* (as I said) they are called

CHAP. XIII. called Serjeants or Servants at Law, also Serjeant of the Coif, (from the white Coif which they wear uppermost at the Solemnization of their Order) but at other times under a black Cap, like the Twelve Judges, because having past this Order, they are then capable of being made one of the Twelve Judges, and to exercise the imployment of a Judge upon emergent occasions.

2. None of all the three Orbs of Professors have a Writ for their Office and Imployment, but the Lord Chief Justice of the *Kings Bench*, (as I have shewn) and these Serjeants at Law. The difference in the Writs are, that in the Writ to the Lord Chief Justice of the *Kings Bench*, (as to his Office) and so in the Patents to the other Justices, (as to their Offices) there is nothing but a *Constituimus*, without any adjunct of Compliment, but in this Writ to the Serjeants at Law, it is *Fideli nostro*; yet in both of their Writs of Summons to a Parliament, they have equal words, *viz. Dilecto & Fideli.*

3. In the Writ of the Lord Chief Justice of the *Kings Bench*, there is no Advice of Council mention'd; but in the Writ to every Serjeant at Law, the words are as in Parliament Writs, *Quia de advisamento concilij nostri*, aud so in the Manda-

Mandatory part of it, *Vobis Mandamus* *firmiter injungend'*, and then under the penalty of a 1000 *l.* to take upon them that Degree; and in their second Writ to be the Kings Serjeant at Law, they have *Vadage*, *Feodage*, *Vesturage*, & *Regardage*, of which I shall speak in my *Annotations*; yet I shall give this hint here, That the word *Investitura* is us'd only in the Patents of Creation of the Lords Temporal, and *Vestura* only us'd in the Patents to the Serjeants at Law, and to no other Degree that sit in the *Lords House* as Peers, or Assistants.

4. That which makes this Degree more eminent is, that by virtue of the first Writ, (to be a Serjeant at Law in general) they continue their Title of Serjeant at Law, *Durante vita*; (though not exprest in the Writ) the other to be the Kings Serjeant at Law is equal with that Writ to the Lord Chief Justice of the *Kings Bench*, and to the other Eleven Justices, *viz.* *Durante beneplacito*; the 3*d.* Writ gives him an interest in Parliament.

5. It is to be noted, That all the twelve Judges before they can take upon them those Offices of Judges, are made Serjeants at Law; so that though they quit those Offices of Judges, and thereby lose the dignity of their Office, yet the dignity

CHAP. XIII. dignity of their Serjeantship still remains during life.

6. It may be here pertinently observed, That though Writs were prepar'd and inroll'd in the *Pettibag* for these two Serjeants, yet whether the Writs were delivered to them, I cannot inform my self, or whether the delivery was declined in respect both of them were chosen Burgesses of the *House of Commons*, (where Sir *John Glyn* did sit during his life, and Sir *John Maynard* during the continuance of this Parliament) or whether they were conniv'd at, as being more ueful in the *House of Commons*, (or to themselves) for being once admitted to sit in the *Lords House*, they might not Plead in other inferior Courts, which had been much to their prejudice.

7. The Kings Attorney is placed in this *Pawn* before the two Serjeants, which was some mistake in the Clerks; and so I find the like misplacings of others in many other *Pawns*; and therefore in this my method, I pursue the order of all such other Solemnities as they usually attend, and of their precedent sitting in the *House of Lords*, (as will be shewn) and so place them here, as they are placed there.

8. As to the Antiquity and number of Serjeants which were formerly Summoned

ed to Parliaments, it is manifest that more or less of them were Summond in most Parliaments of former Kings, *viz.* in the Reign of *Edw.* 3*d.* *Rich.* 2*d.* *Hen.* 5*th.* and *Hen.* 6*th.* (as appears in the Clause Rolls of those Parliaments) and more easily seen in Mr. *Prinns Breviary*, or in the Rolls Chappel; (for it were too great a diversion to recite them here) but those of latter days do appear thus in the *Pettibag*, *viz.* in the 21. *Hen.* 8*th.* there were three Summon'd; but in the 30*th.* none; in the 36*th.* of *Hen.* 8*th.* four; in the first of *Edw.* the 6*th.* three; in the 6. of *Edw.* 6*th.* four; in the 7*th.* of *Edw.* 6*th.* four; in the first of *Mary*, two; and also in the first of *Mary*, two; and in the first and second of *Phil.* and *Mary*, one; in the second and third of *Philip* and *Mary*, one; and in the 4*th.* and 5*th.* of *Philip* and *Mary*, two; in the 28*th.* of *Eliz.* two; in the 30*th.* of *Eliz.* one; in the 35*th.* of *Eliz.* three; in the 39*th.* of *Eliz.* one; in the first of *Jacob.* three; in the 21. of *Jac.* five; in the first *Car. prim.* four; in the 15. *Car.* 1. three; in the 13*th.* *Car.* 2*d.* the two before mentioned; for whom Writs were order'd, but not actually Summond, (as I have shewn.)

CHAP. XIII.

9. In the 39*th.* *Eliz.* the Writs to the three Serjeants are directed distinctly,

Uni,

CHAP XII. *Uni, Uni, & Uni*, but in all the rest, *Servienti ad Legem*, without the addition of *Uni*, nor do I find *Uni* added in any former Writs, before *Henry* the Eighth, but only this, *viz.* 4 *Hen.* 5*th. Johanni Stranguayes, Uno Servienti Regis ad Legem.*

10. And as a peculiar distinction, the Kings eldest Serjeants have the Priviledge to Plead in all Courts of *Westminster* within the Bar, but only in the *Common Pleas*, (where no other Graduats of Law but themselves can Plead, as I have shewn) and there all the Serjeants stand without the Bar.

11. They are also sometimes Assistants to the Judges, and to the Lord Chancellor and Master of the Rolls, and many times in case of age or infirmness of the Judges, they do supply their places, both in the Courts of *Westminster*, and in their Itinerances and Circuits, *Pro hac vice*, and upon death of any of them, if the King think fitting, they are Constituted Judges in their Vacancies, and this by Commission.

12. As to their places in Parliament, they are next the Judges, as shall be shewn in the local part of this Treatise, as also of their Imploymens, *sedente Parliamento.*

Thus having brought the *Servientes ad Legem*, to be *Judices & Magistros legum*, I pass

I pass to the second Degree of the third Orb or Rank, *viz.* the Kings Attorney General. CHAP. XIII.

The Consimilar Writ to the Kings Attorney General.

THis appellation of Attorney is deriv'd from *Tourne* so call'd in *Magna Charta*, which anciently was call'd the *Sheriffs Moot*, or view of *Frankpledge*, and to this day is call'd the *Sheriffs Tourne* from *Turris*, signifying a Tower or Castle where these Courts were kept, and where inquiry is made upon Oath of all things done contrary to the peace of the Countrey, &c. as will be shewn when I come to the *House of Commons*; and then those who did practise to those ends in those and other Courts, were call'd *Ad Tourny's* or *Attourny's*; generally the word doth signifie a Person intrusted to manage other mens Concerns. And this being the most Eminent Trust in managing the Kings Concerns, his Duty, Care and Pains is the greater and more Eminent; he hath also his Patent, *In hæc verba.* SECT. 17.

CHAP. XIII.

Carolus Secundus, &c. *Omnibus ad quos*, &c. *Salutem. Sciatis quod nos de fidelitate & Circumspectione dilecti & fidelis nostri*, G. P. *Mil. plurimum confidentes ipsum* G. F. *Constituimus Ordinavimus deputavimus & assignavimus nostrum Generalem Attornatum in omnibus curijs nostris de Record' in Regno nostro Angliæ Habendum & occupand' officium hujusmodi Generalis Attornat' nostri prefat'* G. F. *quamdiu nobis placuerit percipiend' in & pro officio illo exercend' Vad' Feod' Profic' & Regard' eidem officio pretinend' sive consuet' Dedimus etiam ac tenore presentium damus prefat'* G. F. *plenam potestatem & authoritatem faciend' ordinand' & deputand' tales clericos & officiar' sub seipso in quolibet Cur' nostra quales aliquis alius officium illud proantea habens nomine occupans habuit fecit ordinavit seu deputavit aut facere ordinare seu deputare consuevit eo quod expressa mentio*, &c. *In cujus rei*, &c, *Teste*, &c.

And he hath his Writ of Summons to a Parliament also, *In hæc verba*, *Carolus*, &c. *Dilecto & fideli Galfrido* (which we in *English* call *Jeffery*) *Palmer Militi, Attornato suo generali salutem*, and so *verbatim* according to the Exemplar.

Obser-

CHAP. XIII.

Observations.

1. THat which makes this Assistant the more eminent and remarkable is, That as there is but one Lord Chancellor or Keeper, one Lord Chief Justice of the *Kings Bench*, one Master of the Rolls, one Chief Justice of the *Common Pleas*, and one chief Baron of the *Exchequer*; so there is but one Attorney General: and though those five have Judges and Masters of *Chancery* to assist them; this hath no proper Officer under him, yet hath power to depute Clerks and other Officers to assist him, and is *Singulus in omnibus & omnis in singulis*.

2. Neither these nor any of the Assistants to the *Lords House* before named, have the priviledge of making Proxies either before or in time of Parliament; yet I remember something Equivalent in in the case of *Valentine Elliot*, &c. when upon a Writ of Error brought into the *Lords House*, for reversing of a Judgment given in the *Kings Bench* against the said *Elliot*, Sir *Jeffrey Palmer* being then Attorney General, and indispos'd in his health, and thereby finding himself unfit to manage that Case, Mr. *North*, then a young Professor of the Law, was permit-

CHAP. XIII. ted to appear for the Attorney General, and Plead the Caſe: only here was the difference, had Mr. *Attorney* been there in Perſon, he had ſtood within the Bar and Pleaded; but Mr *North* Pleaded without the Bar, which he manag'd with ſo much Law, Eloquence, and Dexterity, that his Abilities being known, (by uſual Degrees in few years) he was advanc't to his preſent Station of Chief Juſtice of the *Common-Pleas*.

3. This Title of Attorney General began in *Eward* the Firſts time, but I cannot be poſitive when they had their firſt Writs of Summons; but in the 21. 30. and 39. of *Hen.* 8. he had a Writ, and ſo the 1.6.7.*Edw.* the 6. alſo the 1.and 1.of *Mary*, and 2. 3. 4. and 5. *Phil.* and *Mary*, (and in thoſe two laſt Writs he is term'd, *Attornat' Dominorum Regis & Reginæ General'*) and then in the 28. 30. 39. and 43. *Eliz. Attornato Generali*; and ſo alſo the 1. and 21. of King *James*; alſo the 1. and 15. *Carol. primi*; and now 13. *Caroli Secundi*, Sir *Geffrey Palmer*, *Attornato*, and after him none did ſit in the *Houſe of Lords* during this Parliament, except Sir *William Jones* Knt. the Attorneys intervening thoſe two, being ſtill choſen in the *Houſe of Commons*, as will be ſhewn.

Of

CHAP. XIII.

Of the Consimilar Writ to the Kings Solicitor General.

THe words *Attornatus & Solicitator* are us'd in the Civil Laws, as here at the Common Law, for such as do take care to manage or tend other mens Affairs, and there is but one of that Profession (as is before shewn of the Attorney General) but because the Title should be distinguish't from the common sort of such Practisers, as the Kings Attorney hath his Patent and Writ from the King, so hath this, thereupon call'd the Kings Solicitor General, his Patent is, *In hæc verba.* SECT. 18.

C*Arolus Secundus*, &c. *Omnibus ad quos*, &c. *salutem. Sciatis quod nos de gratia nostra speciali ac ex certa scientia & mero motu nostris ordinavimus fecimus & constituimus dilectum & fidelem nostrum*, H. F. *Mil. Solicitatorem nostrum Generalem ac ipsum*, H. F. *Solicitatorem Generalem nostrum per presentes ordinavimus fecimus & constituimus Habendum gaudend occupand & exercend officium illud quamdiu nobis placuerit Percipiend annuatim eidem*, H. F. *pro occupatione & exercic' officij predicti tal' & tant' Vad. Feod. Profic' & commoditat'*

 moditat' qual' & quanta dicto officio debito ſive pertinend prout aliquis alius ſive aliqui alij officium predict' proantea habens ſive occupans habuit vel percepit habuerunt ſive preceperunt in & pro exercitio ejuſdem officij eo quod expreſſa mentio, &c. *In Cujus rei*, &c. *Teſte*, &c.

Obſervations.

THough this Imployment was granted by Patent in *Edward* the Fourths time, yet for want of time I ſhall alſo begin his Writ of Summons, the 21. of *Henry* the Eight; and then *Edward Griffin* being Attorney General, *Goſnold* was Solicitor, and the Writ was, *Hen. Rex*, &c. *Dilecto & fideli ſuo Johanni Goſnold Solicitatori ſuo Salutem Quia*, and ſo *verbatim* according to the Exemplar; in the 36 *Hen.* 8. *William Whorwood* was Attorney General, and *Henry Bradſhaw* Solicitor, and had his Writ the firſt of *Edw.* the Sixth, *Bradſhaw* was made Attorney General, and *Edward Griffin* Solicitor, and had his Writ; and the 6. of *Edw.* 6. *Griffith* was made Attorney, and *Jo. Goſnold* Solicitor, and had his Writ, and both continued ſo till the firſt of *Mary*; and then *William Cordel*, in the room of *Goſnold* was

was made Solicitor, and had his Writ, alſo in another Parliament of that year both had their Writs; in the 1. and 2, 3, and 4. of *Phil.* and *Mary*, and in the 4. and 5. *Phil.* and *Mary*, *Griffith* being Attorney General, *Rich. Weſton* (afterwards Lord Treaſurer) was made Solicitor, *Dominorum Regis & Reginæ*, and had his Writ; in the 38. of *Eliz. Jo. Popham*, afterwards Lord Chief Juſtice, was Attorney, and *Thomas Egerton* (afterwards Lord Chancellor) was Solicitor, and had his Writ, and ſo they continued to the 39. *Eliz.* and then *Edw. Coke* (after one of the Juſtices of the *Common-Pleas*) was made Attorney, and *Tho. Flemins* Solicitor, and had his Writ; and in the 43. Sir *Edw. Coke* was put back to be Solicitor, and had his Writ; and *Thomas Egerton* was Attorney; and in the firſt of *James*, *Edw. Coke* (then Knighted) was again made Attorney General, and *Tho. Flemins* (then Knighted alſo) again made Solicitor, and had his Writ; and in the 21 *Jacobi*, *Thomas Coventry Miles* (after Lord Keeper) was made Attorney, and *Robert Heath* Knt. Solicitor, (after Chief Juſtice) and had his Writ; and both had Writs again the firſt *Car. primi*; and the 15th. *Jo. Banks* Knt. was made Attorney, and *Edward Harbert* Solicitor, and had his Writ.

CHAP. XIII.

CHAP. XIII. But at the Summoning of this Parliament, no Writ was ſent to Sir *Heneage Finch* then the Kings Solicitor, being choſen for the *Houſe of Commons*, and being after made Attorney General, ſtill he continued in the *Houſe of Commons*, till he was made Lord Keeper, and then he was remov'd to the *Lords Houſe* by Writ, as Lord Keeper; and ſo Sir *Francis North* (being the Kings Solicitor) did ſit in the *Houſe of Commons* this Parliament, and was not removed thence till he was made Chief Juſtice of the *Common-Pleas*; ſo that during this Parliament, none (whilſt actually the Kings Solicitors) were Summon'd or did ſit in the *Lords Houſe*; yet I thought fit to inſert this Degree here, (though he be not mention'd in this *Pawn*) becauſe there are ſo many Precedents of his Summons, as are before recited in former Kings Reigns.

Of the Conſimilar Writ to the Kings Principal Secretaries.

SECT. 19. THis Officer of State and Aſſiſtant is plac't the laſt in moſt of the *Pawns*, and brings up the Rear of all the forementioned Aſſiſtants; which poſture is a place of great Honour, both in Civil Solemnities

ties and Martial Imployments; and that it may so appear, in the aforesaid Act of the 31. of *Hen.* the Eighth, none of the other Assistants before recited (except the Lord Chancellor) are so much as mention'd therein, (their precedencies being known in their own Courts from a greater antiquity) but the Secretaries Place is fix't by that Act, *viz.* if he be under the Degree of a Noble Baron, yet it is above all the Assistants and next the Lord Chancellor; if he be of the Degree of a Baron, then above all Barons, or if an Earl, (as in the case of the Lord *Arlington*) then above all of that Degree, unless any of the Superior Officers of State be of that Degree, and then next to him and above the rest.

He hath his Office as Secretary not by Patent, but by delivery of the Privy Signet to him; and so if there be more than one, (as now there are two) each considered as Principal, hath also a Privy Signet delivered to him.

His Parliament Writ in this *Pawn* was thus,

Carolus, &c. *Dilecto & fideli Edwardo Nicolas Militi uno primariorum Secretariorum suorum salutem Quia, &c.* and so *verbatim* according to the last mention'd Exemplar, as an Assistant, and the Title in the *Label* is like the Title of his Writ.

Obser-

CHAP. XIII.

Obſervations.

1. THis Writ agrees with all the former, except in the word *Uni*, and ſo if there be more; (as I have ſhewn in the Writ to the Judges) yet commonly in Superſcriptions, he that is made Chief is Stiled Principal without the word *one*; and the other One of the Principal Secretaries of State.

2. The word *Capitalis* is us'd in the Writs to the two Chief Juſtices and Chief Baron; but to the chief Secretary the word *Principali* is us'd, not only ſignifying the Capital, Firſt, or Chief, but intimating his more immediate Imployment on his Prince, for *Principali* is properly from *Principe*.

3. If there be more Secretaries than one, (as there are ſeldom leſs than two) they divide their negotiations into the Title of Provinces, both in relation to this Kingdom, or Foreign Kingdoms or States; and ſo each of them give an account to the King accordingly, and they have an Office appertaining to them, call'd the Signet Office, where they have four Clerks as their Subſtitutes to perform their Directions, for all Diſpatches both Foreign and Domeſtick, and generally they are of his Majeſties Privy-Council.

Signet.

4. Their

4. Their Implowments in Parliament are either in the *House of Lords* or *House of Commons*, according as they are Summon'd to one, or Elected to the other, and as the King thinks them in either place most useful for his occasions. CHAP. XIII.

5. I need not go back to find the Antiquity of their Summons, for it may be presum'd to be ancient from the Eminency and nature of their Implowments; so it may suffice only to instance here, that in the 36 *Hen.* 8. *William Packet Mil.* had his Writ, *Secretario suo*, and at the same Parliament, *William Petre Mil.* had his Writ, *Secretario suo*, without other addition; in the first of *Edw.* the Sixth, *William Petre Mil.* had his Writ only *Secretario suo*; but in the 6. of *Edw.* the *6th.* the Title alter'd, *viz. Willielmo Petro Mil. Uni primariorum Secretariorum suorum*; and to *Willielmo Cecil alt' primariorum Secretariorum*, and *Jo. Cheke Mil. alt' primariorum Secretariorum*, (so here were three Secretaries Summon'd to this Parliament) and the same three were Summon'd in the *7th.* of *Edw.* 6. and in the first of *Mary*, and 1*st.* of *Mary*, the same *Petre* was Summon'd, *Un' Primariorum Secretariorum Domini Regis*, and *Jo. Bourne Militi alt' Primariorum Secretariorum Domini Regis*; and so the 1*st.* and 2*d.* and 2*d.* and

Secretario. *Uni.* *Alteri.*

CHAP. XIII. and 3d. of *Philip* and *Mary*, the same *Petre* and *Brown* had Writs by the words, *Uni & alteri primariorum Secretariorum Domini Regis*; the 4th. and 5th. *Phil.* and *Mary*, Writs were to *Jo. Broxal*, *Uni primariorum Secretariorum Regis & Reginæ*; the like to the said *Jo. Bourne*, *Militi alt' primariorum*, &c. the 25th. *Eliz. Francisco Walsingham*, *Militi Principali Secretariorum suorum*, and no other Secretary; the 30th. *Eliz. Consiliario suo Roberto Cicil Militi Primario Secretario*, and no other; the 35th. *Eliz.* to the same *Francisco Walsingham*, *Militi principali*, &c. and no other; the 39th. *Eliz. Consiliario Roberto Cicil Primario*, and no other; 43. *Eliz.* none Summon'd; the 1 *Jacobi*, *Johanni Herbert Militi uni Primariorum*; and no other; 21 *Jacobi*, *Georgio Calvert*, *Militi uni Primariorum*, & *Edwardo Conway*, *Militi uni Primariorum*; the 1 *Car. primi*, *Olivero Vicecomiti Grandison uni Primariorum Secretariorum*, & *Johanni Cooke*, *Militi un' Primariorum*, &c. 15 *Caroli primi*, *Francisco Windibanck uni Primariorum*, & *Henr. Vane*, *Militi uni Primariorum*; and so in this 13 *Car. 2di.* the Writ was *Edwardo Nicolas*, *Militi*, *uni Primariorum Secretariorum suorum*; and no other Secretary was Summon'd during this Parliament, the rest being Elected, and accordingly

Principali.

Primario.

ingly did ſit in the *Houſe of Commons*, except the Lord *Arlington*, who ſat as Earl and Secretary in the *Lords Houſe*; and though the word *Primario* is more generally uſed in Writs, yet in Superſcriptions, &c. the word Principal is altogether uſed, as more agreeable (I conceive) to the Idiom of our Language.

CHAP. XIII.

6. The dignity of this Office is ſhewn in their Summons and Place in the *Lords Houſe* according to the Act of *Precedency*; but I muſt ſay ſomething more of the antiquity of the Office, and of the nature of ſuch are imployed in it.

If he be taken for a Scribe, becauſe they write the Kings literal Diſpatches; it had the ſame eſteem among the *Hebrews* that the *Magi* had with the *Chaldeans*, and the *Quindecemviri* among the *Romans*, (which latter were the Expounders of the Secrets of *Sybills* Oracles) Theſe Scribes were uſually ſelected out of the Clergy, and not out of the Laity, ſo that ſuch as were uſed out of the Laicks were call'd *Notarij*, and not Scribes; and ſuch as were us'd by the Clergy were call'd Clerks from *Cleros*, becauſe the Clergy by reaſon of their learning did for the moſt part Guide both Secular and Spiritual Affairs; but the word Secretary (in which Office the Clergy in former times were more commonly

CHAP. XIII. monly imployed than Laymen) doth import ſomething of another nature, being derived from *Secretum*, and that from *Cretum* the Supine of *Cerno*, to ſee or diſcern; ſo by adding *Se* to *Cretum*, it makes *Secretum*, and renders the Perſon imployed in that Office to be one who knows *Se* (*ideſt*) himſelf, and can alſo Judiciouſly diſcern and judge of other mens matters, and yet reſerve the Determination or Execution of them in his own breaſt; and for this tenacity of mind, he is properly call'd a Secretary, and the Kings Secretary, or Secretary of State, as a preſerver of the Secrets of the King and Kingdom for publick and private uſe, till juſt occaſion require their impartments to others; and indeed conſidering the perpetual Deſigns of Princes towards each other, and the Diſcontents and Seditious Humors which are in every Kingdom; there is no quality more requiſite to a Miniſter of State, than a ſecret and reſerved mind, and more particularly to this Officer, his very Title intimating his Duty, in which he ought to be maſter of three Properties; a Prudent Diſpatch, Exquiſite Intelligence, and Secrecy in all; for by theſe (eſpecially the laſt) all Minings and underminings are ſtill diſappointed by the rules of Politick Secrecy; by which Art, Kingdoms are kept

Lord Verulam.

kept in quiet, by quenching fires before they flame; and because this requires not only a great skill but as great a vigilancy, which few are capable to perform; *Bocalini* tells us in his pleasant *Chapter of reforming the World*, that to ease it of this indifatigable trouble, without using so many Meanders; *Apollo* resolved to make a Window in every mans breast, so as at first view, each man might see the thoughts and intentions of each other, and thereby prevent the prejudices which daily arise for want thereof; but before *Apollo* did execute his Resolves, he caus'd the Wise Men of *Greece* with some others of the *Literati* to be Summon'd, and to give their Opinions therein, where *Thales* was the first that press't for it with such Arguments, that *Apollo* was almost confirm'd; but at last he was disswaded by many other Lawyers, Poets, Physicians and Theologicks by more convincing Arguments, shewing that nothing caus'd a greater reverence to those and other Professions, than the mysteries which were contain'd in them, which would make them contemptible, if they should be seen or known by every vulgar Eye, whereupon the Windows were not made.

CHAP. XIII.

7. Now the same reasons which were us'd against making these Windows in the Bodies

CHAP XII. Bodies of Men, may ſerve to oppoſe the Windows too often made in the Bodies of ſuch Councils or Parliaments as are to ſupport a Kingdom, where every Member or Counſellor indeed ſhould be a Secretary of State; becauſe the publiſhing of Conſultations commonly meets with Seditious Tempers, who think nothing is well done but what is done by themſelves, looking meerly on the Fact and Succeſs, not on the Deliberations, Grounds and debated Reaſons of that Fact; for it is not the event which makes the reaſon of managing that Fact to be the leſs Reaſon; for let the event be good or bad, the reaſon is ſtill the ſame; if the Reaſon be good and ſolid, yet the Event bad, it may be ſaid, that it meets with an ill conſtellation; but if the Reaſon be bad and the Event as ill, the diſcovery of theſe do ſtill raiſe a worſe conſtellation; and if the Reaſon be bad and the Event good, (if the bad Reaſon be kept ſecret) the glory of the Event would quickly drown the cenſure of the bad Reaſon, and make the Counſellors ſtand fair; but if divulged, they are ſure not only to loſe the credit of the Event, but double the diſrepute, if both be bad.

Herein ſome men are naturally of a more reſerved temper than others; however thoſe are only fit to be Counſellors and

and Secretaries of State, who have no Windows in their Breast; that is, no ſuch transſparent Eyes, as men may eaſily ſee their diſpoſures of Affairs, but can wiſely keep the Secrets of State from other mens Inſpections: and in Parliaments I conceive ſuch Tempers are very uſeful, for if the People Truſt them, they do well in performing their Truſt; but appealing again to the People, ſhews a diffidence in their own Judgments. CHAP. XIII.

Thus having ſhewn the Kings Warrant in the Front, and the Secretaries Writ in the Rear, and fix't the Noble Lords betwixt thoſe who manage the Laws Divine, and thoſe who are Aſſiſtants in Human Laws, and run through the moſt conſtant Writs which are us'd for Summoning ſuch as are to ſit in a Parliament, either as Eſſential, or Aſſiſting Members thereof; I ſhould now proceed to the *Houſe of Commons*, but I ſhall crave leave; Firſt, To ſpeak of ſome accidentall Writs for Aſſiſtants; Secondly, Of the manner of return of all the aforeſaid Writs; Thirdly, Of ſuch as ſit there without Writ or Patent; Fourthly, Of ſuch as ſit there only by Patent; and Fifthly, Of ſome other Officers who are imployed there by vertue of Patents.

CHAP. XIV.

Of Consimilar Writs and Patents upon Emergent occasions.

1. I Find in Mr. *Prins Breviary*, That he cites many Records long before *Henry* the Eighth; (which I shall not examine, because some of them have been so long disus'd) Of Knights, Justices of *North Wales*, Treasurer of *Carnarvan*, Treasurer of the Kings House, Chancellor of the Exchequer, Deans, Archdeacons, Escheators, (and one *Magister Thomas Tong*, which he takes to be a Master of *Chancery*) that have been Summon'd by Writ to sit in Parliaments in the *Lords House*;) but since *Henry* the Eighth in the Pettibag, several Writs of Assistants were issued, as I have shewn in the 11*th*. Chap. Sect. 9. to shew the Kings Power, some of which were Professors of the Law, and some not.

2. There was another Writ, *viz.* to the Warden of the *Cinqueports*; (which was not constant, but occasional) for sometimes it was directed to an Earl, and sometimes to some one Person under the Degree of a Baron; yet by vertue of the Writ, he was impowr'd

impowr'd to sit in the *Lords House*; but since *Henry* the Fourths time, when that Office was supplied by the Prince of *Wales*, (after called *Henry* the Fifth) who had a Writ with the addition of *Guardian Quinque Portuum*) that Trust hath been committed to some one of the Blood Royal, and from that Writ other Writs are derived to all the *Cinqueports*. CHAP. XIV.

But in respect this Writ (as to a Parliament) is mostly concern'd about Election of 16. Members to serve in the *House of Commons*; I shall refer the Discourse of it to the second part, in that Chapter which particularly treats of the *Cinqueports*.

3. If at any time the Lord Chancellor or Lord Keeper be absent upon just occasion, as when the Lord Keeper *Bridgman* in this Parliament was Sick; a Patent was made for Sir *John Vaughan*, then Lord Chief Justice of the *Common Pleas*, to supply his place, and the like to Sir *Francis North*, Chief Justice of the *Common Pleas* also, &c. and though for the most part this happens in time of Parliament; yet, because it may happen between the time of Summons and the Sitting of a Parliament, (which is the chief design of this part of this Treatise) I have thought fit to enter

CHAP. XIV. the form of that Patent in this place, rather than defer it, *viz.*

CHARLES, &c. *To Our Right Trusty and Welbeloved, Sir* Francis North *Knt. Chief Justice of Our Court of* Common Pleas, *Greeting; Whereas Our Right Trusty and Welboved Councellor,* Heneage *Lord* Finch, *Our Lord High Chancellor of* England, *is often so infirm, that he is not able constantly to attend in the upper House of this Our present Parliament now holden at* Westminster, *nor there to supply the room and place in the said upper House, amongst the Lords Spiritual and Temporal there Assembled, as to the Office of the Lord Chancellor of* England *hath been accustomed: We minding the same place and room to be supplied in all things as appertaineth for and during every time of his absence, have named and appointed you: And by these Presents do Name, Constitute, and Appoint and Authorize you, from day to day, and from time to time, when and so often as the said Lord Chancellor shall happen at any time or times during this present Parliament to be absent from his accustomed place in the said upper House, to Occupy, Use and Supply the said room and place of the said Lord Chancellor, in the said upper House, amongst the Lords Spiritual and*

and Temporal there Assembled, at every such day and time of his absence, and then and there at every such time to do and execute all such things as the said Lord Chancellor of England *should or might do, if if he were there personally present, Using and Supplying the same room; Wherefore, We Will and Command you the said Sir* Francis North *to attend to the doing and execution of the premisses with Effect: and these Our Letters Patents shall be your sufficient Warrant and Discharge for the same in every respect. In Witness whereof, We have caused these Our Letters to be made Patents, Witness our Self at* Westminster *the Nineteenth day of* March, *in the Nine and twentieth Year of our Reign.* CHAP XIV.

Per ipsum Regem propria manu Signat.

And having now dispatch't all the Writs and Patents which concern the Summoning of such as sit in the *Lords House*, it is proper to shew the manner of returning of those Writs, which is usual in all Courts, and ought to be strictly observed here.

Chap. XV.

Of Returns of Writs relating to the Summoning of ſuch as are to Sit in the Lords Houſe.

IN all Judicial Courts from whence Writs do iſſue, there is care taken for their due Returns, as may be ſeen in *Fitz Herbert*, and ſuch Authors who have treated of the nature of Writs and their Returns; but none of them giving a full account of Parliament Writs and Returns, gives me occaſion to inſert this Chapter.

As to the Return of the Writs to the Lords Spiritual, and Temporal and Aſſiſtants, they ought (by every individual Perſon who had a Writ) to be deliver'd to the Clerk of the Parliament before the Houſe Sit, or immediately upon their Entrance into the Houſe, at the Table, and by the ſaid Clerk they are to be kept with the Records of that Houſe.

By the omiſſion of this method many inconveniencies have and may happen to their Succeſſors or Poſterity, and therefore it is wiſht there were more care taken in their due Returns, to which they may be incourag'd, being of ſo little trouble

trouble in the performance. But as to the return of Writs concerning the *House of Commons*, the method consists of much trouble and perplexity, not only from the time of the executing the Writs, but in undue returns, as will be shewn in their proper place.

This Chapter concluding all the Patents and Writs of Summons, and Returns which concern the *Lords House*, (by vertue of which the Persons so Summon'd by Writ do sit there) now I must speak of such as sit there without Patent or Writ of Summons; and first of the Masters of *Chancery*.

CHAP. XVI.

Of the Masters of Chancery.

1. THE Secretaries of State did bring up the Rear of the State Officers, and now the Masters of *Chancery* do bring up the Rear of the Assistants; and though I have spoke something of the Master of the Rolls, partly as chief of the twelve Masters of *Chancery*; yet, there he was considered as Master of the Rolls, (or Records) rather than one of the twelve Masters of *Chancery*, whereof (as I said) he

CHAP. XVI. he is the chief; and theſe twelve are called Maſters in Ordinary.

2. For there are alſo other Maſters in *Chancery*, called Extraordinary, which are of an uncertain number, according to the buſineſſes of the reſpective Counties wherein they are imployed.

3. As for the twelve, they uſually are choſen out of Barreſters of the Common Law, or Doctors of the Civil Law, and eleven of them do ſit in the *Chancery*, or in the Rolls as Aſſiſtants, ſaith Sir *Edward Coke*) to the Lord Chancellor and to the Maſter of the Rolls, every day throughout each Term of the year, and to them are committed Interlocutory Reports, and ſtating of Accounts, and ſometimes (by way of reference to them) they are impowr'd with a final Determination of Cauſes there depending.

4. Theſe twelve have time out of mind, ſat in the *Lords Houſe*; yet have neither Writs nor Patents (for many Ages paſt) impowering them ſo to do; but I conceive, as the Maſter of the Rolls is (as is ſaid by that Inſtitutor) an Aſſiſtant to the Lord Chancellor, the remaining eleven may fairly be ſaid to be Aſſiſtants both to the Lord Chancellor and Maſter of the Rolls, in all or moſt Matters, depending in both

or

or either Courts, and so *Virtute Officij*, they are inclusively capacitated, (by the Writs to the Lord Chancellor, or Master of the Rolls) to be Assistants to them in the *Lords House*, as they are in *Chancery*, without any particular VVrit or Patent to them. CHAP. XVI.

5. Anciently this Title was higher than what Sir *Edw. Coke* affords them; for I find in an old Manuscript in the hands of Sir *J.C.* one of the Masters, (but I have not the opportunity of searching the Records therein mentioned) Intituled, *De Cancellario Angliæ & ejus Cojudicibus, & de authoritate eorum*, and then follows, *viz. In dicta Curia Cancellarij sunt ordinati duodecem Cojudices, viz. Magistri sive Clerici de prima forma ad Robas*, (which in the 13. Chap. I call the first Orb) *pro Arduis negotis Regis & Regni, & Reipublicæ expediendis*, (which agree *verbatim* (and 'tis observable) with the very words of all Writs of Summons to Parliaments) *eidem Cancellario omnino assistentes & secum continuo consedentes*, (which in a manner Intitles them to sit in the *Lords House* with him) and many other matters are mentioned therein, which I shall refer to my *Annotations*, because I cannot now warrantably insert them; but I find in other Books, that anciently they had the care of inspecting

CHAP. XVI. ſpecting all Writs of Summons to Parliaments committed to them, which is now (as I have ſhewn) performed by the Clerks of the Pettibag.

6. As to the Title of *Maiſter*, (from *Magiſter*, and from *Magus* a Wiſeman) it is as ancient as moſt of our borrow'd words from the *Latin*, and was ſtill apply'd to Perſons of Knowledge and other Abilities above the Degrees of Yeomandry.

Amongſt the old *Romans* (as may be read in *Livy*, *Pomponius*, *Aurelius*, and others) they had twelve great Officers, to whom that Title was given, *viz.* *Magiſter Populi*, or Dictator, *Magiſter Equitum*, *Magiſtri Cenſus*, *Magiſter in Auctionibus*, *Magiſtri Epiſtolarum*, *Magiſtri Memoriæ*, *Magiſtri Militum*, *Magiſter Navis*, *Magiſtri Officiorum*, *Magiſtri Scriniorum*, *Magiſter Curiæ*, *Magiſtri Æris*, and many more of a leſſer Rank; for I ſpeak not of *Magiſtri Familiæ* or *Privatæ*, (or as the word is vulgarly applied to its relative word Servant) but as a Title applied to Perſons of Eminency, for their Integrity and Learning; and of theſe there are alſo twelve ſorts with us, (which are found in the Law Books) whereof the firſt we meet with in the Statutes, is the Maſter of the *Mint*, in 2 *H.* 6. *c.* 14. (2.) the Maſter of the Rolls in the firſt of *H.* 7. *Cap.* 20. (for till

till then he was call'd Clerk of the Rolls, or *Custos Archivorum*, and chief Clerk of the *Chancery*, (of which there are twelve, as I said, since which, six chief Clerks, and a greater number of a lesser Form, are there Constituted, whereby they are distinguisht from the ancient Clerks, (now the 12. Masters of *Chancery*) which may be accounted (the Third) sort in point of time mentioned in the Statutes; (the Fourth,) The Master of the Horse in the first of *Edw.* the Sixth; (the Fifth) The Master of the Postern in 2 *Edw.* 6. (the Sixth) The Master of the Kings Houshold in the 32 *H.* 8. (chang'd to the Lord Stuard of the Kings Houshold, (*Charles* Duke of *Brandon* being the first of that Title mentioned in any Statute) (the 7*th.*) The Master of the Court of Wards in the 33 of *Hen.* the 8. (now of no use) (the Eighth) The Master of the Musters, after in the 33 *Eliz.* called Muster Master General; (the 9. 10. 11. 12.) *viz.* The Master of the Armory, the Master of the Kings Jewels, the Master of the Ordinance, (and Master of the Kings Wardrop) are mentioned in the Statute of 39 *Eliz.* not but these Officers were before, but the Statutes (as I said) do not take notice of them till the times that they are quoted in the said Statutes.

Now

CHAP. XVI. 7. Now as the old *Romans* had others which had the Titles of *Magiſtri*, *viz. Magiſtri Univerſitatis vel Societatis*; ſo we in imitation, at *Cambridge* have the Title of *Magiſter* fixt at the head of every Colledge in that Univerſity, (which is an argument of their Antiquity, of which I ſhall ſpeak more) whereas *Oxford* hath but three which bear that Title.

8. It is alſo applied to the Heads of Halls of Companies in *London*, and other Cities; and it hath been formerly applied to all the Members of the *Houſe of Commons*, who were not actually Knights, or Eſquires, or of higher Degrees; but in the *Houſe of Lords*, I do not find it uſed to any, to whom Writs of Summons were ſent to ſit there, except to ſome Priors and Deacons who were ſometimes called *Magiſtri* in their Writs, and others of Religious Orders, call'd alſo in their Writs *Magiſtri*, as alſo to Officers in *Chancery*, *viz.* 49 *Edw.* 3. *Magiſtro Thomæ Tong*, *Officiario Curiæ Cancellariæ*; but whether it was the ſame Office which is now executed by the Maſters of the *Chancery*, *Non Conſtat*; however they were then under the notion of Clerks in an Eccleſiaſtical ſence; but as Writs were ſent to Clerks or Eccleſiaſticks, with the Title of *Magiſter*; ſo in *Henry* the Fourths time, and not

not before, there were Writs sent to Laicks with that Title, and those were Persons of high Quality, *viz.* in the 2. 3. and 6. *Hen.* the 4*th. Magistro Thomæ de la Ware*, (sometimes call'd *Ware* and *Warre*) to attend those Parliaments, and the same *Thomas* was also Summon'd to the Parliaments of the 1. 2. 3. 4. 5. 7. 8. and and 9. of *Hen.* the 5*th. Magistro Tho. de la Ware*, and so to the 1. 2. and 3. of *Hen.* the Sixth; but in the second Parliament of that year, Mr. *De la Ware* was not Summon'd, but one VVrit was *Magistro Johanni Stafford Thes. Angliæ*, and another VVrit, *Magistro Willielmo Alremith Custod. privati Sigilli*. But in the 4*th.* and 6. of *Hen.* the Sixth, both those were left out, and the same *Magistro Tho. de la Ware* Summond again, and for brevity passing to the 36. of *Hen.* the Eighth; and then it was expresly *Roberto Bows Mil. Magistro sive Custod. Rotulorum Cancellariæ*, being then also chief of the twelve Masters of *Chancery*; However Sir *Edw. Coke* saith they are Assistants to the Lord Chancellor, or as the Manuscript saith, *Cojudices*, and thereupon *ex Officio* do sit in the *Lords House*, and the antiquity of the Places allotted them there, (as will be shewn) and their Imployments in every Parliament makes their attendance a kind of Præscription.

CHAP. XVI.

And

CHAP. XVII. And now I proceed to such as sit in the *Lords House* by Patent only, without Tenure, VVrit or Præscription.

CHAP. XVII.

Of the Clerks of the Lords House.

HEre I am to speak of such as have places allowed them in the *House of Lords* by vertue of Patents only, and first of the Clerks; This Title of Clerk from *Cleros*, when the Clergy had (by reason of their great learning) the guidance of Civil Offices, was given as an honour to them; and most of the great Offices, as the Privy Seal, Master of the Rolls, *&c.* had the Titles of Clerks; but now that Title remains to a lower sort, of which there are 26. in number who still retain that Title.

The first, (as to the Progresses of Parliament) is the Clerk of the Pettibag, which is under the Conduct and within the Patent of the Master of the Rolls; (who is the chief of all the Clerks in the *Lords House*, of which Office I have spoke in that Section of the Rolls, and in other places.)

2. The Clerk of the Crown in the *Chancery*, (call'd *Clericus Coronæ in Cancellario*, in his Patent) of whom I have also spoke cursorily in

in ſeveral places) is an Officer to whoſe care many great things are committed, (which may be read in *Compton* and others) but as to what concerns this Subject, I muſt again remind, that all Parliament VVrits which are ſent from the Pettibag, are return'd and kept by the Officer, ſo that the Pettibag gives (as it were) the beginning, this the continuance and ending to a Parliament.

So as this Clerk of the Crown hath three Capacities. Before the Sitting of a Parliament, to receive returns of VVrits which were iſſued from the Pettibag.

And in Parliament to take care according to directions for the iſſuing of Writs in caſe of change or mortality; And in the *Lords Houſe* he firſt reads the Titles of all Bills to be preſented to his Majeſty, of which and other parts of his Duty I ſhall ſpeak more.

3. The third Clerk is term'd in his Patent, *Clericus Parliamentorum*, becauſe he is Clerk in all Parliaments during his life; his imployment here being only converſant about the Affairs of Parliament.

Now in reſpect that all Bills and Matters of State have here their reſult in the *Lords Houſe*, he is the proper Keeper of ſuch Records, (for the *Lords Houſe* is a Court of Record) and to that end his Books are fairly writ, exactly compos'd, according to

CHAP. XVII. to the very words and ſence of that Houſe, and conſtantly perus'd by ſome Lords appointed for that purpoſe, as well for his own juſtification as others ſatisfaction.

He hath alſo an Aſſiſting Clerk allowed him, who is of great uſe and eaſe to him, both of them being well grounded in learning, experience and ability, in the ſafe expediting the concerns of that Houſe, which hath both an Ocean of VViſdom, and curious Rivolets of Honorary punctilios, (not to be omitted by them, ſomewhat different from all other Courts) he hath alſo a Reading Clerk allowed him, who likewiſe attends the Lords Comittees; and theſe are all the Clerks which conſtantly attend in the *Lords Houſe*, and are within the Bar.

4. Of the Clerks of the *Houſe of Commons* I ſhall ſpeak in the ſecond part.

5. As I have ſhewn the Imployments of the Clerks of the *Crown Office* in *Chancery*, ſo (to prevent miſapplications) it is fit to ſhew the Imployments alſo of the Clerk of the *Crown Office* in the *Kings Bench*, who is no conſtant attendant in this *Houſe* or in the *Houſe of Commons*, but only upon contingencies, and then by Order; but more eſpecially in the *Lords Houſe*, for producing, reading, and managing Records concerning VVrits of Error, *Habeas Corpus*, &c.

of

(of which I ſhall ſpeak in order) but his most eminent Imployment is upon the Tryal of Peers, as will be ſhewn. CHAP. XVIII.

Of the 26. Clerks before mention'd, (who ſtill retain that Title,) theſe five which I have named are the chief which are imployed in Parliamentary Matters; but of the other 21. (which may be ſeen in *Lambert*, *Fitz Herbert*, *&c.*) neither the ſix Clerks in *Chancery*, (being Officers of Eminency imployed in that Court bearing that Title, nor are the other Clerks (which are imployed alſo in that Court) in the leaſt (as I know of) ingag'd in the Fabrick of Parliaments. Note that thoſe five Clerks (whom I firſt mention'd) have places allotted them within the Bar of either Houſe, as I ſaid.

And now I muſt ſpeak of other Attendants of another nature, *viz.* the Gentleman Uſher of the Black Rod, and the Serjeant at Arms.

CHAP. XVIII.

Of the Gentleman Uſher of the Black Rod.

THere are but three ways by which the *Houſe of Lords* do ſend any Meſſage to the *Commons*, of two of them I have ſpoken, *viz.* by ſome of the Judges, or by ſome of the Maſters of *Chancery*,

CHAP. XVIII. and the King alſo uſes two ways, *viz.* by his Secretaries, or ſome of the Privy-Council, (when they are Members of the *Houſe of Commons*) both upon ordinary and extraordinary occaſions, or for attending his Perſon upon Addreſſes, &c. But when he hath occaſion to Command the *Houſe of Commons* to attend him in the *Houſe of Lords*, he only ſends this Officer, the manner of which Ceremony I ſhall ſhew in order.

He is call'd the Black Rod, from the Black Staff or Rod (about three foot long tipt with Silver, and guilt with the Kings Arms at one end, and a Lyon Couchant at the other end, and a guilt Knob in the middle) which he carries in his hand; he is always a Perſon of Quality, and born the Kings Subject; and if not a Knight, is made one upon admiſſion to this Office, and hath his Office by Patent; the firſt Grant of it beginning in *Hen.* the 8. time.

1. Before the Sitting of Parliament, he obſerves the Lord Chamberlains directions, in taking care that the *Houſe* be fitted with all things for the Reception of the King, and thoſe who are to ſit there.

2. His Imployment alſo is to introduce Lords into that *Houſe*.

3. And after that *Houſe* is Sat, he hath Imployments concerning the Commitment of Delinquents, &c.

4. He

4. He hath a Seat allowed him, but without the Bar; and to ease him more in these and many other Imployments, he hath an Usher to assist him, call'd the Yeoman Usher, also Door Keepers, &c. as will be shewn. CHAP. XIX.

And so I am come to the last Attendant Officer of Note in that *House*, *viz.* the Kings Serjeant at Arms.

CHAP. XIX.

Of the Kings Serjeant at Arms, Attendant in the House of Lords.

I Have spoken of the *Servientes ad legem* or Serjeants at Law; Now I come to the *Servientes ad arma*, Serjeants at Arms; these were such as amongst the *Romans* were call'd *Satellites Cæsaris*, or a Guard to the Emperor, and sometimes they were call'd *Macerones*, (from whence probably the word Mace might be us'd) which these Serjeant at Arms use to carry before the King, &c.

Of these Serjeants at Arms (for I meddle not with the lower degree in Corporations, sometimes call'd Serjeants of the Mace, or only Serjeants) there are twenty in number, which are call'd the Kings Serjeants at Arms, and these are Created with great Ceremony; for the Person who is to be Created kneeling before the King, the King

 himself

CHAP. XIX. himſelf lays the Mace on the Serjeants Right Shoulder, and ſays theſe words, *Riſe up Serjeant at Arms, and Eſquire for ever*: He hath his Patent for the Office beſides; (of which and of the particulars of his Imployments, *Segar* in his Book of Nobility gives a full account) but of theſe twenty the King appropriates ſixteen to his Perſonal Service, whereof four wait on him every Quarter; the other four are thus diſtributed, *viz.* in time of Parliament one is to attend the Speaker of the *Houſe of Lords*, in caſe he is not Lord Chancellor, another to attend the Speaker of the *Houſe of Commons*; one other to attend the Lord Chancellor, and another the Lord Treaſurer, as well in as out of Parliament.

But in reſpect the Lord Chancellor and Speaker of the *Lords Houſe* is uſually the ſame Perſon, there were but three of the twenty us'd in this time of Parliament, and but two out of Parliament, ſo as the other one or two are reſerv'd for accidental occaſions.

The Serjeant at Arms who attends the *Houſe of Lords* hath the priviledge of carrying the Mace before the Speaker (whether he be the Lord Chancellor or not) within the *Lords Houſe* up to the very Chair of State, and after he hath made his Obeyſances, he lays it down on the firſt

Woolſack

Woolſack by the Speaker, and ſo departs till the Speaker hath occaſion to uſe him again upon the Riſing of the *Houſe*. CHAP. XIX.

And herein methinks the Serjeant at Arms of the *Houſe of Commons* hath more reſpect afforded him than the Serjeant at Arms to the *Houſe of Lords*; for the *Commons* Serjeant hath the freedom to ſtand at the Bar, and hear all Debates, and when weary of ſtanding, hath an eaſie ſeat by the door; but the Lords Serjeant is not permitted to be in the *Lords Houſe* whilſt it is Sitting, nor hath any Station within the Bar, nor Seat without the Bar, as the Gentleman Uſher hath: and yet this Office is more ancient than that, and is not only Serjeant at Arms to the Speaker, and Chancellor (the Parliament not ſitting) but is the chief of the twenty of the Kings Serjeants at Arms; he hath his Duputy, ſo as if there ſhould be occaſion of two, *viz.* for a Speaker and Chancellor, he may ſupply one, and his Deputy the other; and beſides his Deputy he hath alſo other Agents under him, and hath uſe for them; For upon Commitments of Delinquents without door, he is to ſee them forth coming, and in bringing them to the Bar; but upon confinements or Commitment of any Member within doors, that peculiarly belongs to the Gentleman of the Black Rod.

So

CHAP. XIX. So as theſe 2 Officers ſet the firſt wheel of a Parliament in motion; for the Serjeant at Arms conducts the Chancellor or Speaker into the *Houſe of Lords*, the King ſends the Black Rod to the *Commons* to bring up their Speaker, who being confirm'd by the King, goes to his Chair in the *Commons*, uſher'd with the other Serjeants at Arms, and ſo when each Speaker retires from each Houſe, each Serjeant is to each a Conducter.

A Corollary to this Firſt Part.

I Have now ſhewn the General Warrants for Summoning a Parliament, and the particular Writs and Patents impowring thoſe who are to ſit in the *Lords Houſe*; as alſo the Act of Precedency to prevent Diſorders of Places when they meet there, and given a touch of Proxies, and of the words Lords and Peers, and of other Accidental Writs, and of the Returns of their Writs, and of ſome who ſit there without Writs or Patents, and of others who are imployed there meerly by vertue of Patents. And of all theſe I have made ſome Diſcourſes, as well to revive the notions of thoſe who need no other information, as to inform others who have little knowledge therein, but what they gain from the ſhort Memorials of Writers, or from the imperfect Diſcourſes which they glean from ſuch as know ſome things in part, but have not the true Concatenation of the Grandeur of a Parliament.

The

These discourses (and those intended) will (I hope) contain the whole System of this *Constitution.* This part hath applied it self wholly to the Offices, Degrees and Qualities pertinent to the *House of Lords* in general; but as to the particular Persons owning those Offices, Degrees, and Qualities; I reserve them for the Subsequent Parts of this Treatise; that is after I have discours'd of the seven remaining Exemplar Writs in the *Pawn*, which particularly concerns the *House of Commons.*

Viz.

To *Cornwall.* To *Dover*,
To *Cambridge*, To *Lancaster*,
To *London*, To *Chester*,
To *Carnarvan* in *Wales.*

And also shewn the Writs or Precepts derivative of those seven Exemplars, and the manner of Elections and Returns of Writs and Precepts, the Discourse of which will comprehend all the County Shires, Cities and Burroughs; (which have power of Electing Members for Parliaments) I shall then shew you the Places adapted for both Houses to meet in; as also of the Members Summon'd and imployed in both Houses in this Parliament.

After these I shall speak of such Ceremonies as are us'd before any Members be admitted into either Houses; and when they are fixt in both Houses, I shall give an account of the most material passages, as to the renewing of Writs for supply of Members, and other distinct Operations considered as an *House of Lords*, or an *House of Commons*, and in their joynt Operations as *Lords* and *Commons* Assembled in Parliament, and then of their compleat Operations as an intire Parliament, consisting of the King and the three Estates, *viz.* the LordsS piritual the Lords Temporal, and the Commons; and this is more particularly evident, when by passing of Acts, the King confirms what those three Estates do joyntly Operate. And so I conclude with the Kings power of Summoning, Adjourning, Proroguing and and Dissolving of this and all other Parliaments, and what is to be done with Records, Laws, &c. after Dissolution of any Parliament.

And because I could not well reduce the copious matters of so large a Subject into my Discourses, or observations, I shall hereafter add some *Annotations*, as Explanitories and Enlargements to many things which are necessary or convenient to be enlarged or explained.

An

AN
APPENDIX
Being A Diary of the ſe-veral Seſſions of the publick Adjournments, Prorogations, and Proclamations relating to the Parliament which was Summon'd the 18*th*.of *Feb*. 166$\frac{0}{1}$. and Diſloved the 24*th*. of *Jan*. 166$\frac{8}{9}$.

T*HE Kings Warrant, and Writs of Summons for that Parliament were dated the* 18*th. of* Feb. 13 Car. 2*d*. 1660.

Proclamation *contain'd in thoſe Writs, to meet att* Weſtminſter *the* 8*th. of* May, *following.*

Seſsion *the* 8*th. of* May 13 Car. 2*d*. 1661 *at* Weſtminſter, *continued to the* 30*th. of* July *following.*

Acts *Publick* 19. *Private* 21.

Adjourn'd *the* 30*th. of July* 13 Car. 2*d*. 1661 *to the* 20*th. of* November *following.*

Seſsion *the* 20*th. of* Novemb. 13 Car. 2*d*.

1661 *continued to the* 19*th. of* May 14 Car. 2*d.* 1662.

1662. Acts *Publick* 33, *Private* 39.

Prorogu'd *the* 19*th. of* May 14 Car. 2*d.* 1662 *to the* 18*th. of* Feb. 15 Car. 2*d.* 166$\frac{2}{3}$.

The King present.

III. Session *the* 18*th. of* February. 15 Car. 2*d.* 166$\frac{2}{3}$. *continued to the* 27*th.* July 15 Car. 2*d.* 1663.

1663. Acts *Publick* 17, *Private* 19,

Prorogu'd *the* 27*th. of* July 15 Car. 2*d.* 1663 *to the* 16*th. of* March 16 Car 2*d.* 166$\frac{3}{4}$.

The King Present.

IV. Session *the* 16*th.* March 16 Car. 2*d.* 166$\frac{3}{4}$. *continued to the* 17*th. of* May 16 Car. 2*d.* 1664.

1664. Acts *Publick* 8, *Private* 10,

Prorogu'd *the* 17*th. of* May 16 Car. 2*d.* 1664 *to the* 20*th. of* August *following.*

The King Present.

Prorogu'd *the* 20*th. of* Aug. 16 Car. 2*d.* 1664 *to the* 24*th. of* Novemb. *following.*

By Commission.

V. Session *the* 24*th. of* Novemb. 16 Car. 2*d.* 1664 *continued to the* 2*d. of* March 17 Car. 2*d.* 166$\frac{4}{5}$.

1665. Acts *Publick* 12, *Private* 17,

Prorogu'd *the* 2*d. of* March 17 Car. 2*d.* 166$\frac{4}{5}$. *to the* 21*st. of* June 17 Car. 2*d.* 1665.

The King Present.

Proclamation *dated the* 24*th. of* May 17 Car.

Car. 2*d. for the further Proroguing the Parliament from the* 21*st. of* June *to a day that shall be fixt at the actual Prorogation thereof Accordingly.*

Prorogu'd *the* 21*st. of* June 17 Car. 2*d.* 1665 *to the* 1*st. of* August *following.*

By Commission.

Proclamation *dated the* 9*th. of* July 17 Car. 2*d.* 1665 *for further Proroguing the Parliament from the* 1*st. of* Aug. *to the* 3*d, of* Octob. *following Accordingly.*

Prorogu'd *the* 1*st. of* Aug. 17 Car. 2*d.* 1665 *to the* 3*d. of* October *following.*

By Commission.

Proclamation *dated the* 10*th. of* August 17 Car. 2*d.* 1665 *appointing the meeting of the Parliament at* Oxford *in respect the Plague was then at* London, *Accordingly.*

Prorogu'd *the* 3*d. of* Octob. 17 Car. 2*d.* 1665. *at* Oxford, *to the* 9*th. of the same month and place.*

By Commission.

Sesion *at* Oxford *the* 9*th. of* Octob. 17 Car 2*d.* 1665 *continued to the* 21*st. of the same month.*

Acts *Publick* 9, *Private* 1,

Prorogu'd *the* 31*st. of* Octob. 17 Car. 2*d.* 1665 *to meet at* Westminster *the* 20*th. of* Feb. 18 Car. 2*d.* 166⅚.

The King Present.

Prorogu'd *the* 20*th of* Feb. 18 Car. 2*d.*

 166⅚.

1661 *at* Westminster *to the* 23*d.* *of* April 1666.

1666. Proclamation *dated the* 23*d.* *of* April 18 Car. 2*d.* 1666 *for Proroguing the Parliament to the* 18*th.* Sep. *following accordingly*,

Prorogu'd *the* 23*d.* *of* April 18 Car 2*d.* 1666 *to the* 18 *of* Sep. *following*.

By Commission.

VII. Session *the* 18*th.* *of* Septemb. 18 Car. 2*d.* 1666 *continued to the* 8*th.* *of* Feb. *following*.

Acts *Publick* 5, *Private* 5,

Prorogu'd *the* 8*th.* *of* Feb. 19 Car 2*d.* 1667. *to the* 10*th.* *of* October 1667.

The King Present.

1667. Proclamation *dated the* 26*th.* *of* *June* 19 Car. 2*d.* 1667 *to reassemble the Parliament back from the* 10*th.* *of* October *to the* 25*th.* *of* July 19 Car. 2*d.* 1667.

Adjourn'd *the* 25*th.* *of* July 19 Car. 2*d.* 1667 *to the* 10*th.* *of* October *following*.

VIII. Session *the* 10*th.* *of* Oct. 19 Car. 2*d.* *continued to the* 9*th.* *of* May 20 Car. 2*d.* 1668.

Acts *Publick* 15, *Private* 24,

Adjourn'd *the* 9*th.* May 20 Car. 2*d.* 1668 *to the* 11*th.* *of* August *following*.

Proclamation *dated the* 3*d.* *of* July 20 Car. 2*d.* 1668 *for the Parliament to meet the* 11*th.* *of* Aug. *and that they shall and may Adjourn to the* 10*th.* *of* Nov. *following accordingly*.

Ad-

An Appendix.

Adjourn'd *the 11th. of* August 20 Car. 2*d.* 1668. *to the* 10*th. of* Nov. *following.*

Proclamation *dated the* 19*th. of* Sept. 20 Car. 2*d.* 1668. *to meet the* 10*th. of* Nov. *as many of both Houses as may Adjourn themselves to the* 1*st. of* March 21 Car. 2*d.* $166\frac{8}{9}$.

Adjourn'd *the* 10*th. of* Nov. 20 Car. 2*d.* 1668. *to the* 1*st. of* March 21 Car. 2*d.* $166\frac{8}{9}$.

Proclamation *dated the* 18*th.* Dec. 20 Car. 2*d.* 1668. *reciting, that whereas the two Houses of Parliament had Adjourn'd by the Kings directions from the* 10*th. of* Nov. *to the* 1*st. of* March *the King Declares that he will Prorogue them on the said* 1*st. of* March *to the* 9*th. of* October 21 Car. 2*d.* 1669 *accordingly.*

Prorogu'd *the* 1*st. of* March 21 Car. 2*d.* $166\frac{8}{9}$. *to the* 19*th. of* October 21 Car. 2*d.* 1669.

Sesſion *the* 19*th. of* Oct. 21 Car. 2*d.* 1669. *continued to the* 11*th. of* December *following.*

In this Seſſion no bill paſt the Royal aſſent.

Prorogu'd *the* 11*th.* December 21 Car. 2*d.* 1669 *to the* 14*th.* February 22 Car. 2*d.* $166\frac{9}{10}$.

By Commiſſion.

Proclamation *dated the* 23*d. of* Decem. 21 Car. 2*d.* 1669 *requiring the Members*

Dd 4 *of*

of both Houses to attend at the time prefixt at the last prorogation, viz. *the* 14*th*. Feb. 22 Car. 2*d*. $166\frac{9}{10}$. *accordingly*.

X. Session *the* 14*th*. Feb. 22 Car. 2*d*. $166\frac{9}{10}$. *continued to the* 11*th*. *of* April 22 Car. 2*d*. 1670.

1670. Acts *Publick* 8, *Private* 16,

Adjourn'd *the* 11*th*. *of* April 22 Car. 2*d*. *to the* 24*th*. *of* October *following*.

Proclamation *dated the* 21*st*. *of* April 22 Car. 2*d*. 1670 *requiring the Members of both Houses to attend the prefixt time*, viz. *the* 24*th*. *of* October 22 Car. 2*d*. 1670.

XI. Session *the* 24*th*. Oct. 22 Car. 2*d*. 1670 *continued to the* 22*d*. April 23 Car. 2*d*. 1671.

1671. Acts *Publick* 26, *Private* 30,

Progogu'd *the* 22*d*. April 23 Car. 2*d*. 1671 *to the* 16*th*. *of* April 24 Car. 2*d*. 1671.

The King Present.

Proclamation *dated the* 27*th*. Sept. 23 Car. 2*d*. 1671 *declaring the Kings resolution to Prorogue the Parliament from the said* 16 *of* April *to the* 30*th*. *of* October *following Accordingly*.

1672. Prorogu'd *the* 16*th*. *of* April 24 Car. 2*d*. 1672 *to the* 30*th*. *of* October *following*.

By Commission.

Prorogu'd *the* 30*th*. *of* Dec. 24 Car. 2*d*. 1672 *to the* 4*th*. *of* Feb. 25 Car. 2*d*. $167\frac{2}{3}$.

By Commission.

Session

An Appendix.

Sesſion *the* 4*th.* Feb. 25 Car. 2*d.* 167$\frac{2}{3}$. XII.
continued to the 29*th.* March 1673.

Acts *Publick* 10, *Private* 11, 1673.

Adjourn'd *the* 29*th. of* March 25 Car. 2*d.* 1673 *to the* 20*th. of* October *following.*

Prorogu'd *the* 20*th. of* Oct. 25 Car. 2*d.* 1673 *to the* 27*th. of the ſame Month.*

By Commiſſion.

Sesſion *the* 27*th. of* Oct. 25 Car. 2*d.* XIII.
1673 *to the* 4*th. of* November *following.*

No Bills paſt this Seſſion.

Prorogu'd *the* 4*th. of* Nov. 25 Car. 2*d.* 1673 *to the* 7*th. of* January 167$\frac{3}{4}$.

The King Preſent.

Proclamation *dated the* 10*th. of* Decem. 25 Car. 2*d. to require the Members of both Houſes to attend the* 7*th. of* Jan. *following.*

Sesſion *the* 7*th. of* Jan. 25 Car. 2*d.* 167$\frac{3}{4}$. XIV.
continu'd to the 4*th.* Feb. 26 Car. 2*d.* 167$\frac{3}{4}$.

No Bills paſt this Seſſion.

Prorogu'd *the* 24*th. of* Feb. 26 Car. 2*d.* 167$\frac{3}{4}$. *to the* 10*th. of* Novem. 26 Car. 2*d.* 1674.

The King Preſent.

Proclamation *dated the* 1*ſt. of* July 26 Car. 2*d.* 1674 *declaring the Kings pleaſure to prorogue the Parliament to the* 13*th. of* April 1675.

Proclamation *dated the* 3*d. S*eptem. 26 Car. 2*d.* 1674 *for Proroguing the Parliament from the* 10*th. of* Nov. *to the* 13*th. of* April 1675 27 Car. 2*d.* Pro-

An Appendix.

1674. Prorogu'd *the* 10*th. of* Nov. 26 Car. 2*d.* 1674 *to the* 13*th. of* April 1675 27 Car. 2*d.*

By Commiſſion.

XV. Seſſion *the* 13*th. of* April 27 Car. 2*d.* 1675 *continu'd to the* 27*th. of* June *following.*

1675. Acts *Private* 5,

Prorogu'd *the* 4*th. of* June 27 Car. 2*d.* 1675 *to the* 13*th. of* October *following.*

The King Preſent.

XVI. Seſſion *the* 13*th. of* October 27 Car. 2*d.* 1675 *continu'd to the* 22*d. of November following.* No Bills paſt.

Prorogu,d *the* 22*d. of* Nov. 27 Car. 2*d.* *to the* 15*th. of* Feb. 28 Car. 2*d.* 167$\frac{5}{6}$.

1676. Proclamation *dated the* 20*th. of* Dec. 28 Car. 2*d.* 1676 *requiring both Houſes to give their attendance on the* 15*th.* Feb. *next.*

XVII. Seſſion *the* 15*th.* Feb. 28 Car. 2*d.* 1676 *continu'd to the* 16*th. of* April 29 Car. 2*d.* 1677.

1677. Acts *Publick* 10, *Private* 14,

Adjourn'd *the* 16*th. of* April 29 Car. 2*d.* 1677 *to the* 21*ſt. of* May *following.*

The King Preſent.

Acts *Publick* 10, *Private* 14,

Proclamation *dated the* 2*d. of* May 29. Car. 2*d.* 1677 *requiring both Houſes to give their attendance the* 21*ſt. of* May.

Seſsion

An Appendix.

Session *the* 21*st*. May 29 Car. 2*d*. 1677 *continued to the* 28*th*. *of the same Month*.

Adourn'd *the* 28*th*. *of* May 29 Car. 2*d*. 1677 *to the* 16*th*. *of* July *following*.

Adjourn'd *the* 16*th*. *of* July 29 Car. 2*d*. 1667 *to the* 3*d*. *of* December *following*.

Proclamation *dated the* 26*th*. *of* Octo- 29 Car. 2*d*. 1677 *for Adjourning the two Houses of Parliament from the* 3*d*. *of* Dec- *to the* 4*th*. *of* April 30 Car. 2*d*. 1678.

Proclamation *dated the* 7*th*. *of* Decem. 29 Car. 2*d*. *for Adjourning both Houses back from the* 4*th*. *of* April 30 Car. 2*d*. 1678 *to the* 15*th*. Janu. 29 Car. 2*d*. $167\frac{7}{8}$. *requiring the Members of both Houses to attend that day*.

Adjourn'd *the* 15*th*. *of* Jan. 29 Car. 2*d*. $167\frac{7}{8}$. *to the* 28*th*. *of the same Month*.

Session *the* 28*th*. *of* January 29 Car. 2*d*. $167\frac{7}{8}$. *continu'd to the* 27*th*. *of* March 30 Car. 2*d*. 1678.

Acts *Publick* 2, *Private* 13,

Adjourn'd *the* 27*th*. *of* March 30 Car. 2*d*. 1678 *to the* 11*th*. *of* April 30 Car. 2*d*. 1678.

Adjourn'd *the* 11*th*. *of* April 30 Car. 2*d*. 1678 *to the* 15*th*. *of the same Month*.

Adjourn'd *the* 15*th*. *of* April 30 Car. 2*d*. 1678 *to the* 29*th*. *of the same Month*.

Session *the* 29*th*. *of* April 30 Car. 2*d*. 1678 *continu'd to the* 3*d*. *of* May *following*.

Pro-

An Appendix.

Prorogu'd *the* 13*th. of* May 30 Car. 2*d.* 1678 *to the* 23*d. of the same Month.*

By-Commission.

Session *the* 23*d. of* May 30 Car. 2*d.* 1678 *continu'd to the* 15*th.* July *following.*

Acts *Publick* 9, *Private* 12,

Prorogu'd *the* 15*th. of* July 30 Car. 2*d.* 1678 *to the* 1*st. of* August *following.*

By Commission.

Prorogu'd *the* 1*st. of* August 30 Car. 2*d.* 1678 *to the* 29*th. of the same Month.*

By Commission.

Proclamation *dated the* 2*d. of* August 30 Car. 2*d.* 1678 *requiring the Members of both Houses to give attendance on the* 29*th. of August.*

Proclamation *dated the* 8*th. of* August 1678, *declaring that the Parliament shall be prorogu'd the said* 29*th. of* Aug. *to the* 1*st. of* Oct. 30 Car. 2*d.* 1678.

Prorogu'd *the* 29*th. of* August 30 Car. 2*d.* 1678 *to the* 1*st. of* Oct. *following.*

By Commission.

Proclamation *dated the* 25*th.* Sept. 30 Car. 2*d.* 1678 *for the further Proroguing the Parliament to the* 21*st. of* Oct. *in the same Month.*

By Commission.

Session *the* 21*st. of* Oct. 30 Car. 2*d.* 1678 *continued to the* 30*th. of* Dec. *following.*

Acts *Publick* 1, *Private* 0,

Pro-

An Appendix.

Progogu'd *the* 30*th. of* Dec. 30 Car. 2*d.* 1678 *to the* 4*th of* Feb. 31 Car. 2*d.* 1678.

Proclamation *dated the* 24*th. of* Jan. 30 Car. 2*d.* $167\frac{8}{9}$. *wherein the King discharges the Members of both Houses from meeting the* 4*th. of* Feb. 31 Car. 2*d.* 1678 *and declare the Parliament Dissolv'd.*

Dissolution *the* 24*th.* Jan. 30 Car. 2*d.* $167\frac{8}{9}$. *but in the Proclamation His Majesty further Publisheth his pleasure that Writs should be issued for another Parliament to meet the* 6*th. of* March *following,* viz. 31 Car. 2*d.* $167\frac{8}{9}$.

I did design to deferr the Printing of this Diary *till I publish some discourses of the nature of* Sessions, Proclamations, Adjournments, Recesses, Prorogations, and Dissolutions, *but because it will take long time before I shall publish them, some friends did persuad me to add this* Appendix *as very useful to all such as may have any recourse in point of times to matters transacted in this Parliament (of which I chiefly treat) Summon'd the* 18*th. of* Feb. $166\frac{0}{1}$. 13 Car. 2*d. and ended the* 14*th.* January Car. 2*d.* $167\frac{8}{9}$. *and though the dates of Session* &c. *are repeated in several* Paragraphs, *yet it is so ordered for the ease and advantage of him that desires to satisfie himself in the* Chro-

An Appendix.

Chronological *questions of that Parliament, without looking on the* Antecedent *or* Subsequent Paragraphs.

FINIS.

www.ingramcontent.com/pod-product-compliance
Lightning Source LLC
Chambersburg PA
CBHW080224270326
41926CB00020B/4133

* 9 7 8 0 3 6 7 1 8 0 9 0 4 *